Business Law

Marketing means Business

The Chartered Institute of Marketing was founded in 1911. It is now the largest and most successful marketing management organization in Europe with over 20,000 members and 16,000 students throughout the world. CIM is a democratic organization and is run for the members by the members with the assistance of a permanent staff headed by the Director General. The Headquarters of CIM are at Moor Hall, Cookham, near Maidenhead, in Berkshire.

Objectives: The objectives of CIM are to develop knowledge about marketing, to provide services for members and registered students and to make the principles and practices of marketing more widely known and used throughout industry and commerce.

Range of activities: CIM's activities are divided into four main areas:

Membership and membership activities
Corporate activities
Marketing education
Marketing training

Business Law

A complete guide for students of business and marketing

A. A. PAINTER and R. G. LAWSON

*Published on behalf of
the Chartered Institute of Marketing*

Heinemann Professional Publishing

Heinemann Professional Publishing Ltd
Halley Court, Jordan Hill, Oxford OX2 8EJ

OXFORD   LONDON   MELBOURNE   AUCKLAND   SINGAPORE
IBADAN   NAIROBI   GABORONE   KINGSTON

First published 1989
Reprinted 1989

British Library Cataloguing in Publication Data
Lawson, R. G.
Business law: a complete guide for students
of business and marketing.
1. England. Divorce. Law
I. Title   II. Painter A. A. (Anthony Arthur),
1929–   III. Institute of Marketing
344.106′66

ISBN 0 434 91505 X

Photoset by Wilmaset, Birkenhead, Wirral
Printed in Great Britain by
Redwood Burn Limited, Trowbridge, Wiltshire
and Bound by Pegasus Bookbinding, Melksham, Wiltshire

Contents

1 *An outline of the English legal system*

1.1 Introduction

It must be stressed at the beginning of this chapter that it is only concerned with *English* law. The laws and legal systems of Scotland and, to a lesser degree, Northern Ireland are distinct from those of England and Wales. While Scots and Northern Irish law will frequently coincide with that of the rest of the United Kingdom, it must not be assumed that this is always the case.

1.2 How Laws are Made

There are essentially three types of legislation: Acts of Parliament; subordinate legislation, which mainly consists of delegated legislation made by government ministers, local authorities and other bodies under powers derived from Parliament; and the legislation of the European Economic Community (EEC). Parliament is 'supreme', which means that it is not subject to any legal limits on its powers to create, alter or repeal the law. It also means that an Act of Parliament cannot be questioned in, or by the courts: it has to be applied by them.

1.3 Acts of Parliament

While it is going through the parliamentary process, an Act is known as a Bill. Most Bills originate from government departments and have been drafted by parliamentary draftsmen. They will be introduced into either the House of Commons or the House of Lords first, and must receive three 'readings' in each House. The only Bills which cannot be started in the House of Lords are 'money' Bills: this is if the Speaker of the House of Commons gives a certificate to that effect. The annual budget, for example, is a 'money' Bill. Private Members also introduce Bills but these have a very limited chance of ever becoming law. Once a Bill has been accepted by each House, it receives the Royal Assent. Sometimes a Norman French formula is used to signify the assent, though it is not customary today for the monarch to assent in person. The assent is usually just notified to each House by the Speaker of the Commons and the Lord Chancellor (the equivalent of the Speaker in the House of Lords) under the powers provided in the Royal Assent Act 1967.

1.4 Categories of Act

There are three main kinds of Act: public, private and hybrid. Public Acts concern law which will be of general application when it is passed. Private Acts are measures dealing with personal matters or local matters in a certain area of the country only. Hybrid Acts are Public Acts which nevertheless affect private interests in such a way as to render it desirable that part of the procedure for Private Acts should be adopted.

1.5 The Delaying Powers of the House of Lords

The power of the House of Lords to obstruct measures approved by the House of Commons was considerably restricted by the Parliament Acts of 1911 and 1949. The present position may be summarized as follows:

(i) In the case of a Money Bill which has passed the Commons, it shall receive the Royal Assent without the approval of the House of Lords, unless it has been passed by the Lords within one month of being sent to the Lords, provided that the Bill was sent to the Lords at least one month before the end of the session.

(ii) The power of the Lords to reject any Bill attempting to extend the maximum life of Parliament beyond five years is left unimpaired.

(iii) If any other category of Public Bill has been passed in the Commons and rejected in the Lords, is passed again by the Commons in the next session of Parliament but is not passed by the Lords without amendment (except amendments approved by the Commons), the Commons is entitled to forward the Bill for the Royal Assent. The Parliament Acts further provide that at least one year must have elapsed between the second reading of the Bill in the Commons in the first session and the third reading in the Commons in the second session.

(iv) The Parliament Acts do not apply to Private Bills, so the power of the Lords to veto such Bills is untouched.

1.6 Subordinate Legislation

It is very common nowadays for Acts of Parliament to give a body such as a government Minister or a local authority or a public corporation the power to make regulations and to state what punishments are applicable in the event of a breach of those regulations. There is a vast amount of this type of legislation, generally in the form known as Statutory Instruments. The number of Statutory Instruments each year usually exceeds 2000, while the number of Acts of Parliament rarely exceeds 150. Chapter 11 deals with consumer credit, and it will be seen that the one Act of Parliament, the Consumer Credit Act 1974, gave rise to a considerable number of Statutory Instruments. A number of Statutory Instruments have also been made under the Trade Descriptions Act. Another type of subordinate legislation is the byelaw. Byelaws are made by local authorities, public corporations and certain other bodies authorized by Act of Parliament. They are restricted to the locality or undertaking to which they apply. They are not made by Statutory Instrument.

1.7 The United Kingdom and the EEC

The United Kingdom became a member of the EEC on 1 January 1973 after Parliament had enacted the European Communities Act 1972. This Act provided that the Treaty of Rome, which established the EEC in 1957, it to have direct effect in the United Kingdom. The EEC also makes law in the form of Regulations and Directives. As a general rule, it can be said that Regulations automatically become law in each EEC country, while a Directive has to be specifically implemented. This can be done by law such as an Act of Parliament or a Statutory Instrument, but it can be done in any other appropriate way. For instance, EEC Directives on pesticides were at one time implemented in the United Kingdom by a voluntary agreement with the manufacturers, which was a perfectly proper way to implement the relevant Directives.

1.8 Common Law

Legislation is not the only source of law in the United Kingdom. In addition, there is the common law, which is often described as the law made by the judges in deciding cases which come before them where there is no relevant legislation. The law of contract, for instance, and the law of negligence are very heavily dependent on the common law. Legislation is superior to common law, so if there is any conflict between legislation and common law, legislation prevails. Some Acts of Parliament are what are called 'codifying' statutes, that is to say, they do not make new law but codify the existing common law. Two examples are the original Sale of Goods Act 1893 (now replaced by the Sale of Goods Act 1979) and the Supply of Goods and Services Act 1982. The expression 'common law' also includes the so-called rules of 'equity' which are a body of rules developed by the courts of equity (which no longer exist separately) in the nineteenth century. As the name might indicate, the rules of equity were based on fairness. Much of the law of trusts, for example, was created by the courts of equity.

1.9 The Distinction between Civil and Criminal Law

The law of the United Kingdom is usually regarded as falling into two separate branches: civil law and criminal law. Each is based on legislation and common law, though it is probably true to say that the criminal law is based to a larger extent on legislation than is the civil law. Although it will usually be easy to say that a particular matter belongs to one branch as against another, it is very difficult to give a precise definition of the civil or the criminal law which will fit all cases. Criminal cases are called prosecutions and are generally brought by or on behalf of the state in the name of the monarch, or officials who are given the power to prosecute, such as the Director of Public Prosecutions or local trading standards officers. The power of the police to prosecute has largely been superseded by the Crown Prosecution Service established by the Prosecution of Offences Act 1985. In some cases, such as the Trade Descriptions Act 1968, it is possible for injured parties to bring private prosecutions, but these are very rare. If the prosecution in a criminal case is successful, the accused, known as the defendant, can be fined or imprisoned. This is of no direct benefit to the victim of the crime, since the fine is not payable to him, even if the prosecution had been a private one. However, under the Powers of Criminal Courts Act 1973, the courts do have the power to make compensation orders in favour of the victim. Compensation orders are often made in the case of convictions under the Trade Descriptions Act.

In contrast, civil actions are brought by an individual, the plaintiff, against another individual, the defendant.

It should be understood, incidentally, that 'individual' in this context means any 'legal person'. This can cover not just human beings, but also bodies with legal personality, such as partnerships or companies.

If damages are awarded to the plaintiff in a civil action, they are designed to give compensation and not to punish the defendant, though there are a restricted number of instances where punitive damages can be awarded in civil actions, and where they are awarded these too are payable to the plaintiff. Although there are no hard and fast rules as to what categories of law make up the civil law, the following are the most often used: the law of contract; the law of tort (of which negligence is the best-known example); commercial law (agency, sale of goods, consumer credit, negotiable instruments); employment law and company law. Other categories are revenue law, the law of trusts and family law.

The same set of facts can give rise to both criminal and civil cases. A person injured by a car driven negligently can bring a civil action; and a prosecution can also be brought for the road traffic offence. As is explained in 1.10, however, civil and criminal cases are brought in different courts. Under the terms of the Civil Evidence Act 1968, the fact that a person has been convicted of a criminal offence is admissible in evidence in civil proceedings for the purposes of proving that he committed that offence.

1.10 The Court Structure—The Civil Courts

(i) County Courts

The jurisdiction of the county courts is exclusively civil. England and Wales are divided into 285 county court districts, each with its own courthouse, office and staff, which are grouped into 63 circuits. Each circuit has assigned to it one or more circuit judges. Those qualified to be circuit judges are barristers of at least ten years' standing or recorders (*see* 1.11 (ii)) who have held office for three years. Under the provisions of the County Courts Act 1984, the jurisdiction of the County Courts includes (it should be appreciated that all sums mentioned can be changed):

(i) Actions in contract or tort, except defamation, or for money recoverable by statute, where the debt or damages claimed do not exceed £5000. A County Court has jurisdiction over defamation or a claim exceeding £5000 if the parties agree to the jurisdiction, or if the case is remitted to it by the High Court.

(ii) Jurisdiction over actions for the recovery of land where the net annual rateable value does not exceed £1000.

(iii) An 'equity' jurisdiction (*see* 1.8 for an explanation of this term), for example in cases of administration of estates, foreclosure of mortgages and specific performance of contracts for the sale of land, where the amount involved does not exceed £30,000.

(iv) Disputes over the Grant of Probate or Letters of Administration where the net value of the estate is less than £30,000.

Types of jurisdiction under other Acts include (in designated courts): divorce, judicial separation and annulment of marriage cases; guardianship and adoption; bankruptcy; winding-up of companies with a paid-up share capital of not more than £120,000; matters under the Rent, Landlord and Tenant, Housing and Consumer Credit Acts. The procedure in the county courts is simpler, speedier and less costly than in the High Court (*see* 1.10 (ii)). A party who wins a High Court action which should have been brought in the county court may, in certain circumstances, be awarded no costs or costs on the lower county court scale. This rule only applies in cases of contract and tort. Appeals from the county court are to the Court of Appeal (*see* 1.10 (iii)), except in bankruptcy matters where appeal is to the Chancery Division of the High Court (*see* 1.10 (ii)).

(a) Small claims

It is necessary to say a separate word about the county court 'small claims' procedure. A defended action in the county court must be referred to arbitration if the sum claimed or the amount involved does not exceed £500. If referral to arbitration does take place, the hearing takes place before an arbitrator in private and without the formalities normally associated with a trial. The arbitrator will normally be the county court registrar, or deputy registrar, but either party may apply to the registrar for the appointment of any other suitable person. Disputes involving more than £500 can be heard by the 'small claims' procedure if both parties agree. A referral to arbitration of a claim not in excess of £500 may be rescinded by the registrar, on the application of the parties, if the parties are agreed that the case should be heard in court, or if the case involves a difficult question of law or fact or an allegation of fraud, or if it would be otherwise unreasonable for the case to proceed to arbitration. An award made under the 'small claims' procedure is entered as a judgment in court proceedings and is enforceable as such. Each party normally bears his own costs. The county court judge has power, on application, to set the award aside.

(ii) The High Court of Justice

The High Court is staffed by a maximum of 80 judges who are barristers of at least ten years' standing. It is separated into three divisions, each of which handles cases of a different type: the Chancery Division; the Queen's Bench Division; and the Family Division. Each division has both original and appellate jurisdiction, that is to say cases can start in the particular division and appeals can be made to each division from the County Court.

(a) Chancery Division

The Supreme Court Act 1981 assigns a number of matters to the original jurisdiction of this Division, including: the administration of estates of deceased persons;

the execution of trusts; the redemption and foreclosure of mortgages; the rectification and cancellation of deeds; partnership actions; bankruptcy; the sale, exchange or partition of land, or the raising of charges on land; all causes and matters under legislation relating to companies. As for the appellate jurisdiction of the Chancery Division, this is much more limited. A single judge hears income tax appeals from the Commissioners of Inland Revenue. A divisional court of the Chancery Division, which normally consists of two judges, hears appeals from county courts in bankruptcy matters.

(b) Queen's Bench Division

The principal aspects of this Division's original jurisdiction are contract and tort. Commercial matters are dealt with by specialist judges in the commercial court which sits in London, Liverpool and Manchester. Under the Rules of the Supreme Court, this court deals with commercial actions including: 'any cause arising out of the ordinary transactions of merchants and traders and, without prejudice to the generality of the foregoing words, any cause relating to the construction of a mercantile document, the export or import of merchandise, affreightment, insurance, banking mercantile agency and mercantile usage'. The basic features of the commercial court's operations are its speed, and simplicity and flexibility in terms of procedure. The strict rules of evidence may be relaxed and the judges are available at short notice at any stage of the action on the initiative of either party. Disputes can thus be dealt with quickly. Similarly, admiralty matters, such as salvage claims, are heard in this Division by specialist judges, often with lay assessors, in the admiralty court. As far as its appellate jurisdiction is concerned, the Queen's Bench Division may hear certain appeals, including appeals from various tribunals, and it may hear appeals by way of case stated (that is, where the lower court 'states a case' for its consideration) on a miscellaneous collection of civil matters from magistrates' courts, the Crown Court and certain other bodies. Where the appeal is final, or if the court directs, appeals are heard by a divisional court consisting of two or more judges (usually two).

An important aspect of the work of this Division is its supervisory work. The most important aspects of this are the power to issue a writ of habeas corpus, which orders the release of some person held in custody, and to issue the so-called 'prerogative' orders on an application for judicial review against lower courts, tribunals and other decision-making bodies, such as local authorities. These orders are those of *mandamus*, prohibition and *certiorari*. The first is used to compel the body to whom it is directed to carry out a duty imposed on it by law. An order of prohibition or *certiorari* can only be issued in relation to an order or decision made by a body which is under a public duty to 'act judicially' or 'act fairly' in making that decision. This can cover not just courts and tribunals but also such bodies as local authorities which may sometimes be required to act judicially, and other times fairly. The order of prohibition prevents such a body from acting in excess of jurisdiction or otherwise acting improperly. The order of *certiorari* covers much the same area but after such a body had done something and it is desired to review it and, if necessary, quash it on the grounds of exceeding jurisdiction, denial of natural justice, or error of law on the face of the record. Applications for habeas corpus are heard by a divisional court of at least two judges: applications for judicial review are heard by a single judge unless the court directs otherwise.

(c) *Family Division*

With regard to its original functions, this Division deals with all aspects of family law, such as proceedings for divorce, annulment of marriage and judicial separation and ancillary relief, proceedings for the determination of title to property in dispute between spouses, proceedings concerning the occupation of the matrimonial home and wardship of court, guardianship and adoption proceedings. With regard to appellate jurisdiction, this is principally concerned with appeals from decisions of magistrates' courts in domestic and care proceedings. Some of these appeals will be heard by a divisional court of at least two judges.

(iii) The Court of Appeal (Civil Division)

Judges of the Court of Appeal are known as 'Lord Justice'. They must have been judges of the High Court or barristers of fifteen years' standing. The Court of Appeal (Civil Division) hears appeals from the decisions of: all three divisions of the High Court; the decisions of a County Court judge, except in bankruptcy; the decisions of the Employment Appeals Tribunal, Restrictive Practices Court, Lands Tribunal and certain other tribunals. Generally, an appeal must be heard by three members of the Court of Appeal. However, in certain cases, such as appeals from the county court, an appeal may be heard by two members.

(iv) The House of Lords as a court

The House of Lords, when sitting as a court, does so under the terms of the Appellate Jurisdiction Act 1876. This stipulates that, at an appeal, there must be present at least three of the following—the Lord Chancellor, the Lords of Appeal in Ordinary (often called 'law lords') and peers who hold or who held high judicial office (such as ex Lords Chancellors). By convention, peers who do not qualify under any of these heads do not attend meetings of the appellate committee. Law lords must have held high judicial office for at least two years or be practising barristers of not less than fifteen years' standing. The House of Lords hears appeals from the Court of Appeal (Civil Division) provided that leave has been granted by the Court of Appeal or the House itself. There are also the so-called 'leapfrog' appeals from the High Court established under the Administration of Justice Act 1960. Under this procedure, an appeal may be made in most cases direct from the High Court to the House of Lords if: the parties agree to it; the High Court grants a certificate, which it may do only if satisfied that a point of law is involved of general public importance and which relates to the construction of some piece of legislation, or a point on which it considers itself bound by a decision of the Court of Appeal or House of Lords (for the rules as to precedent, see 1.17); and the House of Lords itself gives leave to appeal.

1.11 The Court Structure—The Criminal Courts

(i) Magistrates' Courts

A Magistrates' Court is composed of justices of the peace. Each county is divided into petty sessional divisions, which may be regarded as the Magistrates' Courts districts. There are over 20,000 magistrates. They are not required to have legal qualifications, and they receive only expenses and an allowance for loss of earnings. For legal advice, they rely on their clerk, who will either be a solicitor or a barrister. In inner London and some other city areas, the magistrate is a stipendiary magistrate. He will be a barrister or solicitor of at least seven years' standing, and will be salaried.

As regards the criminal jurisdiction of the Magistrates' Courts, it is important to understand the difference between indictable and summary offences. The former are more serious and are tried in the Crown Court (*see* 1.11 (ii)); the latter are less serious and can only be tried by magistrates. There are, however, a large number of offences, which are 'either way' offences, which can be tried in either court. This is true of most offences under the Theft Act 1968 and of offences under the Trade Descriptions Act 1968. It is estimated that over 96 per cent of criminal cases are tried summarily. Magistrates cannot impose a sentence in excess of six months, except that they may impose consecutive sentences of up to a total of twelve months if the accused has been convicted of more than one offence triable 'either way'. The magistrates also act as examining magistrates prior to a case being heard on indictment in the Crown Court. They have to decide if there is enough evidence on which a reasonable jury, properly directed, could convict.

A person convicted by a Magistrates' Court may appeal to the Crown Court against conviction, sentence, or both, though he can only appeal against sentence if he had pleaded guilty. Appeal will instead be made to the Queen's Bench Division (*see* 1.10 (ii)) by defence or prosecution on the grounds that the magistrates were wrong in law or exceeded their jurisdiction.

(ii) The Crown Court

The Crown Court is divided into six circuits, each circuit covering a large number of towns. The Crown Courts themselves are divided into first-tier, second-tier and third-tier courts. In first-tier courts, sittings of the High Court (*see* 1.10 (ii)) are held for civil cases as well as of the Crown Court for criminal cases. First-tier and second-tier courts are served by High Court and circuit judges and by recorders. Third-tier courts are served only by circuit judges (*see* 1.10 (i)) or recorders, with the result that a few of the very serious crimes, such as murder, cannot be dealt with by them. Recorders are barristers or solicitors of at least ten years' standing.

The Crown Court has exclusive jurisdiction over all offences tried by a jury on indictment. It also has jurisdiction to deal with persons committed for sentence by Magistrates' Courts because their sentencing powers are inadequate, and to hear appeals from Magistrates' Courts against conviction or sentence. Lay magistrates cannot act as judges of the Crown Court by themselves, only with a High Court judge, circuit judge or recorder. They must be part of the Crown Court when it hears appeals from Magistrates' Courts and also when it is sentencing persons who have been committed for sentence by Magistrates' Courts, but the Lord Chancellor has the power to dispense with this requirement. The number of magistrates so sitting must be not less than two nor greater than four.

(iii) The Court of Appeal (Criminal Division)

The Court of Appeal (Criminal Division hears appeals from persons convicted in the Crown Court on indictment. The prosecution has no right of appeal against acquittal. The convicted person may appeal on any of the following grounds: without leave, against conviction on a question of law alone; with the leave of the division, or the trial judge, against conviction on a question of fact alone, or on a question of mixed fact and law; with the leave of the division, against conviction on any other ground which appears to the court to be sufficient; with the leave of the division, against sentence unless the sentence is one fixed by law. In an appeal against conviction, the court will allow the appeal if it thinks that the conviction was, under all the circumstances, 'unsafe or unsatisfactory', or that there was a wrong decision in point of law, or that there was a 'material irregularity' in the course of the trial. However, under the terms of the Criminal Appeal Act 1968, an appeal may be dismissed if the court is of the opinion that 'no miscarriage of justice has occurred', even though the ground of appeal was good. On appeal against sentence, the court may reduce or vary it, provided that the convicted person is not dealt with more severely in the original sentence.

(iv) The House of Lords

The House of Lords can hear an appeal by either the prosecution or the accused from a decision of the Court of Appeal (Criminal Division) or by a divisional court of the Queen's Bench Division (1.12) provided the court has certified that a point of law of general public importance is involved and that court or the House of Lords is satisfied that the point of law is one that should be considered; and either court has granted leave of appeal.

1.12 Courts with Civil and Criminal Jurisdiction

(i) Magistrates' Courts

These have a limited but varied civil jurisdiction which extends over the recovery of certain civil debts, such as income tax, electricity and gas charges, and rates; the grant and renewal of licences; and domestic proceedings. Appeals in civil proceedings generally lie to the Crown Court with a further, or alternative, appeal on a point of law to the Queen's Bench Division (*see* 1.10 (ii)). In appeals from hearings on domestic proceedings, the matter goes to the Family Division (*see* 1.10 (ii) with no alternative of appeal to the Crown Court.

(ii) Crown Court

The civil jurisdiction of the Crown Court itself is principally to hear appeals concerned with betting, gaming and liquor licensing.

(iii) Queen's Bench Division

This has appellate criminal jurisdiction to hear matters by way of case stated from the Magistrates' Courts or the Crown Court (when the Crown Court has itself acted in its appellate capacity). The appeal is heard by a divisional court of two or more judges, and an appeal can only be on the grounds that the original decision was wrong in law or in excess of jurisdiction.

1.13 The European Court of Justice

The European Court of Justice operates under the Treaties of the European Communities, that is to say, the Treaty of Rome, the Treaty of the European Coal and Steel Community and the Treaty of the European Atomic Energy Authority. The Court consists of judges appointed from each of the member states, and they are assisted by Advocates-General, a type of official unknown to the English legal system. It is his task to present the Court with a summary of the law as he judges it to be. Usually, the Court will accept the Advocate-General's submissions, but they need not do so, and do occasionally reject his submissions. The jurisdiction of the Court may be subdivided as follows:

(i) Matters concerning the conduct of member states or of Community institutions, such as hearing complaints brought by the Commission that a member state has failed to fulfil its obligations, as by not implementing a Directive (see 1.7)

(ii) Actions for compensation for wrongful damage caused by the Community institutions or their servants in the course of their duties.

(iii) Disputes between the Communities and their servants.

(iv) Matters of direct concern to litigants or prospective litigants in this country. This covers: preliminary rulings on the interpretation of the Treaties; preliminary rulings on the validity and interpretation of the regulations, directives, decisions and other acts of the institutions of the Communities; and preliminary rulings on the interpretation of certain statutes of bodies established by an act of the Council of Ministers. Where such a question is raised before a court in this country, that court may, if it considers that a decision on the question is necessary before it can give judgment, refer the matter to the European Court of Justice for a ruling. However, where such a point is raised before a court from which there is no appeal, such as the House of Lords, that court must generally refer the matter to the European Court. Once the European

Court has given its ruling on the interpretation of the particular law, it is then the responsibility of the local courts to apply that law as thus interpreted.

1.14 Certain Special Courts and Tribunals

(i) The Privy Council

The Judicial Committee of the Privy Council is the final court of appeal from the courts of some Commonwealth countries. The Committee is normally composed of five law lords (*see* 1.10 (iv)) but judges from Commonwealth countries also occasionally sit. The Privy Council also hears appeals against 'striking-off' from the disciplinary committees of the medical, dental and related professions.

(ii) The Restrictive Practices Court

The Restrictive Practices Court was established by the Restrictive Trade Practices Act 1956, now replaced by the Restrictive Trade Practices Act 1976. The legislation is designed to prevent businesses from entering into agreements which restrict competition or fix prices. The court investigates such agreements to determine if they are contrary to the public interest. The court also deals with questions of resale price maintenance under the Resale Prices Act 1976 and has acquired an additional jurisdiction under the Fair Trading Act 1973 (*see* Chapter 14 for a further discussion of this Act) to consider restrictive agreements in relation to services.

(iii) The Employment Appeals Tribunal

The Tribunal operates under the terms of the Employment Protection (Consolidation) Act 1978. Its jurisdiction is entirely appellate. It can hear appeals on points of law from industrial tribunals under legislation relating to the following: unfair dismissal, redundancy payments, equal pay, sex discrimination, contracts of employment, trade unions and employment protection.

(iv) The Lands Tribunal

The Lands Tribunal was established under the Lands Tribunal Act 1949. It hears: appeals from local valuation courts; cases for the assessment of compensation for the compulsory acquisition of land; applications for the variation, modification or discharge of restrictive convenants under the Law of Property Act 1925.

(v) Other Tribunals

A large number of different tribunals have been created to deal with matters arising under modern legislation, notably under social security legislation. The decision of a tribunal may be challenged by applying to the High Court for judicial review (*see* 1.10 (ii)). Supervision of tribunals is the function of the Council of Tribunals established by the Tribunals and Enquiries Act 1971.

1.15 Arbitration

A dispute may be referred to arbitration in one of three ways: by agreement out of court, by statute or by order of the court. The governing legislation is the Arbitration Acts 1950–79.

(i) Reference by Agreement out of Court

Particularly in commercial matters, the parties to a dispute may prefer to go straight to arbitration. Hence, they may agree before or after a dispute to refer it to arbitration. Many commercial contracts provide for such a reference as do various codes of practice initiated by trade associations. The terms of a contract may well require that disputes be referred for settlement to one of a number of institutions, such as the Court of Arbitration of the International Chamber of Commerce or the London International Arbitration Centre. In order to avoid disputes over the procedure, it has become common practice for arbitration clauses to refer to the United Nations Commission on International Trade Law Arbitration Rules. These Rules provide a framework of procedure which can avoid lengthy disputes on the operation of the arbitration. If a party to an arbitration agreement brings court proceedings, the court may try the case, but the other party may apply to the court for an order staying the proceedings. Where the arbitration is a 'domestic arbitration agreement', the court has a discretion to stay proceedings and will normally do so. In other cases, the court must stay the proceedings unless satisfied that the arbitration agreement is null and void, inoperative or incapable of being performed, or that there is not in fact any dispute between the parties with regard to the matter being referred. The normal position just outlined will not apply if the agreement contains a 'Scott v. Avery' clause. This is an agreement to refer a dispute to arbitration as a condition precedent to action in the courts. Since no right of action in the courts accrues until the arbitration had taken place, non-observance of the clause will provide a complete defence to a court action.

Normally, arbitration is by a single arbitrator. If provision is made for two, they may appoint an umpire and must do so if they cannot agree. The High Court has the power to appoint arbitrators and umpires in default of an appointment by the parties or arbitrators or other persons with the power of appointment. A judge of the Commercial Court may, if in all the circumstances he thinks fit, accept appointment as sole arbitrator or umpire in a case of a commercial character, provided the state of business in the High Court permits him to do so.

An award is final and binding unless the arbitration agreement provides otherwise, and there is no right of appeal to the courts except on a point of law. However, the High Court has power to remit the case for reconsideration. In addition, it may set aside an award where the arbitrator has misconducted himself in proceedings, or where the arbitration or award has been improperly procured.

An award may, by leave of the High Court, be enforced in the same way as a judgment or order of that court, and, where leave is granted, judgment may be entered in terms of the award. If this is done, the award can be enforced in any way allowed in the case of a judgment. Otherwise, the award is enforced by bringing a court action on the award as a contractual debt.

Appeal lies to the High Court on any question of law. Such appeal may be brought by any of the parties, but unless all the other parties consent the leave of the court must be obtained, and this can only be granted if the court is satisfied that the determination of the question of law could substantially affect the rights of one or more parties to the arbitration agreement. In The Nema (1982), the House of Lords held that leave to appeal should not be granted unless it is shown either that the arbitrator has misdirected himself in point of law or that the decision is such that it could have been reached by no reasonable person. Where the question of law concerns the construction of a contract in standard terms, leave should only be granted if the judge considers that a strong prima-facie case has been made out that the arbitrator was wrong in his construction. The test is even stricter where the question of law concerns the construction of a one-off contract. Here, leave should not be granted unless it is apparent to the judge, on a mere perusal of the arbitrator's reasoned award without hearing argument, that the meaning ascribed to the clause by the arbitrator is obviously wrong.

An appeal to the Court of Appeal from the High Court is only possible if: the High Court certifies the question of law to which the decision relates as one of general public importance, or as one which, for some other reason should be considered by the Court of Appeal, and if the High Court or the Court of Appeal itself gives leave to appeal. An appeal may be made to the House of Lords only with the leave of the Court of Appeal or the House itself.

The High Court may determine any question of law arising in the course of a reference to arbitration on the application of any of the parties to the reference. However, unless all the parties consent to the application, the court must not entertain it unless it has the consent of the arbitrators or umpire and it is satisfied that the determination of the question might substantially reduce the parties' costs and could substantially affect the rights of one or more parties to the arbitration agreement. Notwithstanding any agreement of the parties, the High Court is not bound to entertain the application of the parties. Instead, the judge should only entertain it in exceptional circumstances, for example, where the preliminary point of law, if rightly decided, would determine the whole dispute. Subject to the same restrictions as apply to an appeal from the High Court's determination of an appeal following an award, an appeal to the Court of Appeal lies from a decision of the High Court on a preliminary point of law.

Under the Arbitration Act, the High Court must not grant leave to appeal with respect to a question of law, nor may an application for the determination of a preliminary point of law be made without the consent of all parties to the arbitration, if the parties have made a written agreement excluding the right of appeal or the right to a preliminary determination. Such an exclusion agreement may relate to a particular award or may be more general in nature. However, in the case of a purely domestic arbitration, an exclusion agreement is only operative if entered into after the commencement of the relevant arbitration. The same limitation applies where the contract relates to an insurance contract or to a commodity contract, unless the award or question of law relates to a contract which is expressed to be governed by a law other than English law.

(ii) Reference by Statute

Many statutes provide for the reference of certain types of dispute to arbitration. The provisions of the Arbitration Acts apply to statutory references, with certain exceptions, unless the particular statute provides otherwise. Thus, everything, said in 1.15 (i) as to the appointment of arbitrators and umpires, the proceedings, the enforcement of awards and resort to the courts is generally applicable to a statutory reference. However, review by the courts of an award, or of a question of law, in a statutory arbitration cannot be ousted by an agreement between the parties.

(iii) Reference by Order of the Court

Under the provisions of the Supreme Court Act 1981, the High Court may refer any case within its jurisdiction, or any particular issue in such a case, to be tried by an official referee (a circuit judge assigned for such business), a senior officer of the court, such as a master, or (where the issue is of a technical nature requiring specialist knowledge) a special referee. A reference to such an arbitrator can be made even against the wishes of the parties and is particularly likely to be made if: the prolonged examination of documents, or scientific or local examination, is required; or the examination of accounts is required. The award of the arbitrator is entered as a judgment in court proceedings and is binding as such. In certain circumstances, an appeal lies to the Court of Appeal. In addition, the High Court has similar power under the same Act to refer to the same persons as previously mentioned any question in a case or matter before it for inquiry or report. The report may be adopted wholly or partially by the court and, if so adopted, is as binding as a judgment to the same effect.

1.16 Ombudsmen and Trade Conciliation

A number of professional associations have appointed independent ombudsmen who are empowered to settle disputes within their remit. The first such was the Insurance Ombudsman who was established as part of the Insurance Ombudsman Bureau in 1981. This provides a free conciliation service for personal policyholders of member companies. This was followed in 1986 by the Banking Ombudsman who is enabled to make binding awards up to £100,000 in regard to customer complaints brought against the clearing banks and the Scottish banks. The first statutory ombudsman is that established by the Building Societies Act 1986.

Acting under the terms of the Fair Trading Act 1973, the Director General of Fair Trading has encouraged trade associations to establish codes of practice, some of which include conciliation and arbitration schemes for consumers.

1.17 The Doctrine of Precedent

It is fundamental to the way the English legal system operates that lower courts are bound by decisions reached by higher courts. If it were anything different, then the law would be hopelessly uncertain. The hierarchy involved in the doctrine or precedent is as follows.

(i) The House of Lords

Until 1966, the House of Lords was bound by its own decisions. In that year, however, the Lord Chancellor announced that

'too rigid adherence to precedent may lead to injustice in a particular case and also unduly restrict the proper development of the law. They propose therefore to modify their present practice and, while treating former decisions of this House as normally binding, to depart from a previous decision when it appears right to do so.'

(ii) The Court of Appeal (Civil Division)

The Court of Appeal (Civil Division) is bound by its own previous decisions and by those of the House of Lords. However, it is not bound by one of its own previous decisions if that decision is inconsistent with a decision of the Privy Council or the House of Lords.

(iii) The Court of Appeal (Criminal Division)

The Court of Appeal (Criminal Division) is bound by the decisions of the House of Lords and normally by its own decisions. However, an ordinary court of three judges may deviate from previous decisions more easily than the Civil Division because the liberty of an individual may often be at stake. A full court, which generally consists of five judges instead of the usual three, can overrule previous decisions of this division.

(iv) Divisional Courts

It will be recalled from 1.10 and 1.12 above that the Queen's Bench Division, Family Division and Chancery Division can hear appeals in what are called 'divisional courts'. As far as precedent is concerned, such courts are, in civil cases, bound by the House of Lords, the Court of Appeal (Civil Division) but not, since the decision in *R. v. Greater Manchester Coroner, ex p Tal* (1985), by its own decisions. Divisional courts will, though, follow their own decisions where possible but will not do so where convinced that the earlier decision was wrong. In criminal cases, the position may be regarded as the same though there is some argument for saying that since, under the terms of the Administration of Justice Act 1960, there is an appeal direct from the Divisional Court to the House of Lords, that the Divisional Court is not bound by the decisions of the Court of Appeal (Criminal Division).

(v) High Court

A High Court judge is bound by decisions of the House of Lords and the Court of Appeal, but not by other judgments of the High Court, though these will be treated as of great persuasive value.

(vi) Crown Court

A judge sitting in the Crown Court on a criminal case is bound by decisions made in criminal matters by the House of Lords and Court of Appeal (Criminal Division), but not, according to the decision in *R. v. Colyer* (1974) by decisions of the Divisional Court. When sitting on a civil case, the Crown Court is bound by decisions of the House of Lords, the Court of Appeal (Civil Division) and the High Court. A Crown Court is not bound by another Crown Court, though its decisions will again be persuasive.

(vii) County Court and Magistrates' Court

Judgments given in these courts do not give rise to binding precedents, if only because they are very seldom reported. They are, however, bound by decisions of the courts considered above.

(viii) Privy Council

The decisions of the Privy Council do not bind itself and are only persuasive authority in English law because it only hears appeals from other Commonwealth countries.

(ix) The European Court of Justice

In those areas where the European Court of Justice is the ultimate court (*see* 1.13), its decisions bind all English courts. The European Court does not itself observe the doctrine of precedent, but it does lean in favour of consistency with previous decisions.

1.17 Law Reports

The system of precedent described in the previous paragraph depends on a good system of law reports, that is to say, publications which contain the more important decisions given by the courts. Although law reporting has been in existence since at least the time of Bracton in the thirteenth century, it was not until 1865 that law reporting became formalized. A body was established called the Incorporated Council of Law Reporting, which is a joint committee of the Inns of Court, the Law Society and the Bar Council. Their reports are simply known as the Law Reports and they have priority in court because the judge who heard the case sees and revises the report before publication. In 1953, the Council began to publish the reports on a weekly basis in what are known as the *Weekly*

Law Reports. There are in addition a large number of private publications, of which the *All England Law Reports* are probably the best known.

1.18 The Legal Profession

(i) Barristers

Barristers conduct cases in court and generally draft the pleadings which outline the way in which a case is to be conducted. Barristers have an exclusive right to be heard in the House of Lords, the Court of Appeal, the three divisions of the High Court with the exception of certain bankruptcy matters; and only barristers can appear in the Crown Court except in those cases which have come to it by way of appeal from a Magistrates' Court or where the accused has been committed to the Crown Court for sentence. Both barristers and solicitors may appear in the County Court and the Magistrates' Court. Call to the English Bar is within the prerogative of the four Inns of Court: Lincoln's Inn, Gray's Inn, the Inner Temple and the Middle Temple. The Inns are unincorporated societies governed by Masters, who are judges or senior barristers, and call to the Bar is by the Benchers. The Bar as a profession is represented by the Bar Council. Barristers cannot form partnerships, but work together in chambers, sharing rent and expenses.

(ii) Solicitors

A solicitor deals with the general public and is very much a businessman who advises clients on legal, financial and related matters. Much of his work relates to probate, the drafting of wills and the like, and to conveyances of land. The solicitor had now lost his monopoly of conveyancing which can also be carried on by licensed conveyancers. The distinction between barristers and solicitors is most marked in the matter of litigation. The solicitor's function is to prepare the case, ascertain the facts, and arrange for the presence of the necessary witnesses and any documents which may be required. He also conducts any disputes over costs which may be awarded after judgment. Regarding advocacy, the solicitor has a right to be heard in County Courts and Magistrates' Courts, and may also be heard in bankruptcy matters in the High Court and Divisional Court. Unlike barristers, solicitors are normally members of a partnership or are employed by a partnership. The Law Society is responsible for this branch of the legal profession.

(iii) Legal Executives

Legal executives are qualified legal assistants in solicitors' offices who, while working under the control and authority of a solicitor, possess a high degree of expertise in their chosen field. Their professional body is the Institute of Legal Executives. Fellows of the Institute have a right of audience before the County Court in regard to unopposed applications for an adjournment, and an application for judgment by consent where there is no question as to the applicant's entitlement to judgment or its terms.

1.19 Law Officers

(i) The Lord Chancellor

The Lord Chancellor is the Speaker of the House of Lords and the head of the judiciary in that he is the chief judge in the country and also controls the administration of the courts of law. He advises the Crown on the appointment of judges, is responsible for the appointment of Justices of the Peace, and advises on the appointment of Recorders and Stipendiary Magistrates. Unlike the Speaker of the House of Commons, he may take part in debates and may vote in all divisions, but he has no casting vote. The office is political and the holder sits in the Cabinet.

(ii) The Attorney-General

The Attorney-General is almost always a member of the House of Commons and will be a member of the governing party. He represents the Crown in civil matters and prosecutes in important criminal cases. He is the head of the English Bar, and points of professional etiquette are referred to him. He also advises government departments on legal matters, and the courts on matters of parliamentary privilege. He can institute litigation on behalf of the public, for example, to stop a public nuisance or the commission of a crime. Generally, individuals do not have a sufficient interest in law (know as *locus standi*) to bring an action in such cases. Where a person does not have sufficient interest to initiate proceedings himself, he may ask the Attorney-General to take proceedings. If the Attorney-General does act in this way, the action is known as a 'relator action', and the relator, that is to say the private individual, is responsible for the court costs. If the Attorney-General refuses to act, no court can compel him to do so.

(iii) The Solicitor-General

Like the Attorney-General, the Solicitor-General is almost always a member of the government party in the House of Commons. Despite his title, he is a barrister. His duties are similar to those of the Attorney-General and he is in many ways his deputy. The Law Officers Act 1944 provides that any functions authorized by the Attorney-General may be discharged by the Solicitor-General if the office is vacant, of if he is unable to act because of absence or illness, or where the Attorney-General authorizes the Solicitor-General to act in any particular manner. Both law officers are precluded from private practice.

(iv) The Director of Public Prosecutions

The Prosecution of Offences Act 1985 states that the Director of Public Prosecutions is to be appointed by the Attorney-General and must be a barrister or solicitor of at least ten years' standing. His functions are listed in s.3 of that Act as follows:

(*a*) To take over the conduct of all criminal proceedings (except in relation to proceedings specified by the Attorney-General) instituted on behalf of a police force.

(*b*) To institute and have the conduct of criminal proceedings in any case where it appears to him that:

1. the importance or difficulty of the case makes it appropriate that proceedings should be instituted by him; or
2. it is otherwise appropriate for proceedings to be instituted by him.

(*c*) To take over the conduct of all binding over proceedings instituted on behalf of a police force.

(*d*) To take over the conduct of all proceedings begun by summons issued under s.3 of the Obscene Publications Act 1959 (forfeiture of obscene articles).

(*e*) To give, to such extent as he considers appropriate, advice to police forces on all matters relating to criminal offences.

(*f*) To appear for the prosecution, when directed by the court to do so, on any appeal under:

1. section 1 of the Administration of Justice Act 1960 (appeal from the High Court in criminal cases);
2. Part I or Part II of the Criminal Appeal Act 1968 (appeals from the Crown Court to the criminal division of the Court of Appeal and thence to the House of Lords); or
3. section 108 of the Magistrates' Court Act 1980 (right of appeal to Crown Court) as it applies by virtue of subsection (5) of s.12 of the Contempt of Court Act 1981, to orders made under s.12 (contempt of Magistrates' Courts).

(*g*) To discharge such other functions as may from time to time be assigned to him by the Attorney-General.

(v) Crown Prosecutors

Crown prosecutors were established by the Prosecution of Offences Act 1985. The Act gives them all the powers of the Director of Public Prosecutions as listed in the preceding paragraph, but they can only exercise those powers under the direction of the Director. The Act provides that Crown prosecutors shall have in any court the rights of audience enjoyed by solicitors (*see* 1.18 (ii) and may also be granted additional rights by the Lord Chancellor as to appearing in the Crown Court.

2 Contract

2.1 The Categories of Contract

Contracts may be broadly divided into two categories. A specialty contract, alternatively known as a contract by deed, is a written promise which is signed, sealed and delivered. Generally speaking, no further requirements are needed for such a contract to be fully enforceable. For present purposes, this is a category of relatively minor importance, and it is not discussed further in this chapter. The most important category is the simple contract. For such a contract to be enforceable, the following conditions must be fulfilled:

(i) Parties must have legal capacity.
(ii) There must be offer and acceptance of that offer.
(iii) There must be an intention to create legal relations.
(iv) There must be consideration.

It should be appreciated that these are requirements which have been developed as common law principles, and they are not to be found in any statute.

2.2 Legal Capacity

Where an agreement is entered into by a mentally disordered or drunken person at a time when he could not understand the nature of the contract, he can avoid the contract provided his state was known, or should have been known, to the other side. However, any such person will be required to pay for necessaries.

(i) Minors

A minor is a person who has not yet reached eighteen, Family Law Reform Act 1969, s.1. At common law, a minor is obliged to pay for necessaries and he is also bound by a contract of service or apprenticeship. Such a contract, however, when construed as a whole must be of such a nature that it is substantially for the minor's advantage. A minor is also bound, unless he repudiates it during infancy or within a reasonable time of reaching his majority, by a contract under which he acquires an interest in some subject matter of a permanent nature, for example, a subject matter to which continuous or recurring obligations are incident. The most obvious example is a contract for a lease. A minor cannot take a legal estate in land (Law of Property Act 1925, s.1 (6); Settled Land Act 1925, s.27 (1)) but a lease which is for a term of years does convey to him an 'equitable' title (that is, something short of a full legal title) for the agreed period. In all other cases, a contract made by a minor is ineffective unless he elects to confirm it after his majority. The Infants Relief Act 1874 used to bar ratification of such contracts, but this Act was repealed by the Minors' Contracts Act 1987. The 1874 Act also used to provide that certain contracts made by a minor were absolutely void, so that they could not even be ratified on majority, but this provision too was repealed by the 1987 Act.

The Minors' Contracts Act also provides that where a contract cannot be enforced against a minor, or he repudiates the contract, because he was a minor when the contract was made, this does not affect the validity of any guarantee given in respect of that contract. A further provision in the Act stipulates that, where a minor has acquired property under a contract which is unenforceable against him, or which is enenforceable against him because of his minority, he may be required by the court where it is 'just and equitable' to return the property, or property representing that which he has acquired.

(ii) Companies

Where a company has been incorporated under the Companies Act 1985, it can only pursue those objects which are set out in its memorandum of association. A contract which relates to an object not defined expressly or by implication in the memorandum is void. However, the Act also provides, by virtue of a provision first contained in the European Communities Act 1972, that anyone dealing in good faith with a company shall be entitled to rely on a transaction decided on by the directors of the company, even though it is outside the capacity of the company, as though it actually were within its capacity.

2.3 Offer and Acceptance

It is a necessary prerequisite to a binding contract that one party should have made a firm offer and that that offer should have received an unequivocal acceptance. An offer must, however, be distinguished from what is usually called 'an invitation to treat'. An invitation to treat is not an offer, and so cannot be accepted so as to give rise to a binding contract. For instance, the display of goods in a shop is not an offer by the shopkeeper to sell: it is an invitation to shoppers to make an offer to buy which the shopkeeper can accept or reject at his discretion (*Pharmaceutical Society of Great Britain v. Boots Cash Chemists*, 1953; *Fisher v. Bell*, 1961). It is for this reason that a shopper can never demand to buy goods which are accidentally priced lower than their true price (though the circumstances may be such as to show a false pricing offence, see Chapter 10).

Example

An enquiry about a parcel of land sent by telegraph said: 'Will you sell us Bumper Hall Pen. Telegraph lowest cash price.' The reply was that the lowest price was £900, and this elicited the response: 'We agree to buy Bumper Hall Pen for £900 asked by you.'

Held: The statement as to the lowest price was not an offer to sell, but merely a statement of what the price would be if the owners were prepared to sell.

(Harvey v. Facey, 1893)

(i) Rules Governing Acceptance

Acceptance may be oral, written or implied by conduct. It must also be absolute and unqualified and, once acceptance is complete, it cannot be withdrawn. Because the acceptance must be absolute and unqualified, it is the case that a counter offer or a conditional acceptance automatically rejects the original offer which cannot be revived by a purported subsequent acceptance.

Example

A farm was offered for sale at £1000. A counter offer was made at £950, but two days later the intending buyer offered the original £1000. The seller refused to sell.

Held: No binding contract had come into existence since the counter offer of £950 had destroyed the original offer to sell which could not be revived by the second offer to buy for the full asking price.

(Hyde v. Wrench, 1840)

However, a mere enquiry is not a counter offer. A company offered to sell iron at £2 a tonne. The company to whom this offer was made asked if the sellers would accept £2 for delivery over two months, or, if not, the longest limit available. No reply was received and a telegram was then sent accepting the original offer. It was held that the request for information was only that and was not a counter offer. The original offer could still therefore be accepted.

Where an offer is accepted 'subject to contract', this indicates that the parties are not prepared to be bound until a formal contract is prepared and signed by them (*Eccles v. Bryant and Pollock*, 1948). Where in a written agreement, the words 'provisional agreement' are used, the courts are likely to construe this as a binding agreement which is later to be replaced by a formal contract.

In the so-called 'battle of the forms', each party purports to accept the other party's offer but each does so on his own terms and conditions of contract. In fact, each such acceptance amounts to a counter offer, since it is not an unqualified acceptance. In *Butler Machine Tools Co. Ltd v. Ex-Cell-O Corporation (England) Ltd* (1979), sellers quoted a price for certain machinery. That offer was stated to be subject to certain terms and conditions which 'shall prevail over any terms and conditions in the buyer's order'. The buyers placed an order on their own terms and incorporated at the bottom of the order was a tear-off acknowledgement of receipt of order which stated: 'We accept your order on the terms and conditions stated thereon.' The sellers returned this tear-off slip. The Court of Appeal held that the buyers' order was a counter-offer which destroyed the original offer. However, the sellers by completing and returning the slip had accepted that counter-offer. If the seller had not returned the slip, then the probable result would have been that there would have been no contract until the goods were delivered and accepted by the buyer. If the seller had not attempted to reimpose his own terms, then the contract would have been on the buyer's terms. It was suggested by Lord Denning in that case that there may be circumstances in the 'battle of the forms' where, if the parties were under the impression that they had reached a binding agreement, it would be more sensible to try to construct a contract out of both sets of terms.

(ii) Lapse of Offer

An offer must be accepted within a reasonable time. If the acceptance is made after the lapse of a reasonable time, the offer is deemed to have lapsed and so cannot be accepted. Just what is a reasonable time is a question of fact to be decided in all the circumstances of the case.

Example

A person offered to buy shares in June and this offer was accepted in November. *Held*: This was after a reasonable time had passed and that the offer had therefore lapsed.

(*Ramsgate Victoria Hotel Co. v. Montefiore*, 1866)

Example

An offer was made in January to take over certain liabilities. That offer was accepted in November.
Held: About four months was a reasonable time and that, since longer had elapsed before acceptance, the offer had lapsed and could not be accepted. If a party promises to hold an offer for a certain time, and the other side gives nothing in return for that promise, it can be revoked at any time before the deadline.

(*Chemco Leasing v. Rediffusion*, 1987)

(iii) Communication of Acceptance

Where a contract is made face to face, then the rule is that the acceptance must reach the person making the offer. This has been extended to those cases where, with the aid of technology, the parties are to all intents and purposes negotiating face to face.

Example

A London company telexed another company in Amsterdam with an offer to buy goods from them. The latter accepted the offer also by telex received in London. *Held*: The contract was made in London because that was where the acceptance was received.

(*Entores Ltd v. Miles Far East Corpn*, 1955)

The same decision was reached in *Brinkibon v. Stahag Stahl und Stahlwaren-handelgesellschaft* (1983) where an offer was made by telex in Vienna and accepted by a telex sent from London. The contract was held to be made in Vienna.

The rule that an acceptance must be communicated to the offeror will not apply if it is clear from the circumstances of the case that the person making the offer is waiving any right to a personal reply, and is subject to any particular mode of acceptance imposed by him. The rule is also displaced where communication is through the post. In such a case, the acceptance is complete when the letter is posted even though it might not reach its intended destination.

Example

A letter offering to sell goods was posted on 2 September. On 5 September, the buyer posted his acceptance. It reached the seller on 9 September. The day before, however, the seller had sold the goods to a third party.
Held: A binding contract had been made when the letter of acceptance was posted on 5 September.

(Adams v. Lindsell, 1818)

However, if the party making the offer stipulates that the acceptance must reach him, then even if the letter of acceptance is posted, there is no acceptance until that letter is received (*Holwell Securities Ltd v. Hughes*, 1974).

(iv) Revocation of Offer

An offer can be revoked at any time before acceptance, provided the party making the offer has not entered into a binding agreement to keep it open for a specific time (that is, has been given consideration in return for his promise to keep the offer open, *see* 2.5). To be effective, however, that revocation must be communicated to the other side. It can be sufficient for knowledge of the revocation to be obtained indirectly. An agreement was made to sell property, the offer to be kept open until Friday. On Thursday, the buyer learned that the seller was intending to sell the property to a third party. That day he accepted the offer. It was held that he could not accept the offer because by then he knew that it had in effect been revoked (*Dickinson v. Dodds*, 1876).

2.4 Intention to Create Legal Relations

It must be clear from the terms of the agreement that the parties intended to create a binding legal relationship. It will normally be the case that purely domestic or social arrangements (such as an agreement to entertain friends for dinner) will not be intended to create a legal relationship. A contract between businesses, however, will be intended to be binding unless they expressly agree otherwise.

Example

The relevant document stated: 'This arrangement is not entered into . . . as a formal or legal agreement and shall not be subject to legal jurisdiction in the Law Courts . . . but is only a definite expression and record of the purpose and intention of the parties concerned.'
Held: The intention to create a legal relationship had been expressly excluded. The pools companies also place on their coupons statements to the effect that the relationship subsisting between them and their clients is binding in honour only.

(Rose, Frank & Co. v. Crompton Bros, 1923)

2.5 Consideration

The requirement that a contract must be supported by consideration means that each party must give something, or do something, to or for the other. In a contract for the sale of goods, for example, the buyer gives money, the seller provides goods. It has long been established that the consideration provided by one party need not be anything like commensurate in value with the consideration received.

Example

A widow had been promised by her husband that she should have the house in which she lived or £100. The executors promised to convey the house to her provided she paid £1 a year in rent and kept the house in good repair. The executors breached this agreement.

Held: The court said that £1 a year rent was 'something of value in the eyes of the law'.

(Thomas v. Thomas, 1842)

It follows from decisions such as this that if a person makes an offer, for example, to sell land, and further offers to keep the main offer open for a set time, the subsidiary offer can be converted into a binding contract by the provision of some nominal sum (*see* 2.3 (iv)).

(i) Categories of Consideration

Consideration is usually divided into the following categories: executory, executed and past. Only the latter is insufficient. Executory consideration arises where a promise is made in return for a promise, as where the buyer and seller of goods agree on the future delivery of goods on credit. The whole transaction remains for the future. Executed consideration would arise where, for example, a person advertises a reward for the return of a lost dog. The finder of the dog accepts the offer by returning it and the performance of the required act constitutes the required, and in the circumstances executed, consideration. An example of past consideration is provided by Re *McArdle* (1951). A number of children, by their father's will, were entitled to a house after their mother's death. During the mother's life, one of the children and his wife lived with her in the house. The wife made various improvements to the house, and at a later date all the children signed a document addressed to her, stating that 'in consideration of your carrying out certain alterations and improvements to the property, we hereby agree that the executors shall repay to you from the estate, when distributed, the sum of £488 in settlement of the amount spent on such improvements'. The Court of Appeal held that, as all the work on the house had in fact been completed before the document was signed, this was a case of past consideration and that the document could not be supported as a binding contract.

(ii) Agreeing to Perform Existing Duties

If a party agrees no more than to do what he is already contractually obliged to do, or is obliged to do by law, then this promise to do such thing is not consideration.

Example

A ship's captain promised the remaining crew that if they worked the ship home, they would be paid the wages of those who had deserted.
Held: The seamen were bound to do this anyway, they had given no consideration for the promise.

(Stilk v. Myrick, 1809)

Example

A defendant was sued by the plaintiff, an attorney, for 6 guineas which he alleged had been promised to him for attending as a witness in a case.
Held: The duty to attend was imposed by law and so no consideration had been given for the promise.

(Collins v. Godefroy, 1831)

However, if something more is promised then that will amount to consideration.

Example

Mine owners who feared violence asked for police protection greater than the authorities thought necessary.
Held: The company were bound by their promise to pay since the police had provided additional protection. This is why football clubs have to pay for the police presence at their grounds.

(Glasbrook Bros Ltd v. Glamorgan C.C., 1925)

It is also the case that payment of a smaller sum than that owed under a contract is not consideration for payment of the whole sum, unless there is some consideration for the smaller sum, such as an agreement to pay the smaller sum now instead of paying the full sum some time hence when it actually falls due.

Example

Builders carried out work for the defendants who held up payment knowing that the builders were close to bankruptcy. The defendants offered £300 in satisfaction of a debt of £482. The builders accepted this and then sued for the balance.
Held: By putting unfair pressure on the builders, the defendants could not hold that there was consideration for accepting the smaller sum, and so the builders were entitled to the balance.

(D & C Builders v. Rees, 1965)

(iii) The Position of Third Parties

The doctrine of privity of contract means those who are not the actual parties to the contract have no right to sue on it.

Example

A father entered into an agreement with his son's father-in-law whereby each was to pay a sum of money to the son. The father-in-law never paid and the son brought an action against the executors of his father-in-law's estate.

Held: Even though the contract was for the benefit of the son, he was not a party to the contract and could not sue on it.

(Tweddle v. Atkinson, 1861)

Example

A coal merchant contracted to sell his business to his nephew, one of the terms of sale being that the nephew would pay his wife, if she survived him, £5 a week. The nephew paid just one week's instalment to the widow then refused to pay. *Held*: She had no personal right to sue on the contract to which she was a third party.

(Beswick v. Beswick, 1968)

(iv) Promissory Estoppel

The doctrine of promissory estoppel has been used as a way of avoiding some of the harsher aspects of the rules as to consideration.

Examples

In *Central London Property Trust Ltd v. High Trees House Ltd* (1947), the plaintiffs leased a block of flats to the defendants. The following January, because of the war, the plaintiffs reduced the rent. Early in 1945, the plaintiffs claimed that they were entitled to the full rent agreed in 1939. The court agreed that they could claim the full rent for the future, but that they could not claim it retrospectively even though there was no consideration for the reduction. The rule adopted in the case was that where A makes a promise to B intending legal consequences and that B should act on the promise, which he does, then A should not be allowed to go back on his promise and enforce his strict legal rights with retrospective effect. The doctrine, however, acts only as a defence and not as a cause of action. In *Combe v. Combe* (1951), a wife started proceedings for divorce and obtained a decree nisi. The husband then promised to allow her £100 per annum free of tax as permanent maintenance. The wife did not apply to the Divorce Court for maintenance, but this action was not at the husband's request. The decree was made absolute. The annual payments were never made and the wife sued on the promise. The Court of Appeal dismissed the wife's action:

'The principle stated in High Trees . . . does not create new causes of action where none existed before. It only prevents a party from insisting upon his strict legal rights, when it would have been unjust to allow him to enforce them, having regard to the dealings which have taken place between the parties.'

2.6 The Terms of a Contract

Those terms which the parties actually agree on are known as the express terms of the contract. The contract may also, however, contain implied terms which are those terms implied by law. Statute sometimes implied terms into a contract, as is the case with contracts for the sale of goods (see Chapter 3). Terms will also be implied if they are customary in the trade (*Harley & Co. v. Nagata*, 1917) and the courts will also imply such terms as may properly be implied from all the circumstances of the case. For instance, the courts will imply a term where this is necessary to give the contract business efficacy.

Examples

In *The Moorcock* (1889), the contract permitted the plaintiff to unload his ship at the defendants' jetty. The court implied a term to the effect that the defendants agreed that the river bed, so far as reasonable care could provide, was not in a condition which would damage the ship when she grounded at low tide, as both parties realized she would. Under doctrine of business efficacy, the courts have implied into a contract between a driving school and a customer that any car provided would be covered by insurance (*British School of Motoring v. Simms*, 1971) and that where a contract for the transfer of a footballer provided that an extra sum should be paid when he had scored 20 goals that he was to be given a reasonable opportunity to score the goals (*Bournemouth and Boscombe Athletic Football Club Co. Ltd v. Manchester United Football Club Ltd*, 1980).

(i) Incorporating the Terms of a Contract

The mere fact that parties have drafted a set of terms does not of itself mean that those terms are a part of the contract. Before this can be said to have been done, those terms must have been incorporated into the contract. This is most easily achieved by proof that the other side signed a document which contained the particular terms.

Example

A contract for ordering an automatic slot machine was signed by a customer.
Held: She was bound by the terms even though she had not read them. If the document containing the terms is unsigned, then it is necessary to show that the other party had had notice of the terms.

(*L'Estrange v. Graucob*, 1934)

Example

A couple arrived at a hotel and made their booking at reception. In their room, there was a notice containing certain terms.
Held The notice was presented to the parties after the contract had been made and thus had no effect.

(*Olley v. Marlborough Court Ltd*, 1949)

Example

A driver obtained a ticket from an automatic machine before entering a car park. The court ruled that the driver had accepted the offer of a space for his car when he placed his money in the appropriate slot.
Held: The terms on the ticket came after the contract was made and so did not bind the driver.

(*Thornton v. Shoe Lane Parking Ltd*, 1971)

It has yet to be decided whether a party is bound by terms in a contract, even if they are presented to him before the contract is made, when he is incapable of withdrawing from the contract. A person at the front of a line of cars queuing for a car park space at an automatic barrier effectively has no choice but to proceed with the contract, since he can hardly turn back if he decides that he does not like the particular terms. The question was not specifically answered in *Thornton v. Shoe Lane Parking Ltd*, though the court did seem to be of the opinion that a person would not be bound in such circumstances.

It will always be a question of fact as to whether terms have been brought to the attention of the other side. However, it seems clear that it is insufficient if they are reproduced on a document which cannot be regarded as contractual.

Example

The plaintiff hired deckchairs from a pile stacked near a notice. A person hiring the deckchairs was given tickets which he retained for inspection.
Held: The terms printed on the tickets were not part of the contract since no reasonable person would have considered that the tickets were anything other than a receipt for the money.

(*Chapelton v. Barry UDC*, 1940)

It should be appreciated that it is not necessary to reproduce the full, or any, terms of the contract on the particular document. Terms can be incorporated by reference; that is to say, it would be acceptable for the document to say that the agreement is subject to a company's terms. Just such a phrase is often used, commonly with a rider to the effect that a copy of these terms is available on request. Provided the notification of this incorporation follows the rules set out above, then the terms are incorporated into the contract. This is so even if the other party does not ask for a copy of the contract (*Smith v. South Wales Switchgear Ltd*, 1978).

(ii) Notice of Onerous Terms

In the case of *Spurling v. Bradshaw*, it was said, without a specific decision being made on the point, that where a clause was particularly onerous or unusual, it should be in some way especially drawn to the attention of the other party otherwise it would not be binding. This was first made the actual grounds for a decision by the Court of Appeal in *Interfoto Picture Library Ltd v. Stiletto Visual Programmes Ltd* (1987). Following a telephone conversation, certain pictures were delivered by hand in a bag. The contract was made when the arrival of the bag was acknowledged over the telephone. One bag also contained a delivery note on which were printed the terms of the contract. One of these terms was agreed by the court to be exceptionally onerous. It was held that although the delivery note was part of the contract, this particular term had no effect because it had not been drawn specifically to the relevant party's attention.

(iii) Categories of Contract Term

It is traditional to divide the terms of a contract into conditions and warranties. A condition is a major term of a contract, while a warranty is a minor one. The precise relevance of this will be made clear when dealing with remedies for breach (see page 37). Simply because a term is called a condition of the contract does not mean that it is a condition in the strict sense (*Schuler AG v. Wickman Machine Tool Sales Ltd*, 1974). If a term has been classified as a condition of warranty (as by the Sale of Goods Act, see Chapter 3), that classification will of course be applied. Again, if a term has been previously classified by the courts in a binding case, that categorization will be followed (*The Mihalis Angelos*, 1971). If neither aid to interpretation is present, the courts will instead construe the term in the light of the intention of the parties. However, in *Hong Kong Fir Shipping Co. Ltd v. Kawasaki Kisen Kaisha* (1962), it was said that, it there is no precise statutory or judicial classification of the contract term, then the term will be classified as an intermediate term, and the remedies available to the injured party will depend on the gravity of the breach.

(iv) Exclusion and Limitation Clauses

An exclusion clause is a clause by which a party seeks to exclude his liability for breach of contract. A limitation clause is one whereby a party seeks to limit his liability in the event of breach. The courts have never been favourably disposed to such clauses, particularly exclusion clauses, and have always taken the line that they must be strictly construed against the party in whose favour the clause was drawn, particularly if the clause seeks to exclude liability for negligence.

Example

The plaintiff hired a cycle on the terms that 'nothing in this agreement shall render the owners liable for any personal injuries to the riders of the machine hired.'
Held: While this clause would protect the defendants from liability in contract, it would not protect them against liability in negligence.
(*White v. John Warwick & Co. Ltd*, 1953)

Example

The relevant clause ran: 'The company is not responsible for damage caused by fire to customers' cars on the premises'.
Held: Although the court held that the term was not in fact part of the contract (*see* 2.6 (i)), it was held that although the defendants' liability could only be in negligence, the clause did not cover them since it could be read simply as a warning that the defendants would not be responsible for a fire caused without negligence.
(*Hollier v. Rambler (AMC) Ltd*, 1972)
In *Smith v. South Wales Switchgear Ltd*, it was said that a clause would be apt to cover liability in negligence only if that word, or some acceptable synonym was used.
While these cases remain valid precedents, much of the work of controlling exclusion and limitation clauses has been taken over by the Unfair Contract Terms Act 1977. With regard to negligence liability, the simple rule laid down by s.2 is that no term can exclude or restrict such liability where the negligence has resulted in death or personal injury. Where the negligence results in any other

category of loss, such as damage to personal property, then an exclusion or limitation clause will be valid if it passes the test of reasonableness (*see below*). Section 4 provides that a consumer cannot be made to indemnify another party for that other party's negligence except where the indemnity clause is reasonable. Section 5 provides that where consumer goods are defective because of the negligence of a manufacturer or distributor, nothing in any guarantee can exclude or restrict liability for loss or damage caused by the negligence.

A separate set of rules is laid down in s.3 where the contract is on written standard terms or is made with a consumer. If such a contract contains any of the following terms, such term will be valid only if reasonable: clauses seeking to exclude or restrict liability for breach; clauses seeking to allow a substantially different performance from that which was reasonably expected; and clauses seeking to allow no performance at all.

Section 11 of the Act says that whenever the reasonableness test is applied, it is assumed to be unreasonable until the contrary is proved. The person relying on the clause will have to show that in all the circumstances of the case, the clause was a reasonable one to incorporate bearing in mind all circumstances which were, or ought reasonably to have been in the contemplation, of the parties when the contract was made.

Example

A surveyor's contract contained a term which disclaimed any kind of assurance as to the accuracy or validity of the report. The survey was carried out negligently and the purchase went ahead.
Held: Where a survey was prepared in the knowledge that it would be forwarded to the purchaser, who was likely to rely on it without commissioning a further report, it would not be fair or reasonable to allow reliance on that clause.

(*Smith v. Bush*, 1987)

2.7 Mistake

It has become traditional to divide 'mistake' into three categories: common mistake, where both parties make the same mistake; mutual mistake, where the parties misunderstand each other and are at cross purposes; and unilateral mistake, one party is mistaken and the other knows, or is presumed to know, that the mistake has been made.

(i) Common Mistake

The basic position is that a common mistake does not affect the validity of the contract unless the mistake is such as to eliminate the very subject matter of the contract.

Examples

In *Galloway v. Galloway* (1914), for example, a separation deed was declared a nullity because it was made on the basis of the common mistake that the parties were in fact married when they were not. In such cases, the courts will, however, in the exercise of their equitable jurisdiction set aside the agreement on terms that are just and fair. In *Cooper v. Phibbs* (1867), X agreed to take a lease of a fishery from Y, although, unknown to both parties, it already belonged to X. The House of Lords set the agreement aside, but only on terms that Y should have a lien on the fishery for such money as he had spent on its improvement. Indeed, the courts have made it clear that they will use their equitable jurisdiction where the common mistake is not one that eliminates the subject matter of the contract. In *Grist v. Bailey* (1967), the plaintiff agreed to buy the defendant's house subject to an existing tenancy. The value of the house with vacant possession was about £2250 but the price was fixed at £850 since both parties wrongly believed that the tenancy was protected by legislation. The court held that the contract was a valid one but dismissed the plaintiff's action for specific performance of the contract on terms which required the defendant to enter a fresh contract to sell the house at the appropriate price.

(ii) Mutual Mistake

Where the parties misunderstand each other, and so make a mutual mistake, the question for the court to answer is whether a reasonable third party would take there to be a binding contract or not.

Examples

In *Wood v. Scarth* (1858), the defendant offered to let a public house to the plaintiff. After an interview with the defendant's clerk, the offer was accepted. The defendant intended that a premium should be paid in addition to the rent and believed that the clerk had made this clear. The plaintiff believed that his only duty was to pay the rent. It was held that the parties had not so misunderstood each other that a contract could not be said to have been formed. In *Scriven Bros & Co. v. Hindley & Co. (1913)*, the dispute concerned an auction where the auctioneer was to sell hemp and tow. The catalogue specified lots of 47 and of 176 bales. It did not make it clear that the latter contained tow. The same shipping mark was entered against each lot. Samples of each lot were on view, but the plaintiff did not inspect these as he had already seen samples of the hemp. The defendant, believing that both lots were of hemp successfully bid an extravagant price for the 176 bales of tow. Witnesses said that tow and hemp had never been landed from the same ship under the same mark. The confusion in this case was such that the court held that no contract had come into existence.

(iii) Unilateral Mistake

Where the unilateral mistake is fundamental to the agreement, then the courts will rule that that mistake means in effect that no contract has come into existence.

Example

In *Webster v. Cecil* (1861), the defendant, who had already refused to sell his land for £2000 offered to sell it for £1250. The plaintiff accepted by return of post. The defendant immediately realized that he had mistakenly written that price for £2250 and gave notice of his error. Knowledge of the mistake was clearly to be imputed to the plaintiff and the contract was held to be without effect.

Many of the cases under unilateral mistake involve cases of mistaken identity. The position appears to be that such contracts will be void when the innocent party to the contract thought he was dealing with someone else and that the identity of the person he thought he was dealing with was central to the contract.

Examples

In *King's Norton Metal Co. Ltd v. Eldridge* (1897), a person called Wallis set up business at Hallam and Co., and stated on his letterhead that he had various foreign factories. On this paper, he ordered goods from the plaintiffs which he later sold to the defendants. The plaintiffs claimed the goods back from the defendants on the ground that their contract with Hallam was void since they mistakenly believed that the firm existed. It was held that this argument failed because they must have intended to contract with the writer of the letter since they could not have relied on the credit of a non-existent person. They were unable to show that they meant to contract with Hallam, and not with Wallis, for there was no other entity in question. Such contracts can be set aside for misrepresentation (*see* 2.8), but not if an innocent third party, as here, has obtained the goods. In *Ingram v. Little* (1961), the plaintiffs sold their car to a person who claimed he was a Mr Hutchinson with an address in Caterham. One of the plaintiffs checked the telephone directory and found that there was such a person with such an address. The sale went through. The Court of Appeal held that on the facts of the case, the plaintiffs had only meant to deal with Mr Hutchinson and so the contract was void.

2.8 Misrepresentation

A misrepresentation can only be actionable if it is a false statement of a fact which induces the other party to enter into the particular contract. Merely to state an opinion as to how many sheep a piece of land could carry was not, for example, a misrepresentation of fact (*Bisset v. Wilkinson*, 1927).

Examples

In *Horsfall v. Thomas* (1862), the plaintiff was asked to make a gun to a particular specification. The gun was duly delivered and burst in use due to a defect which had been concealed. The defendant was held liable for the price of the gun. He had never inspected it and so the misrepresentation as to its soundness could not have affected his decision to accept it. Similarly, in *Smith v. Chadwick* (1884), a prospectus contained a false statement that certain important people were on the board. The plaintiff admitted, however, that he had been in no degree influenced by this claim. The misrepresentation, therefore, was held to have no effect. Silence can amount to a misrepresentation if it distorts a positive representation. In *With v. O'Flanagan* (1936), a doctor wished to sell his practice to the plaintiff. In January, he stated that his income was £2000 a year. Between January and

May, when the contract was entered into, the practice fell substantially. The silence as to the drop in income was held to amount to a misrepresentation.

(i) Innocent Misrepresentation

A representation is innocent if it was made in the genuine belief that it was true and with good grounds for that belief. A contract may be rescinded in such a case, but the plaintiff has no right to claim damages though he has a right to recover expenses which he was obliged to incur by the contract itself (*Whittington v. Seale-Hayne*, 1900). The position has been affected by s.2 (2) of the Misrepresentation Act 1967 which allows the court to order the contract to remain binding and for damages to be awarded instead.

(ii) Negligent Misrepresentation

A representation is made negligently where it is made by a person who believes it to be true but with no good grounds for that belief. The Misrepresentation Act, s.2 (1), gives the victim of a negligent misrepresentation the right to damages in addition to the right to rescind which has has in any event. In fact, the common law had also, independently of the Act, reached the stage whereby the victim of a negligent misrepresentation could claim damages (*Hedley Byrne & Co. Ltd v. Heller & Partners Ltd*, 1964). It is more prudent to sue under the Act since an allegation of negligence is deemed correct until the contrary to proven. If the case were brought at common law, the allegation of negligence would have to be proved on the balance of probabilities. Under s.2 (2) of the Act, the court may order the contract to remain binding but for this to be compensated in damages.

(iii) Fraudulent Misrepresentation

A misrepresentation is made fraudulently when it is 'made knowingly, or without belief in its truth, or recklessly, careless whether it be true or false' (*Derry v. Peek*, 1889). In such a case, the plaintiff may claim damages and rescind the contract. The position is not affected by the Misrepresentation Act.

(iv) Loss of Right to Rescind

The victim of any category of misrepresentation will lose his right to rescind where he affirms the contract with full knowledge of the misrepresentation.

Example

A lorry was misrepresented as being 'in exceptional condition'. Two days after purchase, defects appeared and the plaintiff accepted an offer to pay half the costs of repair.
Held: This amounted to affirmation of the contract.

(*Long v. Lloyd*, 1958)

It is also not possible to rescind a contract if the parties cannot be restored to their precontractual position.

Example

A syndicate sold a nitrate mine to a company under a contract with misleading terms. The company sued for rescission of the contract.
Held: Since the mine had been worked by the company, the parties could not be restored to their original position and so the contract could not be rescinded.

(*Laguanas Nitrate Co. v. Laguanas Syndicate*, 1899)

Where an innocent third party has obtained an interest in the subject matter of the contract, it cannot be rescinded.

Example

The plaintiffs contracted with A for the purchase of 50 tonnes of iron which A had obtained by fraud from the defendants who delivered it to the plaintiffs on A's instructions. The plaintiffs paid A on receipt, but the defendants seized the iron when they discovered they had been defrauded.
Held: Their seizure was wrongful as they could not avoid the contract with A after the goods had come into the hands of an innocent third party, the plaintiffs.

(*White v. Garden*, 1851)

Finally, the right to rescission will be lost on the grounds of unreasonable delay.

Example

A painting believed by both parties to be a Constable was found five years later not to be by that painter.
Held: Too long a period had lapsed since the sale to allow rescission.

(*Leaf v. International Galleries*, 1950)

(v) Excluding Liability

Section 3 of the Misrepresentation Act provides that a contract term excluding or restricting liability for a misrepresentation is valid only if it satisfies the reasonableness test laid down in the Unfair Contract Terms Act (*see* 2.6 (iv)).

Example

Particulars of sale at an auction misrepresented the position as to planning permission. The buyer successfully bid for the property but later sought to rescind the contract on the grounds of misrepresentation.
Held: The sellers were held not entitled to rely on an exclusion clause since the plaintiff had had no chance to check for himself as to the accuracy of the claim in relation to planning permission. In such a case, it would not be reasonable to allow the sellers to rely on the clause.

(*South Western General Property Co. v. Marton*, 1983)

2.9 Frustration

The basic rule is that contractual obligations are absolute, so that a party cannot plead that events which have happened after the contract was agreed on have had the effect of ending all obligations under the contract. For example, when a shipowner agreed to load his ship with certain goods at a place in West Africa, he was liable in damages even though those goods were unobainable (*Hills v. Sughrue*, 1846). However, there are certain exceptions to this rule.

Example

A music hall was hired to the plaintiff but was destroyed before it was put into use.
Held: The contract was frustrated.

(*Taylor v. Caldwell*, 1863)

Example

A pianist agreed to play at a concert. He became ill and informed the organizer. The organizer sued the pianist for the loss of the postponed function.
Held: The pianist's illness frustrated the contract.

(*Robinson v. Davison*, 1871)

Example

The defendant hired rooms in Pall Mall to view the coronation procession of Edward VII. When the coronation was cancelled because of the King's illness, the defendant refused to pay the balance of the rent.
Held: The viewing of the procession was the basis of the contract, and so the contract had been frustrated.

(*Krell v. Henry*, 1903)

Example

In contrast, a boat was chartered to see the royal naval review at Spithead and cruise round the fleet. The review did not take place once the coronation was cancelled and the boat owner sued for the hire price.
Held: The contract had not been frustrated since the fleet remained in position, and so the charge was due.

(*Herne Bay Steam Boat Co. Ltd v. Hutton*, 1903)

(i) The Law Reform (Frustrated Contracts) Act 1943

When a contract is frustrated, all future obligations under it are discharged. The Law Reform (Frustrated Contracts) Act 1943 further provides:

(*a*) All sums paid under the contract before discharge may be recovered.
(*b*) If the person who received payment under the contract has incurred expenses in carrying it out he may retain or recover from the payer all or part of the expenses where the court thinks just.
(*c*) All sums payable under the contract cease to be payable.
(*d*) Any valuable benefits obtained from the other party's actions under the contract must be paid for where the court thinks just.

The Act can be excluded by express agreement and in any event does not apply to charter parties, carriage of goods by sea, agreements for the sale of specific goods which perish before the risk has passed to the buyer, and insurance contracts. The common law which applies to such contracts provides:

(*a*) Both parties are discharged from all obligations not yet accrued.

(*b*) If the price, or any part, has been paid, it can be recovered if there has been a total failure of consideration.

(*c*) If there is a total failure of consideration, no part of the price can be retained for expenses incurred.

(*d*) Payments made cannot be recovered if there has been only a partial failure of consideration.

(*e*) It is not possible to compel one party to pay for a benefit received where the contract was to perform one indivisible service and nothing had been received.

2.10 Remedies

Reference has been made above (*see* 2.6 (iii)) to the subdivision of contract terms. In the case of a breach of condition, or an intermediate term which is treated as a breach of condition, the innocent party will be entitled to rescind the contract and to claim damages (for exclusion and limitation clauses, *see* 2.6 (iv)). The right to rescind is lost in the same way as it is in relation to misrepresentation (*see* 2.8 (iv)). In the event of a breach of warranty, the plaintiff is only entitled to damages. Contract damages are based on putting the injured party in the position he would have occupied if the contract had been properly performed. This is, however, subject to the rule that the defendant is only liable for the loss which he contemplated as a probable result of the breach (*Hadley v. Baxendale*, 1854). In *Victoria Laundry (Windsor) Ltd v. Newman Industries Ltd* (1949), a laundry business ordered a new boiler. The boiler was delivered many weeks late and in a damaged condition. The plaintiff was entitled to loss of normal business profits but not to compensation for the loss of certain exceptional contracts since the latter were not in the defendants' contemplation at the time the contract was made.

Contracts often contain clauses which specify the amount of damages to be paid in the event of a breach. If these clauses genuinely try to estimate the loss, they are known as liquidated damages clauses and are valid. If, however, they are meant to act as a penalty in the event of a breach, they are known as penalty clauses and cannot be enforced.

Example

Manufacturers supplied tyres to dealers under an agreement whereby the defendants agreed not to sell below list price, nor to supply certain persons, and to pay £5 for each breach.
Held: The sum was enforceable as a genuine pre-estimate of loss, as the fixed figure was not extravagant.

(*Dunlop Pneumatic Tyre Co. Ltd v. New Garage and Motor Co. Ltd*, 1915)

Example

A dealer agreed not to sell any car or parts below list price, nor to resell to dealers or to exhibit cars bought under the agreement. In the event of a breach, £250 was to be paid by the dealer.

Held: The sum was a penalty and so could not be enforced.

(Ford Motor Co. (England) Ltd v. Armstrong, 1915)

The victim of a breach of contract must mitigate his loss by doing all that is reasonable in the circumstances of the case. If an employee is wrongfully dismissed, he can recover damages for loss of wages, but he must reduce his loss by seeking new employment (*Brace v. Calder*, 1895).

The courts also have the discretion whether or not to order a party to perform his contract by use of a decree of specific performance. An order will only rarely be given. The plaintiff must be able to show that: damages would not be an adequate remedy; enforcement of the order would not require constant supervision by the court; the contract is enforceable by both parties; and the plaintiff himself has acted fairly and equitably. The courts also have the discretionary remedy of an injunction. A prohibitory injunction enforces a negative promise (such as not to sell a particular item), while a mandatory injunction orders a person to undo what he has already done in breach of contract. An injunction will not be granted if the circumstances would not allow an order of specific performance.

2.11 Assignment

All rights under a contract can be assigned under the terms of the Law of Property Act, s.136. To be effective, the assignment must be in writing, signed by the person making the assignment, be absolute and not solely by way of charge. Express notice must be given to the debtor, trustee or other party from whom the assignor could claim. If these formalities are not complied with, then the assignment is equitable only. Notice should be given to any third party affected so that priority is gained over any subsequent assignee without notice of the assignment. Contracts of a personal nature, such as a contract to write a book, cannot be assigned.

3 Sale of goods and supply of services

3.1 Introduction

Contracts for the sale of goods have been regulated since the enactment of the Sale of Goods Act 1893. This Act, however, was what is called a 'consolidating' Act since it did not actually create any new law, but consolidated the law which had been developed by the courts over the years before. That is why many of the cases cited as sale of goods precedents date from the nineteenth century. The 1893 Act was amended many times in recent years, and eventually it was itself repealed and consolidated by the Sale of Goods Act 1979. Because the 1979 Act is, as will be seen from this brief history, really much older that would seem, it is now being examined by the Law Commission to see what changes are necessary to make it more in tune with modern needs.

The Sale of Goods Act only concerns, of course, actual contracts of sale. Section 2(1) defines these as contracts where the property (or ownership) of the goods passes to another for a money sum. In short, contracts are contracts of sale only if they involve a straight exchange of money (which will include any form of money equivalent, such as a cheque or a credit card) for goods. This means for example that part-exchange transactions, where (often in the motor trade) a buyer offers goods and money in exchange for goods, are not contracts of sale. Contracts of barter, where goods are exchanged for goods, are not contracts of sale. Nor are contracts where some service is attached to the supply of goods. For example, a contractor might be employed to install a central heating system. The home owner becomes owner of the radiators, boilers and pipes which are installed, but the contract was not one of sale. This is because the contract also contained a service element, that is the installation of the system. Until 1982, these other contracts were subject to common law rules which were, in effect, identical to the statutory rules contained in the Sale of Goods Act. In 1982, however, the Supply of Goods and Services Act was passed, and this now covers those other types of contract just referred to. As we shall come to see, the relevant parts of the Sale of Goods Act and of the Supply of Goods and Services Act are identical.

A separate mention needs to be made of contracts of hire purchase and of contracts of conditional sale. Although they look the same, and in practical terms are the same, they are legally different. In a contract of hire purchase, the customer only rents or hires the goods for the agreed period. At the end of that period, he has an option whether or not to buy the goods for a nominal sum. He always does, of course. The payment of the 'option money' is usually spread over the regular instalments. The point to be noted is that, technically, the customer is not committing himself to buying the goods when he enters the contract, only to hiring them for the stated period. For that reason a contract of hire purchase is not governed by the Sale of Goods Act. Instead, it is subject to the terms of the Supply of Goods (Implied Terms) Act 1973 which are, in their relevant parts, absolutely the same as the Sale of Goods Act. In a contract of conditional sale, the customer pays the price off in regular instalments, but commits himself at the very beginning to buying the goods. Unlike a hire purchase contract, he has no option once the contract has been made. Although the difference between a conditional sale and a contract of hire purchase is really only a technicality, it is enough to mean that a conditional sale contract is governed by the Sale of Goods Act, whereas, as just seen, a hire purchase contract is not.

Although there are three separtate Acts governing the different types of contract, we have seen that their relevant terms are absolutely identical. For the rest of this chapter, we shall refer to all three as 'the Acts', and it will be understood that this is a reference to the Supply of Goods (Implied Terms) Act 1973, the Sale of Goods Act 1979 and the Supply of Goods Act 1982. It should also be understood that the material dealt with below deals only with the major provisions of the legislation, and that the Sale of Goods Act contains much more than either of the other two Acts. For instance, the 1979 Act provides that goods must be delivered within a reasonable time if no time is agreed (s.29 (3)), or if no price is agreed on, then a reasonable price must be paid (s.8 (2)). There are no equivalent provisions in the other Acts, but the same rules nevertheless apply by implication of the common law.

3.2 Conformity with Description

The Acts require, as a condition of a contract (that is a major term) that the goods supplied must conform to any description given in the precontract negotiations. The relevant provisions are contained in s.9 of the Act of 1973, s. 13 of the Act of 1979 and s.8 of the Act of 1982. This covers both oral and written descriptions, and also 'self-applied' descriptions, such as the packaging of the goods. This rule applies even if the contract is a purely private transaction. If, therefore, the contract is for white paint, and blue paint is delivered, the goods do not conform to their description. Examples can, of course, become much more complicated than that.

Examples

In *Ashington Piggeries Ltd v. Christopher Hill* (1972), herring meal was sold which was contaminated with a substance which made it unsuitable for feeding to mink, although this was what the buyer wanted it for. The House of Lords ruled by a majority that the herring meal had been correctly described as 'herring meal' although it was not suitable for its intended purpose. On the other hand, in *Pinnock Bros v. Lewis and Peat Ltd* (1923), the contract was for the sale of copra cake. The goods which were delivered were a mixture of copra cake and castor beans. The Court of Appeal ruled that the quantity of beans so changed the nature of the product that it no longer corresponded to its description of 'copra cake'. These cases illustrate how difficult it can sometimes be to decide whether or not goods do correspond to the description which has been given to them. The decision was not, however, hard to make in *Raynham Farm v. Symbol Motor Corporation* (1987). A car was sold as a 'new car' when, some months before, it had been badly damaged by fire in the Netherlands after being exported from the United Kingdom. It was brought back to this country and a great deal of repair work was done to it. The court agreed that a certain amount of very minor damage, if repaired, might not stop a car being described as 'new', but the damage suffered by this car, however good the quality of the repairs, did prevent it from being described as 'new', if only because there would always be a lurking doubt that the fire had caused additional damage which could not have been detected.

3.3 Merchantable Quality

The Acts state that all goods supplied under the contract must be of 'merchantable quality'. The relevant provisions are found in s.10 (2) of the Act of 1973, s.14 (2) of the Act of 1979 and s.9 (2) of the Act of 1982. This provision only applies if the contract is made in the course of a business. According to the Acts:

> 'Goods of any kind are of merchantable quality . . . if they are as fit for the purpose or purposes for which goods of that kind are commonly bought as it is reasonable to expect having regard to any description applied to them, the price (if relevant) and all the other relevant circumstances'.

Examples

To illustrate the meaning of 'merchantable quality', we can first look at the decision of the House of Lords in *B. S. Brown & Son Ltd v. Craiks Ltd* (1970). The buyers ordered a quantity of cloth. The sellers thought it was wanted for industrial purposes, but the buyers wanted it for making dresses. It turned out to be unsuitable for the buyers' purposes. The contract price was 36.25d a yard, which was higher than would normally have been paid for industrial cloth but not substantially higher. In fact, the sellers resold some of the cloth for 30d a yard. The House of Lords ruled that on these facts the cloth was of merchantable quality. If the market value of the cloth had been, say, only 15d a yard, then in all probability the cloth would not have been held to have been of merchantable quality.

Another example is *Bernstein v. Pamson Motors (Golders Green) Ltd* (1987). A new Nissan Laurel broke down when the buyer had had it for just three weeks and when he had only driven 140 miles (220 km). The engine had seized up when the car was being driven on a motorway. The High Court held that the car was not of merchantable quality. There were two main reasons for this decision. First, although the car had been repaired 'as good as new', there would always be a doubt as to the area of potential damage arising because the engine had seized up. The other reason, which was the main reason for the decision, related to safety. The court pointed out that if the engine had seized up while the driver was in the fast lane, he would have been unable to control the car and a nasty, even fatal accident could well have happened. Mr Bernstein, however, was not allowed to reject the car but was limited to getting compensation in damages (*see* 3.11).

The Acts provide for two ways in which a buyer can lose his right to goods of merchantable quality. These are: if the defects were pointed out to the buyer before the contract was made; or if the buyer examined the goods before the contract was made and should have seen the particular defects.

3.4 Reasonable Fitness for Purpose

The Acts state that the goods supplied under the contract must be fit for the buyer's purpose where the buyer makes known, expressly or by implication, any particular purpose for which he wants the goods. This requirement only applies where the contract is made in the course of a trade or business. Where the goods only have one normal purpose, the seller will be taken to know what the goods are wanted for. If, on the other hand, the goods are wanted for a purpose which is out of the ordinary, the seller must be specifically advised.

Example

In *Griffiths v. Peter Conway Ltd* (1939), the buyer contracted dermatitis from a coat bought from the seller. The buyer had, however, an abnormally sensitive skin and a normal person would have suffered no adverse reaction. The Court of Appeal ruled that the required use was so special that the buyer should have advised the seller in advance. Since she had not, she had no claim.

The Acts provide that the buyer will lose his right to goods which are reasonably fit for the purpose if he did not rely on the skill or judgment of the seller, or if he did rely on the seller's skill or judgment but when it was unreasonable for him to do so. It has been said that in the usual case of goods being purchased from a retailer, 'the reliance will be in general inferred from the fact that a buyer goes to the shop in the confidence that the tradesman has selected his stock with skill and judgment' (*Grant v. Australian Knitting Mills*, 1936). On the other hand, if a buyer orders goods under a brand name, and does so in such a way as to make it clear that he is doing so because goods under that name are the only goods he wants, then he cannot be said to be relying on the seller's skill or judgment.

3.5 Strict Liability

The seller's liability under those parts of the Acts discussed in 3.2, 3.3 and 3.4 are strict; that is to say, the seller is liable however free of blame he might be.

Example

In *Frost v. Aylesbury Co. Ltd* (1905), a bottle of milk was contaminated by the presence of a bacillus. The seller was still liable under the Sale of Goods Act even though the presence of the bacillus could not then have been discovered by the use of any care or diligence by him.

3.6 Title

The Acts provide that the seller must have the right to sell the goods. If the buyer has to return the goods because there has been a breach of this requirement, he will be able to claim back his entire purchase price and will not have to give any allowance for the period of use he has had of the goods.

Examples

In *Rowland v. Divall* (1923), the buyer bought a car from the defendant which he then resold to a third party. It was then discovered that the defendant had no right to sell the car which was repossessed from the third party. The buyer returned the full price to the third party, and then claimed the amount of his own purchase price from the defendant. The Court of Appeal held that he could recover the whole of the price and that the defendant was not entitled to set-off anything for the four months' use the third party had had.

In *Butterworth v. Kingsway Motors Ltd* (1954), a person took delivery of a car under a hire purchase agreement. In the belief that she could sell it provided that she kept on making the payments, she did sell it. The car was then sold several times. It was eventually sold to the plaintiff who used it for very nearly a year. The hire purchase company then discovered what had happened and sought to repossess it. The plaintiff then sought to recover his entire purchase price. The court ruled that he was entitled to do this, even though just one week later the last instalment was paid in the hire purchase contract.

The Acts also state that the goods must be free of any undisclosed encumbrance or charge and that a buyer must enjoy quiet possession of the goods, except where his quiet possession is disturbed by an encumbrance or charge of which he has been told.

Examples

In *Mason v. Burningham* (1949), a typewriter was sold by someone who had no title to it. It was repossessed from the buyer who was held entitled to claim damages for breach of his right to quiet possession. The buyer could also have sued for breach of the provisions discussed above.

In *Healing (Sales) Pty Ltd v. Inglis Electrix Pty Ltd* (1968), the seller of goods gave the buyer 60 days to pay. Before that period was up, the seller repossessed them. This was held to be a breach of the buyer's right to quiet possession.

In *Lloyds & Scottish Finance Ltd v. Modern Cars and Caravans (Kingston) Ltd* (1966), a debtor sold a caravan which he had bought, but for which he had not paid, and which had already been 'seized' (though not physically removed) under a court order. The buyer was entitled to claim that the goods were subject to a charge or encumbrance which had not been disclosed to him.

In *Microbeads AC v. Vinhurst Road Markings Ltd* (1975), the seller sold to the buyer certain equipment to be used in road markings. A third party obtained a patent over the equipment after the contract was made. Patent law enabled the patent owner to take possession of the equipment. This was held to infringe the buyer's quiet possession.

The Acts provide that none of the foregoing provisions apply where the circumstances of the contract make it clear that the seller is providing only such title as he or a third party might have. When goods are sold under a distress warrant, for example, it is usual to sell merely the 'title and interest' of the debtor, whatever that might be. Where the circumstances do show that only a limited title is being offered, the buyer still has two rights granted by the Acts: that the seller has disclosed all charges and encumbrances of which he is aware; and that none of the following will disturb the buyer's quiet possession—the seller, a third party (where the circumstances of the contract were that the seller would transfer only such title as a third party might have), or a person claiming through either the seller or a third party except under a charge or encumbrance which was disclosed to the buyer.

3.7 The Rights of the True Owner in the case of Sales without Title

The basic rule is that where a seller sells goods to which he has no title, the true owner is entitled to claim them back from the buyer even if the latter bought in entirely good faith. This rule is often known by its Latin tag: '*Nemo Dat Quod Non Habet*'. With regards to contracts of sale, this is specifically stated in the Sale of Goods Act. In other cases, this is the position which exists at common law. There are, however, a number of exceptions to the rule which allow the innocent buyer to retain the goods against the true owner. These are explained below. These exceptions, where they are to be found in the Sale of Goods Act, may also be considered as restating the common law.

(i) According to ordinary principles of law, a seller can pass a valid title if he is acting as the owner's agent and is acting within his actual or usual authority.

(ii) The owner loses his rights if he is precluded by his conduct from setting up his title. This is known as the doctrine of 'estoppel'.

Examples

In *Eastern Distributors v. Goldring* (1957). A, as part of a plan to deceive a hire purchase company, signed and delivered forms to B which enabled B to represent that he had A's authority to sell a car belonging to him. The Court of Appeal held that A was 'estopped' from setting up his title against the party who had bought the car from B. In *Central Newbury Car Auctions Ltd v. Unity Finance Ltd* (1957), a person offered to buy from the plaintiffs a car on hire purchase terms. He gave a car in part-exchange, but it was later discovered that this car was subject to a hire purchase agreement. He drove away in the car he was obtaining on hire purchase, but some time later, his hire purchase proposal was in fact turned down by the relevant finance company. The car was later discovered in the possession of a person who had bought it in good faith. The case for estoppel was based on the fact that the owner had allowed the car to be driven away complete with its registration book. The Court of Appeal held that there was no estoppel in this case and that the true owner was entitled to the return of the car. The registration book is not a document of title and did in fact contain a warning that the person in whose name the car is registered may not be the owner.

(iii) There is the special rule for sales made in 'market overt'. A market overt is every open, public and legally constituted market. Every shop in the City of

London is a market overt. The goods must be such as are usually sold in the market and the sale must be open and between the hours of sunrise and sunset (*Reid v. Commissioner of Metropolitan Police*, 1973).

Example

The hirer of a car under a hire purchase agreement tried to sell it by auction in Maidstone Auction Market but failed to do so. He later sold the car privately in accordance with the custom of the market. The hire purchase company sought the return of the car from the person who had bought it in good faith.
Held: As the custom of the market had been followed, the purchaser had obtained a valid title against the owner.

(Bishopsgate Motor Finance Corpn v. Transport Brakes, 1949)

(iv) Where a person with a 'voidable' title sells the goods to a person in good faith before the true owner renders his title void, the purchaser obtains a good title. A contract will be voidable, for example, where the goods were obtained from their true owner by some fraudulent act, such as a person being allowed to pay by cheque by pretending to be someone other than who he really is.

Example

An owner advertised his car for sale, and sold it to a person who claimed to be a certain actor. The vehicle was later sold to a person who bought it in good faith. In the meantime, the cheque given by the fraudulent party bounced.
Held: He had obtained a voidable title which had not been made void by the time he sold the car. The purchaser therefore acquired a valid title.

(Lewis v. Averay, 1971)

Example

A car was obtained by false pretences and then sold and resold. Before the various sales, however, the fraud was discovered and the true owner informed both the police and the Automobile Association.
Held: These acts rendered the voidable title void and, since they had been done before any further resale, the true owner was entitled to recover his property.

(Car and Universal Finance Co. Ltd v. Caldwell, 1965)

In *Newtons of Wembley Ltd v. Williams* (1964), it was held by the Court of Appeal that where the owner of a vehicle obtained by false pretences had taken all possible steps to trace the offender, and had issued a 'stop' notice to the Hire Purchase Information Bureau, this was enough to render the contract void.

(v) Both the Factors Act 1889, and the Sale of Goods Act, in terms which are effectively identical, provide that the seller who retains possession of the goods after the sale and who makes a further sale, pledge or 'other disposition' to a second buyer who takes them in good faith passes a good title to that second buyer.

Example

In this case, A Ltd, who were dealers in vehicles, sold a number to the plaintiffs under a 'display agreement' whereby A Ltd remained in possession of the cars in display in the showroom. They were paid 90 per cent of the price and were authorized to sell the vehicles as agents for the plaintiffs. A Ltd got into financial difficulties and the plaintiffs revoked their authority to sell, but A Ltd still went ahead and sold a number of vehicles to purchasers who took them in good faith. *Held*: The purchasers obtained a valid title against the plaintiffs to whom the vehicles had first been sold.

(*Pacific Motor Auctions Pty Ltd v. Motor Credits (Hire Finance) Ltd*, 1965)

Example

G bought a car from the defendants, paying the price with a cheque that was not met. He then sold the car to a finance company, the plaintiffs in this case, but retained possession of the car as he had induced the plaintiffs to accept a hire purchase proposal for the benefit of an accomplice. Subsequently, the defendants, with the consent of a G, retook the car from him.
Held: The defendants were protected as against the plaintiffs. So far as the plaintiffs were concerned, G was a seller who remained in possession. Moreover, the retaking of the car by the defendants was a 'disposition' by G to them inasmuch as it amounted to a rescission of the contract between them and, therefore, it revested the property in the defendants.

(*Worcester Works Finance Ltd v. Cooden Engineering Co. Ltd*, 1972)

(vi) Both the Factors Act and the Sale of Goods Act provide that a buyer who is in possession of goods, but who is not yet the owner, can pass a good title to anyone who buys from him in good faith. Under the terms of the Consumer Credit Act 1974, this does not, however, apply to conditional sales where the buyer in possession is a private consumer and the amount of credit extended to him does not exceed £15,000. The provisions of the Acts will, however, apply if the buyer is a business or if the credit exceeds £15,000.

Example

Goods were bought under the terms of an agreement which committed the buyer at the outset to a purchase, but which allowed him to pay off the price in instalments (a conditional sale).
Held: A further sale by him after he had obtained possession, but before he became owner, passed a good title to a person who bought in good faith. This decision would not be the same today but only because the goods were within the £15,000 limit. The principle of the case is still entirely valid.

(*Lee v. Butler*, 1893)

One particular problem which has arisen in the interpretation of the Factors Act and the Sale of Goods Act comes from this problem. If a thief steals goods from the owner and then sells them to a third party, it is plain that the Acts cannot apply since the thief is obviously not a buyer in possession. If the third party then sells to a fourth party, it could be argued that the fourth party does get a good title because the third party clearly is a buyer in possession. However, the House of Lords in *National Employers Mutual General Insurance Association Ltd v. Jones* (1988) ruled that because the thief had never any title to the goods, he could not be said to have 'sold' the goods to the third party who therefore could not be said to be a buyer in possession. The absence of a genuine contract of sale on the part of the thief would mean, the House of Lords said, that however many further sales of the goods there might be, none of the buyers down the line could be treated as buyers in possession.

(vii) The Factors Act provides that a mercantile agent who is in possession of the goods with the consent of the owner can pass a good title in the goods to someone who takes them in good faith, even if he is not authorized to sell them. A mercantile agent is someone who, in the ordinary course of his business, has authority to sell or buy goods, or to raise money on the security of goods. A typical mercantile agent is the car dealer. Another is an auctioneer.

Example

A car owner delivered his car to a dealer for a sale at not less than £575. The dealer sold to a buyer at £340 who took the car in good faith. The agent defaulted with the purchase price and the original owner sued to recover the price from the purchaser.
Held: As the dealer a mercantile agent in possession with the owner's consent, the purchaser had obtained a good title.

(*Folkes v. King*, 1923)

Example

A car owner left his car with a dealer to see what offers would be made, but the dealer was not authorized to make a sale. Right from the outset, however, the dealer had intended to sell the car if he could. He did indeed eventually sell it to a third party.
Held: Even though the dealer had obtained possession from the owner by deception, that still amounted to him having possession with the consent of the owner. Because of that, the good faith third party acquired a valid title.

(*Pearson v. Rose and Young*, 1951)

(viii) Under the terms of the Hire Purchase Act 1964, where a person sells to a private consumer a car which he is buying under a hire purchase agreement or under a conditional sale agreement (for the difference between the two types of contract, *see* 3.1), the title in the car will pass to the purchaser so long as he buys in good faith and without notice of the seller's defect in title.

3.8 Leasing Contracts

The Supply of Goods and Services Act 1982 also covers contracts for the hire or rental of goods. It has to be understood that a hiring contract is very different from a hire-purchase contract (*see* 3.1). Under a hiring contract, possession of the goods passes to a party for a specified period, and during that time he is entitled to use the goods in accordance with the contract. However, unlike a hire-purchase contract, the aim is not to buy the goods, and the hired goods return to the owner when the contract has run its course. The relevant provisions of the Act with regard to description, merchantable quality and reasonable fitness for purpose are, with two exceptions, identical to the provisions discussed above. The first exception is that, in relation to leasing contracts, there is no requirement that the goods are free from any undisclosed charge or encumbrance. The second is that there are no provisions enabling the owner of the goods to pass only a limited title.

3.9 Exclusion Clauses

Up until 1973, it used to be possible for the seller to 'contract out' of or exclude the provisions of the Sale of Goods Act relating to title, description, merchantable quality and reasonable fitness for purpose. In that year, Parliament enacted the Supply of Goods (Implied Terms) Act which imposed certain restrictions on the use of exclusion and limitation clauses. The latter are clauses which admit liability, but not to the full extent of the other party's loss. The relevant provisions are now contained in the Unfair Contract Terms Act 1977. This first states that no contract term can exclude or limit liability in relation to any of the provisions relating to title considered in 3.6 above. With regard to the provisions relating to description, merchantable quality and reasonable fitness for purpose, the Act distinguishes between sales by a business to a business, and sales by a business to a private consumer. In the former case, an exclusion or limitation clause will be valid if and only if the seller can prove that it is reasonable in all the circumstances of the case. In the latter case, an exclusion clause or limitation clause is automatically void and of no effect. Indeed, under the terms of the Consumer Transactions (Restrictions on Statements) Order 1976, it is a criminal offence for a business to include in a contract any terms which are automatically void in this way.

The foregoing provisions apply equally to hire purchase contracts, but they do not apply to such other contracts as contracts of barter, contracts of part exchange and contracts where a service is provided in addition to the goods. In such cases, the Supply of Goods and Services Act 1982 provides that liability in relation to the provisions as to title cannot be excluded or limited. Where goods are leased, the provisions as to title can be excluded or limited only if the particular clause can be shown to be reasonable. As far as the provisions as to description, merchantable quality and reasonable fitness are concerned, the distinction is again drawn between contracts with businesses and contracts with private consumers. In the former case, the particular clause is valid if it can be shown to be reasonable; in the latter case it is automatically void. However, in this latter case, there is no criminal offence committed by including an automatically void clause in the contract.

3.10 Passing of Property and Risk

The rule under the Sale of Goods Act is that property passes under the contract when the parties intend it to pass. However, since the parties may not always show their intention, the Sale of Goods Act lays down five Rules for determining when the property in the contract goods passes to the buyer. At that point, the buyer becomes the real owner. These Rules express the common law and may be taken to cover contracts within the Supply of Goods (Implied Terms) Act 1973 (*see* 3.1). The basic rule also laid down in the Sale of Goods Act, and again at common law, is that any damage to, or deterioration in, the goods is at the risk of the person who has property. It is, however, possible, and it is often found in business contracts, for the parties to say in the contract that risk will pass at a specific time, regardless of when property passes. It is also possible for the parties themselves to say when property is to pass, and if they do the Rules will not apply. In the absence of any indication in the contract, however, the Rules will apply and they are set out below. It should be understood that references to 'specific goods' are references to goods which have been specifically identified as the very goods which the buyer will be getting (for example the same car that the purchaser has just test driven); while 'unascertained goods' are those described generally, and where any item will do so long as it conforms to the description (such as an order for goods seen in a catalogue).

Rule 1

Where there is an unconditional contract for the sale of specific goods, in a deliverable state, the property passes to the buyer when the contract is made. Goods are in a deliverable state when they are in such a state that, under the terms of the contract, the buyer would be bound to take delivery of them (see further on this, Rule 2).

Example

In *Dennant v. Skinner and Collom* (1948), an auctioneer knocked down a van to the highest bidder. He paid by cheque and was allowed to drive the car away on signing an undertaking that property would not pass until the cheque was met. The cheque was not met, but it was still ruled that property had passed. This was because property passed when the contract was made, and this was when the car was knocked down to the buyer. The undertaking was signed after that had happened.

Rule 2

Where the contract is for the sale of specific goods, and the seller is bound to do something to put the goods into a deliverable state, property passes when that thing is done and the buyer has been notified.

Example

Sellers sold an engine which was bolted to the factory floor. It was the seller's task to dismantle it after detaching it from the floor.
Held: In these circumstances property had not passed when the contract had been made.

(*Underwood Ltd v. Burgh Castle Brick and Cement Syndicate*, 1922)

Rule 3

Where a contract is for the sale of specific goods in a deliverable state, and something, such as weighing, has to be done before the price can be determined, property does not pass until that thing is done and the buyer has been notified. This Rule only applies, however, where the particular thing has to be done by the seller.

Example

Cocoa was sold to the buyer who resold it to a third party. This party was to weigh it to determine how much the buyer owed the original seller.

Held: The fact that the weighing was not to be done by the seller excluded the operation of the Rule.

(*Nanka-Bruce v. Commonwealth Trust Ltd*, 1926)

Rule 4

This covers the case of specific goods supplied on sale or return terms or something similar. Property passes when the buyer adopts the transaction, or when he keeps them after the date for return, or, where no date is fixed, he keeps them for more than a reasonable time.

Example

A car was left with dealers, but with no time limit given. The car was unsold for three months, despite several requests during this period by the owner for the car's return.

Held: Property in the car passed to the dealers as it had not been returned in a reasonable time and they were liable for the price.

(*Poole v. Smith's Car Sales (Balham) Ltd*, 1962)

Rule 5 (1)

This deals with a contract for the sale of unascertained or 'future' goods (these being goods which are yet to be made). Property passes to the buyer if they are in a deliverable state and have been unconditionally appropriated to the contract by either party with the assent of the other. Assent may be express or implied and may be given before or after the act of appropriation.

Rule 5 (2)

This gives as an instance of unconditional appropriation the delivery of the goods by the seller to the buyer or to a carrier for transmission to the buyer, where the seller has not reserved any right of disposal.

Example

Here 140 bags of rice were sold, the bags being unascertained. The buyer paid by cheque and asked for a delivery order which was duly sent for 125 bags. The seller said that the balance was awaiting delivery at his place of business. The buyer waited for a month for the remaining bags, but they were found to have been stolen.

Held: Property had passed since the seller had appropriated the balance of fifteen bags to the contract and the buyer had agreed to this by his conduct.

(*Pignatoro v. Gilroy*, 1919)

Example

The seller sold 600 boxes of frozen kidneys out of a consignment of 1500. The buyer's carrier took delivery the next day of the 600 boxes when the delivery note was handed over.

Held: The property had passed under Rule 5 (1) as there had been an unconditional appropriation of goods to the contract.

(*Wardar's Import & Export Co. Ltd v. W. Norwood & Sons Ltd*, 1968)

Because a buyer who has property in the goods is their complete owner, this means that the seller cannot use the goods as security against payment. The goods become the buyer's property and they cannot be repossessed from him even if he defaults in payment. It has therefore become common for business contracts to contain retention of title clauses (sometimes known as 'Romalpa' clauses after the case in which they achieved prominence, namely *Aluminium Industrie BV. v. Romalpa Aluminium Ltd*, 1976). Under such a clause, which can take many forms, the seller will stipulate that the property will remain his until the buyer has paid all sums outstanding under the contract. In the so-called 'all monies' clause, the seller goes a stage further and stipulates that the particular goods do not become the buyer's property until he has paid all sums outstanding under the particular contract and all other contracts between them. Often, the seller will also stipulate that the goods must be marked and identified as being his goods, and that any monies received by the buyer if he disposes of them must be paid into a separate account. By securing his title until all relevant sums have been paid, the seller is able to repossess the goods in case the buyer defaults. Where the goods sold to the buyer remain unused and identifiable, it was held in *Clough Mill Ltd v. Martin* (1984) that the retention clause did not create a charge over the goods so it did not need to be registered under the Companies Act 1985 to ensure its validity. The Court of Appeal did indicate (though they did not have to make a definite decision) that if the goods become incorporated in, or used as material for, other goods, that could create a charge over those other goods which would only be valid if registered.

It should be noted that, even where a buyer obtains goods subject to a retention clause, the buyer is still capable of selling them on because he is a buyer in possession (*see* 3.7).

3.11 Remedies for Buyers

Where the seller is in breach of the requirements of the Acts as to passing a good title, conformity with description, fitness for purpose and merchantable quality (see 3.2–3.4 and 3.6), the buyer is entitled to terminate the contract, and so recover the price if this has already been paid, and claim damages. The buyer can, however, lose his right to reject, but not his right to claim damages, if he has 'accepted' the goods. In law, he has accepted the goods if any of the following occurs:

1. He 'intimates' acceptance of the goods (this has to be more than merely acknowledging receipt).

2. He performs an act which is inconsistent with the ownership of the seller after he has had a chance to examine the goods.

3. He retains the goods for more than a reasonable time without indicating that he is rejecting them.

Example

A sold barley to B by sample, delivery to be at a named railway station. B inspected it at the station and then resold to C. C rejected it as not being in accordance with the sample, and B also attempted to reject the barley as against A.

Held: B's act of inspection and his ordering the transmission to C was an acceptance and he could not later reject the goods.

(*Perkins v. Bell*, 1893)

Example

The buyer in the case cited in 3.3, although he won his case that the car was not of merchantable quality, lost his right to reject because, having had the car for three weeks and driven some 140 miles (220 km), he had had the goods for a reasonable time without giving notice of rejection.

(*Bernstein v. Pamson Motors (Golders Green) Ltd*, 1987)

The damages to which a buyer is entitled in the event of breach will compensate him for the loss which arose naturally from the breach. In the case of non-delivery, both the Sale of Goods Act and the common law generally state that this will amount to the difference between the contract price and the higher cost, if any, of buying the equivalent of those goods in the market. If damage is caused by defective goods, the buyer will be able to claim compensation for the normal loss which resulted from the breach, even if the precise scale of the loss was larger than could have been anticipated.

Example

The sellers sold a feeding hopper to a pig farmer. When installing it, the sellers failed to open the ventilator with the result that the pig feed inside went mouldy. The pigs became ill and this triggered off a much more serious illness from which many of the pigs died. The value of these pigs was in the region of £10,000.
Held: Although the gravity of the illness could not have been foreseen, the seller could reasonably have anticipated that the contents of the hopper would become mouldy and that this might cause illness to the pigs.

(*Parsons (Livestock) Ltd v. Uttley, Ingham and Co. Ltd*, 1978)

A seller will be liable for loss of resale profits only when he knew, or ought reasonably to have known, the buyer intended to resell those goods.

Example

The sellers sold a cargo of corn to the buyers who then resold it. The sellers failed to deliver.
Held: The buyers were entitled to their loss of resale profits. The sellers knew that the corn was for resale since that was actually envisaged in the terms of the contract itself.

(*Re R. and H. Hall and W. H. Pim (Junior) and Co's Arbitration*, 1928)

A final remedy open to the buyer is that of specific performance. This is a court order directed to the seller ordering him to perform the contract. However, a buyer has no right to such an order, since it lies entirely within the discretion of the court. The court will generally not grant an order where damages will be adequate compensation and will usually insist that there must be something unique about the particular goods before it will order specific performance.

Examples

In *Sky Petroleum v. VIP Petroleum* (1974), buyers requested an order to prevent the sellers from breaking a contract which they had with the buyers to supply them with all their petroleum requirements for ten years. Because of the very unusual state of the oil market at the time, the court ruled that damages would not be adequate compensation and gave the buyers the order they wanted.

In *Societé des Industries Metallurgiques SA v. Bronx Engineering Co. Ltd* (1975), the Court of Appeal refused to order a seller to deliver a machine, although it was over 220 tonnes in weight, cost some £270,000 and could only be bought in the market with a nine to twelve months' delivery date.

3.12 Remedies for Sellers

If property in the goods has passed (*see* 3.10), the seller is entitled to claim the purchase price, both under the Sale of Goods Act and at common law. He is also entitled to the price if a date was given for payment and that date has passed, whether or not property has also passed. It is only in these circumstances that the seller can recover the price. If the buyer simply refuses to accept the goods, and such circumstances are inapplicable, the seller has to claim damages instead. The damages which the seller is entitled to cover the normal loss which arises from the breach. This will allow him to recover the difference between the contract price and the sale price in the market if this is lower.

An unpaid seller is also given certain rights over the goods. These are set out below:

(i) Lien

This is the seller's right to retain the contract goods which are in his possession. It only applies to the contract goods; the seller cannot retain other goods belonging to the buyer which have been paid for even though other goods have not. It is a right to retain the goods until the price is paid. A lien is lost if the seller delivers the goods to a carrier for transmission to the buyer without reserving the right of disposal; if the buyer or his agent obtains lawful possession of the goods; or if the seller waives the lien. The exercise of a lien does not of itself put an end to the contract.

(ii) Stoppage in transit

The right to stop goods in transit can only be exercised where the buyer has become insolvent, that is to say where he has ceased to pay his debts in the ordinary course of business, or is unable to pay debts as they become due. The unpaid seller may exercise his right to stop goods in transit either by taking possession of the goods or giving notice to the carrier. On being given such notice, the carrier must redeliver according to the directions of the seller. The exercise of the right to stop in transit does not of itself put an end to the contract. The right to stop goods in transit comes to an end when the transit ends. This will be when: the buyer or his agent takes delivery of the goods from the carrier, even before arrival at their destination; the carrier or his agent informs the seller that he holds the goods as warehouseman for the buyer, the goods having arrived at their destination; the carrier or his agent wrongfully refuses to deliver to the buyer or his agent; if the carrier acknowledges that he holds the goods for the buyer but keeps them after they have reached their destination; or if the goods, in certain circumstances, are delivered to the master of the buyer's ship. If the goods are rejected by the buyer, and the carrier retains possession, transit is not at an end even if the seller has refused to take the goods back.

(iii) Resale

Although it will normally be a breach of contract for the unpaid seller to resell the goods, there are three cases where he is entitled to resell: where the right to resale was expressly reserved in the contract of sale; where the goods are perishable; and where the unpaid seller gives notice to the buyer of his intention to resell and the buyer does not tender the price within a reasonable time. In these cases, the seller can resell and claim for any loss caused by the buyer's breach of contract. The exercise of the right to resell in these cases rescinds the original agreement and the unpaid seller may keep any profit made on the resale.

Example

On 6 May, the seller sold to the buyer a Vanguard and a Ford Zodiac for a total of £850. The buyer put down a deposit of £25 but refused to pay the balance. The buyer was told that if the balance was not paid by 11 May, the seller would resell the cars. They buyer failed to answer and the Vanguard was sold on 24 May for £350, but no purchaser could be found for the other car. The seller claimed the balance of the purchase price of £475 plus the cost of advertising the cars. The Court of Appeal refused to allow this claim since resale of the Vanguard rescinded the whole contract. The correct remedy was to award the seller damages. These were assessed at the total contract price, £850, less the £25 deposit, less the £350 received for the Vanguard, less an agreed value for the Zodiac, £450, plus the advertising costs of £22.50. The total damages awarded therefore came to £47.50.

(Ward v. Bignall, 1967)

4 *Agency*

4.1 Definition

Agency is based on the principle that one who acts through another is deemed in law to have acted in person. It is the legal relationship which exists between two persons, one of whom, the agent, is employed by the other, the principal, to bring the principal into a legal relationship with a third party.

4.2 Capacity

An agent can be appointed to effect any transaction for which the principal has capacity (the capacity to contract is dealt with in Chapter 2). A mentally disordered person can appoint an agent to purchase or obtain necessaries; and a minor can appoint an agent to buy necessaries or make a beneficial contract of employment for him. In addition, under the terms of the Minors' Contracts Act 1987, a minor can ratify on reaching his majority any contract which would not be binding against him as a minor. This will apply to the ratification of contracts made through an agent.

Anyone not suffering from mental incapacity can be appointed an agent. A minor can act as an agent in a transaction which he would not have been able to make on his own behalf.

4.3 Appointment of Agent

(i) Express Appoinment

Express authority may be given by a principal to his agent orally or in writing, and in the latter case it may be under hand or under seal. If the authority is given under seal it is known as a power of attorney. Under the Powers of Attorney Act 1971, such documents must be signed and sealed by the principal, or by his direction and in his presence. In this latter case, two witnesses are required. If the agent has to execute a deed his appointment must itself be by deed. It should be noted, though, that even if the agent is not appointed by deed he can validly execute a deed if he does so in his principal's presence and by his authority. In addition, s.53 of the Law of Property Act 1925 provides that, subject to exceptions, an interest in land cannot be granted or disposed of except by writing signed by the person creating of it or by his agent authorized in writing.

(ii) Appointment by Implied Agreement

If parties conduct themselves in their relationships with each other that it may be reasonable to suppose that they have agreed to act as principal and agent, then that is what they are. For instance, the agent of an insurance company may also be held to be the agent of the party seeking cover if the circumstances warrant such an implication. Factors which have been found relevant in determining whether an agency has been created by implied agreement are whether one party acts for another at that other's request and whether commission is payable.

(iii) Agency by Estoppel

Estoppel means that a person who has allowed another to believe that a certain state of affairs exists, with the result that another person has relied on that belief, cannot later say that the true state of affairs is different. In the context of agency, this means that a person who, by words or conduct, has allowed another to appear to be his agent, with the result that third parties deal with him as agent, cannot afterwards repudiate this apparent agency if so to do would injure third parties.

Example

The owner of a house asked his wife to put it into the hands of estate agents with a view to sale. She had no authority to instruct the estate agents to enter into a binding contract but a contract was made, signed by the plaintiff as purchaser and by the agents as 'agents for the vendor'. Subsequently, the owner treated the plaintiff as the purchaser, allowing him to engage a builder to carry out repairs to the house, but the owner then refused to complete the contract of sale.
Held: When the owner learned that the plaintiff believed that he was under a binding obligation to him, the owner was then obliged to disclose that there was no such obligation. The failure to disclose that his wife had acted without authority amounted in all the circumstances to a representation that she was the owner's agent, so he was therefore estopped from asserting that the contract had been entered into without authority.

(*Spiro v. Lintern*, 1973)

(iv) Ratification

If a person without previous authority purports to make a contract with a third party on behalf of another, then that person may ratify the contract and adopt it. The effect of this ratification is to establish the relationship of principal and agent between the unauthorized person who made the contract and the person who ratified it. The contract then becomes binding on the principal. There are certain requirements for ratification.

(a) The contract must have been made expressly on behalf of the intended principal.

Example

A firm instructed an agent to buy corn at a certain price. Without authority, the agent bought at a higher price. The agent bought in his own name, even though he intended it to be a purchase on a joint account with the firm.

Held: (by the House of Lords): The firm purported to ratify the contract, but this was of no effect since the agent had not professed to be acting as agent when he made the unauthorized purchase at the higher price.

(Keighley, Maxted and Co. v. Durant, 1901)

(b) The principal must be in existence and have due capacity at the date of the contract.

Example

L. Newborne arranged a contract for the purchase of tinned meat for a company he was forming. The contract was signed 'Leopold Newborne Ltd, Leopold Newborne, Director'. The company, when formed, tried to enforce the agreement.

Held: The company could not do this as when the agreement was made it was not in existence. Newborne himself incurred no rights or liabilities as he signed his name not as an agent but simply to show his responsibility in fixing the signature of the company. It should be noted that s.36 (4) of the Companies Act 1985, repeating the provisions of s.9 (2) of the European Communities Act 1972, states that:

'Where a contract purports to be made by a company, or by a person as agent for a company, at a time when the company has not been formed, then subject to any agreement to the contrary the contract has effect as one entered into by the person purporting to act for the company or as agent for it, and he is personally liable on the contract accordingly.'

(Newborne v. Sensolid (Great Britain) Ltd, 1954)

(c) Ratification must be within any period of time fixed for ratification and in the absence of any fixed period, ratification must be within a reasonable time. It is also the case that ratification must be before the date when the contract is intended to become effective. In *Grover and Grover Ltd v. Mathews* (1910), a contract of fire insurance had been taken out on a person's behalf, but without his authority. That person attempted to ratify the agency after a fire had taken place. The purported ratification was held to be ineffective.

(d) Void contracts are not ratifiable. If the directors of a company purport to make a contract which is outside their power, it cannot be ratified by the shareholders of the company even after altering the memorandum of association to increase their powers. However, by s.9 (1) of the European Communities Act 1972, now s.35 (1) of the Companies Act 1985, in favour of a person dealing with a company in good faith, any transaction decided on by the directors shall be deemed to be one which it is within the capacity of the company to enter into.

(e) A purported principal can only ratify if he is aware of all the material facts, or can be shown to have adopted the purported agent's acts, whatever they were. For instance, if without authority one person agrees to sell another's goods for £100, but then tells the owner that he has sold them for £200, any ratification by the owner will be ineffective if made without knowledge of the true facts.

(v) Agency of Necessity

In certain limited circumstances a person may be bound by a contract made on his behalf without authority and which he declines to ratify. For instance, the master of a ship, in times of emergency, may contract for provisions and urgent repairs and bind the shipowners to the contract.

Example

A railway company carried a horse to its destination. There was no one to receive it and the company had no appropriate accommodation. The horse was therefore placed with a stable keeper and the railway company paid the charges.
Held: The company had acted in an emergency as an agent of necessity and was therefore entitled to claim an indemnity from the owner of the horse.

(*Great Northern Rail Co. v. Swaffield*, 1874)

For a valid agency of necessity to exist, the purported agent must be in a position where it is impossible to contact the purported principal.

Example

For instance, a consignment of tomatoes was sent from Jersey to London. A strike at Weymouth meant that the goods were delayed for two days. On unloading, the company found that they were bad, so they were sold locally without first obtaining instructions from the party to whom they were consigned.
Held: The company was liable in damages to the principal as they should have got in touch with him before selling the consignment. In any case, any action taken or contract made must have been reasonably necessary in the circumstances and taken in good faith in the interest of the principal.

(*Springer v. Great West Railway*, 1921)

The former law, that a deserted wife was an agent of necessity with an authority to pledge her husband's credit, was abrogated by the Matrimonial Proceedings and Property Act 1970.

(vi) Authority of the Agent

An agent may bind his principal in contract by virtue of actual or apparent authority. Apparent, or ostensible authority, is an authority which has not been given by the principal, but which the law regards the agent as possessing notwithstanding the principal's lack of consent.

Example

The principal employed a manager to run a shop. He regularly paid the plaintiff for goods ordered by the manager for sale in the shop. When the manager left the shop he ordered more goods from the plaintiff.
Held: The principal was liable to pay since he had given the manager authority to buy on his behalf in the past and had not informed the plaintiff that this authority had come to an end.

(*Summers v. Solomon*, 1857)

4.4 The Duties of the Agent

The duties of an agent depend primarily on the contract of agency if there is one. Subject to any such express terms, the agent owes a number of implied duties or obligations to his principal. It is the agency relationship as such that gives rise to these obligations so that, as a general rule, they fall as much on the gratuitous agent as on the paid agent.

(i) Obey the Principal's Instructions

If a paid agent agrees to make a particular contract for his principal, he is in breach of contract if he fails to do so.

Examples

In *Turpin v. Bilton* (1843), an insurance broker agreed for consideration to obtain a contract of insurance on the plaintiff's ship, but he failed to do so. The ship was lost and the broker was held liable to the plaintiff. In *Fraser v. B. N. Furman (Productions) Ltd* (1967), insurance brokers agreed for consideration to effect an employer's liability policy and failed to do so. The employer was held liable for £3000 damages in an action brought against him by an employee for breach of the Factories Act, and the Court of Appeal held that the brokers must indemnify the employer in that sum for breach of contract.

(ii) Exercise Care and Skill

An agent, whether paid or gratuitous, is required by law to exercise due skill and care. In the case of paid for agents, this is now laid down by s.13 of the Supply of Goods and Services Act 1982, and is laid down by common law in the case of gratuitous agents.

Example

In *Keppel v. Wheeler* (1927), agents were employed to sell a block of flats and received an offer from one party which was accepted 'subject to contract'. The agents later received a higher offer but, instead of telling the owners, arranged a resale from the earlier party to the later after the original sale to the earlier party was effected. It was ruled that the agents had acted in breach of their duty to obtain the best price available, and that duty included passing on details of better offers until a binding contract was concluded.

(iii) Act Personally

Unless he has been given an express instruction to that effect, an agent is required to act personally. He may not delegate his duties to anyone else. Delegation may be implied from trade usage or from having been authorized in the past between the same parties. If a client instructs a country solicitor, that solicitor is impliedly authorized by his client to delegate work, such as work concerning litigation in

London, to London agents. An agent may also delegate a purely ministerial duty such as a duty to sign letters.

(iv) Fiduciary Duties

Fiduciary duties are those duties which an agent owes to his principal as a matter of good faith. An agent has four main such duties.

(a) Conflict of interest

The agent must not allow his own personal interests to conflict with those of his principal. If the agent breaks this duty, the principal may set aside any transaction made with the agent and claim any profit made by the agent.

Example

A became aware that B wanted to obtain shares in a certain company and told B that he could acquire them for him at £3 a share. A deal was agreed at that price. Later B learned that A was himself the owner of the shares at the time of the transfer, having just bought them at £2 a share.
Held: A was required to pay B the £1 difference.

(Kimber v. Barber, 1872)

(b) Secret profits and bribes

If an agent, in the course of the agency, and without his principal's knowledge and consent, makes a profit for himself out of his position, or out of property or of information with which he is entrusted, he must account for this profit to his principal. Thus, an agent may not accept commission from both parties to a transaction, nor, for example, keep for himself the benefit of a trade discount while charging his principal the full price.

(c) Not to misuse confidential information

It is a breach of the duty of good faith for an agent to use information, acquired while acting as an agent, for his own personal advantage or for the benefit of a third party. This applies even after the agency ceases.

(d) To account

There is a duty on the agent to keep proper accounts of all transactions, and to keep 'agency money' apart from his own.

4.5 The Rights of the Agent

Subject to the express terms of the agency agreement, an agent has a right to claim from his principal an indemnity against all expenses or loss incurred in acting on the principal's behalf.

Example

Solicitors instructed stockbrokers to sell certain shares. The stockbrokers made a contract to sell the shares but incurred a liability to the intended purchaser because the solicitors' client declined to execute a transfer of the shares. It was held that the stockbrokers were entitled to claim an indemnity from the solicitors, the amount of the indemnity being the cost of obtaining substituted stock for the intended purchaser.

(*Hichens, Harrison, Woolston and Co. v. Jackson & Sons*, 1943)

Where there is a contract of agency, the agent may be entitled to be paid for his services. He will, however, be entitled to the remuneration only if he has performed precisely and completely all the obligations in his contract. If he does part of what is required, but not all of it, then he is not entitled to payment unless the contract provides to the contrary. Where the contract provides for the exact amount of remuneration, that is the amount payable. If the contract only provides for the agent to be paid, but does not specify the exact amount, then a reasonable sum has to be paid. This is so at common law and by virtue of s.15 of the Supply of Goods and Services Act 1982. The mere occurrence of the transaction which the agent is commissioned to effect does not entitle him to remuneration. The occurrence must be brought about by the agent unless the contract provides that he is to be paid however the desired result occurs.

An agent who has suffered loss or incurred liabilities in the course of carrying out authorized actions for his principal is entitled to be reimbursed or indemnified by his principal. However, he has no right to reimbursement or an indemnity for losses or liabilities arising because of breaches of duty, such as failing to comply with his instructions, or in carrying out an illegal transaction or a transaction rendered void by statute.

4.6 The Duties of the Principal

The principal is under a duty to pay any agreed commission and remuneration and not to prevent or hinder the agent from earning it. The duty to pay the remuneration, however, will only apply where the agent has been the direct, effective or efficient cause of the event on the occurrence of which the principal has agreed to pay the agent remuneration. It is irrelevant to the payment of the remuneration that the principal has derived no benefit from the agent's acts. So long as the agent has performed what he was employed to do, and has not been at fault in failing to benefit his principal, the latter will be bound to pay the agreed remuneration.

Examples

In *Fisher v. Drewett* (1879), the agent was employed to get a mortgage for his principal's property. A third party was found ready to advance the money, but the mortgage could not be made because the principal had no title. It was held that the agent was entitled to his remuneration, despite the fact that the principal had derived no benefit from the act. The agent had done what he was employed to do. On the other hand, the agent would not be entitled to his commission if he had not performed what the agency contract required him to do, even if the principal's conduct had prevented the agent from achieving this, so long as the principal's conduct was legitimate under the contract, as where the principal accepted a higher offer from another purchaser, or the principal was entitled to reject the offer of a loan from a third party introduced by the agent, in accordance with his task of finding a lender, on the ground that the terms of such loan was unacceptable (*Francis v. Bond Street Brokers Ltd*, 1967).

Even if there is an agreement to pay remuneration and the agent has obtained what the principal wanted, there may be no liability to pay the agreed remuneration. This will be so where the transaction on which the agent was employed was illegal. The same applies in respect of an agency connected with a gaming or wagering transaction. But the liability to pay remuneration depends on whether the agent knew the undertaking was illegal. In *Haines v. Busk* (1814), commission was recoverable by a broker for procuring freight, even though the charter party arranged by the broker was illegal. This was because, although to make it legal the charterer had to obtain certain licences (which had not been done), the broker did not have to obtain the licences but was entitled to rely upon the charterer's doing so. Similarly, the agent will be unable to receive remuneration when he has acted in breach of his duties under the contract of agency, or is otherwise guilty of misconduct. Thus, if the agent has acted in an unauthorized way, as by selling property by private contract instead of by auction as agreed, he cannot recover the commission, even though there may be a custom permitting him to recover his commission, so long as such custom is not known to the principal.

(i) The Principal's Duty to Indemnify the Agent

The principal's duty to indemnify his agent against losses, liabilities and expenses incurred in the performance of the undertaking may be expressly stated in the contract of agency, but more often it is implied. Hence, the extent of his liability depends on the nature of the agreement between the parties, and the kind of business in which the agent is employed.

Examples

In *Adams v. Morgan & Co.* (1924), the business carried on by the agent for the principal was such that it could be implied that the principal would indemnify his agent in respect of payments of supertax. However, the agent will not be entitled to claim an indemnity if he has not acted within his express, implied or usual authority, or if he has acted unlawfully, in breach of duty or negligently. In *Barron v. Fitzgerald* (1840), the agent was employed to effect insurance on the principals' lives. He was given authority to do so in the names of the principals, or in his, the agent's, own name. He did so in the name of X and then claimed an indemnity. It was held that the principals were not so liable since the agent had exceeded his authority. Similarly, in *New Zealand Farmers' Co-operative Distributing Co. Ltd v. National Mortgage and Agency Co. of New Zealand* (1961), an agent was not entitled to recover expenses which were incurred through his lack of knowledge and skill as regards the transaction in respect of which he was employed.

4.7 The Principal and the Third Party

(i) Rights of Principal against Third Party

The rights of the principal against the third party depend to a considerable extent on whether the principal was disclosed or undisclosed. A disclosed principal is one of whose existence the third party was aware at the time of contracting, whether or not the third party knew his name. An undisclosed principal is one of whose existence the third party was unaware at the time of contracting. With regard to a disclosed principal, the general rule is that he can sue the third party. The third party is not discharged by settling with the agent unless the principal has by his conduct induced the third party so to do, or unless the agent had authority to receive the payment. The third party cannot set off against the principal any debt which the agent may owe to the third party. Where the principal is undisclosed, he also can sue the third party. That right, however, is limited as follows:

(*a*) An undisclosed principal is not allowed to intervene where this would be inconsistent with the terms of the contract.

Example

A person signed a charterparty as 'owner'.
Held: This meant that only he was owner, so the undisclosed principal could not intervene.

(*Humble v. Hunter*, 1842)

(*b*) If the party can show that he wanted to deal with the agent and with no one else, the undisclosed principal cannot intervene.

Example

A person agreed to underwrite a new issue of shares by a company.
Held: This contract involved such reliance on the business reputation and integrity of the underwriter that his undisclosed principal was not allowed to enforce it.

(*Collins v. Associated Greyhound Racecourses Ltd*, 1930)

(*c*) An undisclosed principal can only sue the third party subject to any defences which the third party has against the agent. This rule is clearly necessary for the protection of the third party who thinks that he is dealing with the agent alone. Thus, if the agent owes money to the third party, the debt can be set off against the principal by the third party, and if the third party pays the agent he can rely on the payment against the principal.

(ii) Liability of Principal to Third Party

The general rule is that, disclosed or undisclosed, the principal is liable to the third party. An undisclosed principal will not be liable, however, if the true construction of the contract is that the agent is solely entitled and liable under it. The principal cannot set off against the third party any money owed to him by the agent. If the principal gives the agent the money with which to pay the third party, but the agent fails to pay it over, the principal remains liable to the third party. He must seek out his creditor and see that he is paid. The principal is only discharged by payment to the agent if such payment is made at the third party's request, or if the third party looked to the agent for payment and so induced the principal to settle with the agent.

4.8 The Agent and the Third Party

The general rule is that the agent is neither liable under, nor entitled to enforce, a contract which he makes on behalf of his principal. However, there are a number of exceptions:

(*a*) An agent is liable under the contract if he in fact intended to undertake personal liability. An agent who is described in a written contract as a party to it and signs it without qualification is liable under it even though the third party knew that he was contracting as agent (*Basma v. Weekes*, 1950). It was at one time thought that the inference that the agent intended to contract personally must be drawn whenever he acted on behalf of a foreign principal, but it is now recognized that this fact is only one of many to be taken into account when determining whether the agent had any such intention.

(*b*) An agent may be personally liable or entitled if that is the usual course of business either between particular parties or in relation to a particular class of agents.

(*c*) Where the principal is undisclosed, the agent is both entitled and liable, but this rule does not apply where the agent uses words of representation and the principal is only unnamed.

(*d*) An agent may purport to act on behalf of a principal when he is in fact acting on his own behalf. If he purports to act on behalf of an unnamed principal, he can enforce the contract for his own benefit. If, however, he purports to act for a named principal, he can only enforce the contract after giving the third party due notice that he acted on his own behalf. Even then, the agent will not be allowed to sue if this would prejudice the third party. These safeguards are necessary as the third party may have relied on the attributes of the named principal when making the contract. Where the alleged principal is non-existent, it will be easier to infer that the agent intended to assume personal liability.

Examples

In *Kelner v. Baxter* (1886), promoters were personally held liable on a contract made by them on behalf of a company which had not then been formed. Section 36 (4) of the Companies Act 1985 now provides that

'Where a contract purports to be made by . . . a person as agent for a company, at a time when the company has not been formed, then subject to any agreement to the contrary the contract has effect as one entered into by the person purporting to act . . . as agent'.

The principle of Kelner's case extends, of course, beyond the problems of unformed companies.

(*e*) An agent who enters into a contract under seal is liable on it, even if he is known to be contracting as an agent (*Schack v. Anthony*, 1813). In the case of a seal executed under a power of attorney, however, s.7 (1) of the Powers of Attorney Act 1971 has the effect of making the donor of the power liable.

(*f*) There are certain statutory exceptions. Under s.44 (1) of the Insolvency Act 1986, an administrative receiver appointed by debenture holders, who is deemed to be the agent of the company, is nevertheless personally liable on a contract into which he enters in carrying out his functions, except in so far as the contract provides otherwise. Under s.5 of the Partnership Act 1890, a partner who contracts on behalf of the partnership is jointly liable with the rest of the partners on that contract.

(*g*) If a trade custom, not inconsistent with the contract, makes an agent liable on a contract, the courts will give effect to that custom (*Barrow and Bros v. Dyster, Nalder and Co.*, 1884).

(*h*) Under s.26 of the Bills of Exchange Act 1882, an agent will be personally liable on a negotiable instrument if he signs his name as a party to the instrument, unless he indicates that he is signing on behalf of a principal.

(i) Agent's Sole or Joint Liability

Where the agent is liable on the contract, the question will arise whether the principal is also liable. If the agent was acting for an undisclosed principal, then agent and principal are jointly liable. This may also be the case where an agent incurs personal responsibility under a contract made on behalf of a disclosed principal (*The Swan*, 1968). Where the agent and principal are jointly liable, then the third party may elect which one to sue. This election may be express or implied. An implied election will only occur if a third party with full knowledge of the relevant facts indicates clearly which party he intends to hold liable on the contract. What consitutes an implied election is a question of fact: beginning legal proceedings, demanding payment, and debiting an account are all relevant but not conclusive factors. Under s.3 of the Civil Liability (Contribution) Act 1978, the mere fact that judgment has been obtained against one person is not a bar to proceedings against another who is jointly liable, though it could possibly still amount to an election.

(ii) Agent's Liability on a Collateral Contract

If there is a collateral contract between the agent and the third party, this is separate from the main contract between the principal and the third party and can be separately sued upon. At a sale by auction, there is a collateral contract between buyer and auctioneer under which the auctioneer undertakes to give the buyer possession. The buyer is also liable under this contract to pay the price of the thing sold.

(iii) The Agent's Implied Warranty of Authority

If a person acts as agent, knowing that he has no authority, he is liable to the third party for breach of warranty of authority if he has represented to the third party that he has such authority (*Collen v. Wright*, 1857). Purporting to act as agent constitutes a representation of authority unless the third party knew or ought to have known of the lack of authority (*Halbot v. Lens*, 1901). Even if an agent genuinely and reasonably believes that he has authority, when he has not, he may be liable for breach of the warranty.

Examples

In *Yonge v. Toynbee* (1910), an agent acting on behalf of his principal was held liable when, entirely unknown to him, his authority had been terminated by the insanity of his principal. The agent will not, however, be liable if the representation of authority is a mistake as to law and not fact. In addition, there is no breach of the warranty if an agent acts without authority in circumstances where his principal would be bound. In *Rainbow v. Howkins* (1914), an auctioneer who was authorized to sell a horse, subject to a reserve price, sold it without reserve. It was held that he was not in breach of the implied warranty, since the buyer could have enforced the contract on the ground that the auctioneer had apparent authority to sell without reserve. Similarly, an agent would not be liable for breach of the implied warranty if he did an unauthorized act which the principal later ratified.

4.9 Types of Agent

Factors and Mercantile Agents

A factor, now commonly referred to as a 'mercantile agent' is defined by s.1 of the Factors Act 1889 as a person 'having in the customary course of his business as such agent authority to sell goods or to consign goods for the purpose of sale, or to buy goods, or to raise money on the security of goods'. Under s.2 of the Act, any sale, pledge or other disposition of goods by a mercantile agent in possession with the consent of the owner passes a good title in those goods to a good faith third party even though the owner had not consented to the particular disposition.

(ii) Brokers

A broker has been defined as

> 'An agent employed to make bargains and contracts between persons in matters of trade commerce and navigation. Properly speaking, a broker is a mere negotiator between other parties. . . . He himself . . . has no possession of the goods, no power actual or legal of determining the destination of the goods, no power or authority to determine whether the goods belong to buyer or seller or either.' (*Fowler v. Hollins*, 1872.)

For instance, stockbrokers deal with stocks and shares; insurance brokers deal with policies of insurance; credit brokers arrange credit for those who wish to obtain goods. Other brokers deal with the hiring of ships on charter parties. Stockbrokers will fall within the Financial Services Act 1986, insurance brokers within the Insurance Brokers (Registration) Act 1977, and credit brokers within the Consumer Credit Act, 1974.

(iii) Auctioneers

Auctioneers are agents whose ordinary business is to sell goods by public auction. They are not always given possession, but when they are then they are mercantile agents (*see* 4.9 (i)). Auctioneers are agents for both parties. The auctioneer can be sued in conversion by the true owner if the seller of the goods lacks proper title.

(iv) Shipmasters

A shipmaster is the captain or similar officer of a ship who has been appointed to conduct the voyage of the ship to a favourable conclusion. He has wide authority in his conduct of the affairs of the ship with respect to its navigation, control of the crew and passengers, and handling of the cargo. In consequence of emergencies, his authority may be considerably widened with regard to the disposition of the ship itself or its cargo under the doctrine of agency of necessity. (*see* 4.3 (v)).

(v) Estate Agents

An estate agent who is instructed to negotiate the sale of a house by private treaty has no authority, unless it is agreed to the contrary. Despite his title, he is not an agent in the normal sense of the word in that he does not usually act as the vendor's agent. However, estate agents have been held liable to their clients for breach of fiduciary duties, failure to exercise reasonable care and skill, or for the unauthorized appointment of a subagent. They have also been held liable to third parties, as well as their principals, where the agent has been guilty of a negligent misrepresentation with respect to property with which the agent has been dealing on the client's behalf. In *Sorrell v. Finch* (1977), it was ruled that an agent possessed no authority to receive and accept a deposit from a potential buyer with the result that the vendor was not liable to the buyer who had lost his deposit by reason of the estate agent's impropriety. The profession is regulated by the Estate Agents Act 1979 under which the Director-General of Fair Trading may bar persons from estate agency work.

(vi) Solicitors

In the exercise of their profession, solicitors frequently involve those employing them in legal responsibility for the agreements made on their behalf in and out of court. However, it has been held that a solicitor has no implied authority on behalf of his client (*Singer v. The Trustees of the Property of Munro*, 1981); but a client's solicitor and counsel do have implied authority, as between themselves and the client, to compromise a suit without reference to the client for instructions, so long as such a compromise did not include matters that were collateral to the intended action, and they were also invested with apparent authority as between themselves and the opposing litigants, to compromise such suit without proof of authority (*Waugh v. H.B. Clifford and Sons*, 1982). It has also been ruled that, in a contract for the sale of land, knowledge acquired by the purchaser's solicitors is to be imputed to the purchaser himself (*Strover v. Harrington*, 1987).

(vii) Del Credere Agents

These are agents who, in return for an extra commission, undertake responsibility for the due performance of their contracts by persons whom they introduce to their principals.

(viii) Confirming Houses

When a supplier receives an overseas order, it is usual for the order to be confirmed by a person in the supplier's country. This person, a 'confirmer', is personally liable to the supplier if the buyer fails to carry out the contract.

Example

Buyers in Turkey placed orders for radio sets with British manufacturers, the order being confirmed by C. After part of the goods had been received, the buyers refused to accept the balance.
Held: C was liable to the exporter in damages for the non-acceptance by the buyer.

(*Sobell Industries Ltd v. Cory Bros and Co. Ltd*, 1955)

(ix) Advertising Agents

Despite their popular title, advertising agents are not agents at all but independent principals in their own right, a fact recognized by their professional body which is known as the Institute of Practitioners in Advertising. This was established in the case of *Emmett v. De Witt* (1957). It was conceded by defendant advertisers that certain sums were due in respect of particular advertising. These sums were paid into court, but no further concession was made as to whether the plaintiff agency was in fact a principal or an agent. It was held that it was the

> 'Custom of the advertising trade in England that advertising agents who agree to procure the publication of their customers' advertisements in newspapers or otherwise and place orders for such publication with the publishers contract as principals with their customers and/or the publishers.'

This means that if an advertising agent becomes insolvent owing money to a media owner, the owner cannot look to the advertiser for payment. Again, if the advertiser becomes insolvent, the agency still has to pay the media owner, even though the agency will not be reimbursed by the advertiser.

4.10 Termination of Agency

Where the agency is contractual, it may be for a fixed term, or it might specify a period of notice. If neither is the case, the agency agreement can be determined on the giving of reasonable notice, this being a question of fact depending on all the relevant circumstances. If notice is given in breach of the agreement, the innocent party is entitled to damages, but the agency relationship is still at an end. If the principal effectively brings the agency to an end, as by closing down the relevant business, this determines the agency. Whether the agency can then claim damages depends on whether there was a breach of an express term of the agency or of an implied term.

Examples

In *French & Co. Ltd v. Leeston Shipping Co. Ltd* (1922), agents who arranged the charter of a ship for eighteen months were to be paid commission on the basis of a monthly chartering fee. The charterers bought the ship after four months, thereby terminating the charter contract. It was held that the agents were not entitled to claim the commission which they would have earned if the charter had continued for the full eighteen months. On the other hand, in *Turner v. Goldsmith* (1891) a manufacturer agreed to employ a salesman for five years. After two years his factory was destroyed. It was held that the manufacturer was not released from his obligation to provide the agent with a chance to earn commission, so that the agent was awarded damages.

(i) Death

The death of either party determines the agency whether the survivor has notice of the death or not. Dissolution of a company or partnership has the same effect.

(ii) Bankruptcy

The principal's bankruptcy terminates the agent's authority. The bankruptcy of the agent makes him unfit to perform his duties.

(iii) Insanity

At common law, agency is determined by the supervening insanity of the principal or agent.

(iv) Powers of Attorney

The Powers of Attorney Act, 1971, provides that a power of attorney expressed to be irrevocable, and given to secure a proprietary interest of, or the performance of an obligation owed to, the donee of the power shall not be revoked by the donor without the consent of the donee, or by the donor's death, incapacity or bankruptcy, so long as the interest or obligation secured by it remains in being. The Act also protects third parties who deal in good faith with the donee of a power which is expressed to be irrevocable and to be given by way of security. A third party is entitled to act in reliance on the power unless he knows that it has been revoked by the donor with the consent of the donee. The Enduring Powers of Attorney Act 1985 makes provision for powers of attorney executed in a prescribed form and express to continue in spite of the donor's supervening mental incapacity. Such an enduring power is not revoked by such incapacity, but when such incapacity occurs the power is in effect suspended until registered by the court. Once an enduring power has been registered, it can no longer be revoked by the donor; it can only be revoked with the consent of the court.

(v) Authority Coupled with an Interest

An authority coupled with an interest cannot be revoked. The authority must be given for valuable consideration, or under seal, to secure some interest of the agent which exists independently of the agency. The rule only applies if the authority was intended for the protection of the interest; it cannot apply where the interest arose after the creation of the authority. Thus, in *Smart v. Sandars* (1848) an agent to whom goods were entrusted for sale later advanced money to the owner. His authority did not thereby become irrevocable.

(vi) Apparent Authority

Notice to the agent does not terminate apparent authority. Notice must be given to a third party to have effect. A principal's insanity terminates his agent's actual authority, but a third party who goes on dealing with the agent without notice of the insanity may be able to sue the principal on the ground that the agent still had apparent authority.

4.11 Effect of Termination

Termination normally brings to an end an agent's authority to act on behalf of the principal. This is true even if the termination is wrongful and gives the injured party a claim in damages. Termination also brings to an end the relationship of principal and agent, *inter se*, so that after termination no fresh rights between them can arise out of that relationship. On the other hand, rights and liabilities which have accrued before termination are not affected by termination. An agent who continues to act for his former principal after termination may become liable to a third party for breach of warranty of authority (*see* 4.8 (iii)).

5 *The protection of intellectual property*

5.1 The Basic Rule

It is a basic rule of English law that ideas cannot be protected. Monopolies in ideas are looked on with disfavour, the view being that it is in the public interest that ideas should be exploited to the full irrespective of the fact that this might leave the originator of the idea without reward.

Example

The plaintiff had the idea of publishing a drawing of a hand making a cross on a ballot paper, thus instructing the illiterate how to vote.
Held: He was unable to prevent another party from publishing a similar drawing since the idea itself could not be protected (*Kennick v. Lawrence*, 1890).

However, statute law has intervened in many areas of what is now generally called intellectual property to protect certain specific categories of such property. The student should realize, though, these statutes only serve as exceptions to the rule, so that if there is an area of intellectual property not covered by them or the tort of passing of, the basic rule described in this paragraph prevails.

5.2 Patentability

Section 1 of the Patents Act 1977 requires the following conditions to be satisfied before a patent is granted:

(i) The invention is new.
(ii) It involves an inventive step.
(iii) It is capable of industrial application.

An invention is taken to be new if it does not form part of the state of the art. This is defined in the case of an invention as including all matter, whether a product, a process, information about either or anything else, which has at any time before the priority date (that is, the date of filing the application) of that invention been made available to the public within or outside the United Kingdom by written or oral description, by use or in any other way. The state of the art also includes matter contained in an application for another patent which was published on or after the priority date of the application if:

71

(i) That matter was contained in an application for that patent both as filed and published.

(ii) The priority date of that matter is earlier than that of the invention.

With regard to the inventive step, the invention will be lacking this if it was obvious at the priority date to a person skilled in the art to perform the steps performed by the patentee for the purpose of achieving the object achieved by the patentee. If, on the other hand, an inventor achieves a particular object in a way which would not have been obvious to the person skilled in the art, then there is an inventive step. If it was obvious that a particular step should be taken for a particular purpose, a person taking that step, whether or not with the object of performing that purpose may nevertheless be deemed to have made an invention if he achieves some special and unexpected result or finds special and unexpected properties.

An invention is taken to be capable of industrial application if it can be made or used in any kind of industry including agriculture. An invention of a method of treatment of the human or animal body by surgery, therapy or diagnosis is not included as capable of industrial application. However, this does not prevent a product consisting of a substance or composition being so treated merely because it is invented for use in any such method of treatment.

There is also a list of matters excluded by the Act from patentability as being essentially intellectual: scientific theories; mathematical methods; computer programes; aesthetic creations of all sorts.

5.3 Patent Protection

Application for patents are made to the Patent Office, usually with the help of patent agents, and once granted a patent lasts for a maximum of 20 years. The patent has, however, to be kept in force during that period by the payment of annual renewal fees. Section 60 of the Act states that a person infringes another's patent if, without the consent of the patent holder:

(i) Where the invention is a product, he makes, disposes, uses or imports the product or keeps it for disposal or otherwise.

(ii) Where the invention is a process, he uses or offers it for use in the United Kingdom knowing, or where it would be obvious to a reasonable person in the circumstances, that its use without the patent holder's consent would be an infringement.

(iii) Where the invention is a process, he disposes or offers to do so, uses or imports any product obtained directly by means of that process or keeps it for disposal or otherwise.

It will also constitute infringement where a person (other than the patent holder), while the patent is in force and without the holder's consent, supplies or offers to supply in the United Kingdom any of the means, relating to an essential element of the invention, for putting it into effect, to a person other than a licensee or other entitled person when he knows or should reasonably know that those means are suitable and intended for putting the invention into effect in the United Kingdom.

5.4 Licensing

If the patent is valid, the manufacture, import, sale or use of a patented article, or of articles made by a patented process or machine, are each only lawful if the patent holder gives permission for them. This permission is known as a 'licence'. Subject to certain exceptions, a patent holder can charge what he likes for the licence and make what rules he likes for its exercise. Under EEC law, if a licence is granted to manufacture a patented article in one EEC country, that licence cannot stop the licensee selling the item manufactured in other EEC countries. United Kingdom law states that a licensee cannot normally be compelled to buy unpatented materials from the licensor (though he may be given preferential terms if he does); and the licensee cannot be stopped from putting an end to the licence once the original patents have expired, though he can on occasions be required by the licence to stop manufacturing if he does.

An application can be made to the Patent Office for a compulsory licence on the ground that a patent is being misused, as where the patent is being used to prevent all use of an invention. An application cannot be made for three years after the patent has been granted. The successful applicant will have to pay a proper royalty.

5.5 Designing Round a Patent

In practice, the patent agent who devises the specifications to be incorporated in a patent application tries to guess what features of the new product are going to be important to its success, and makes claims to cover whatever combinations of those features are not found in earlier specifications. If he makes the right decision, the patent should be valid and difficult to 'design round'. If the agent makes the wrong decision, it will be later found either that he has claimed something only trivially different from the subject of an earlier patent (in which case the new patent will be invalid for obviousness; *see* 5.2) or that the patent has been confined to items having some features that are not essential, in which case rivals may be able to avoid infringing the patent by omitting that particular feature.

One way to avoid a patent is to go back to earlier patents. This could place the owner of the latest patent in a difficulty because, if his own patent is not all that different from those which came before, then his own will be invalid. For example, when the Schick shaver first came onto the market, it was protected by a valid US patent. Shortly afterwards, several makes of shaver came to the market closely resembling designs proposed by earlier patents. However, the change in the shaver introduced by the rivals of Schick differed too much from the earlier patent.

5.6 Remedies for Infringement

The usual procedure in any action for infringement is for the issue of liability to be decided first. If the patent holder does win, he is given a 'certificate of contested validity'. He then has to choose between being compensated according to the damage which the infringement has done to his own business; or, instead, to have paid over to him the profits made by the infringer for the infringement. In either case, only the damage suffered or the profits made in the six years immediately prior to the issue of the writ in the action and since the issue of the writ can be awarded. If he elects to have damages, the court will order an inquiry into how much the infringement has injured the patent holder. However, an infringer can escape damages if he can show that, at the time of infringement, he was not aware, and had no reasonable grounds for supposing, that the particular patent was in existence. As to the measure of damages, the patent holder is entitled to exact compensation for any monetary damage which he has actually suffered which can be fairly attributed to the infringement.

When it comes to the alternative of taking an account of profits, it is the infringer's profits that matter, not those of the patent holder. These are harder to assess, the result being that, in practice, an account of profits is not often requested. Innocent infringement of a patent is probably a defence, but this is not entirely clear.

5.7 Employee Rights

The Patents Act 1977 regulates the rights to employees' inventions and compensation of employment for certain inventions. Notwithstanding any rule of law, an invention made by an employee shall, as between himself and his employer, be taken to belong to the employer if:

(i) It was made in the course of the normal duties of the employee or in the course of duties falling outside the normal duties, but specifically assigned to him, and the circumstances in either case were such that an invention might reasonably be expected to result from the carrying out of his duties.

(ii) The invention was made in the course of the duties of the employee and at the time of making the invention, because of the nature of his duties and the particular responsibilities arising from the nature of the duties, he had a special obligation to further the interest of the employer's undertaking. Any other invention made by an employee, shall, as between himself and the employer, be taken for those purposes to belong to the employee.

Where it appears to the court or the controller of patents on application by an employee that the latter has made an invention which belongs to the employer for which a patent has been granted, that the patent is of outstanding benefit (having regard, not exclusively, to the size and nature of the employer's undertakings) then, if it is just on the facts to award compensation to the employee, the court or controller may do so on the basis of securing for the employee a fair share of the benefit which the employer has derived or might be reasonably expected to derive from the patent or from its exploitation.

5.8 Patenting Abroad

The following countries belong to the European Patent Convention: Austria, Belgium, Switzerland, West Germany, France, the United Kingdom, Lichtenstein, Luxembourg, the Netherlands and Sweden. The European Patent Office is in Munich. If an applicant wishes to take out a patent in at least three of these countries, he can make a single application through the Office. This facility has considerably reduced the attractiveness of the purely United Kingdom application. There is presently no single patent for the whole territory of the EEC.

International applications can also be made under the terms of the Patent Co-operation Treaty which covers some 40 countries. This system is supervised in Geneva by the World Intellectual Property Organization. An application made to a national Patent Office will be handed to a foreign office specializing in the particular subject matter. Eventually, the application will be passed to those countries which adhere to the Treaty in which the applicant wants patent protection.

5.9 Copyright

The present law on copyright is governed by the Copyright Act 1956. But a word of warning is necessary: as this book was going to press, a major Bill reforming the law of copyright was proceeding through Parliament. Readers would be well advised to check the latest position for themselves.

5.10 Copyright Works

Sections 2 and 3 of the 1956 Act give copyright protection to all 'original' literary, dramatic, musical and artistic works. The test is the originality of the work, not its quality. Copyright exists independently of any formalities such as registration; it is enough merely to produce an original work.

5.11 Period of Copyright

The periods of copyright protection are as follows:

(i) Literary, dramatic and musical works—until 50 years from the end of the year in which the author died or publication, whichever is later.

(ii) Artistic works—until 50 years from publication in the case of a photograph, until 50 years from the death of the author or publication, whichever is later, for an engraving; 50 years from the death of the author for other artistic works.

(iii) Films (this includes a television programme)—until 50 years from registration of a British film under the Cinematograph Films Act registration provisions, otherwise 50 years from publication, that is release of copies of the film.

(iv) Sound recordings—until 50 years from publication, that is, issue to the public of records or tapes.

(v) Broadcasts—both the BBC and IBA have a special copyright in their own broadcasts, which lasts for 50 years from the first broadcast.

5.12 Copyright Protection

The Act lists the following as restricted by the existence of copyright in an artistic work:

(i) Reproducing it in any material form.
(ii) Publishing it.
(iii) Including the work in any television broadcast.
(vi) Causing a television programme which includes the work to be transmitted to subscribers to a diffusion service.

In the case of musical, literary and dramatic works, the following will count as infringing copyright:

(i) Reproducing the work in any material from.
(ii) Performing the work in public.
(iii) Publishing the work.
(vi) Broadcasting the work.

In the case of sound recordings, the Act prevents any person from making a record embodying the recordings; from causing the recording to be heard in public; and from broadcasting the recording. For cinematograph films, the following are restricted: taking a copy; causing the film to be seen or heard in the public; broadcasting the film; causing it to be transmitted to subscribers to a diffusion service.

5.13 Infringement of Copyright

Copyright is infringed whenever any of the acts referred to in 5.12 is done, which has the effect either of a complete reproduction of the copyright work or is alternatively a reproduction of a 'substantial part'.

Examples

In the case of *Ladbroke (Football) Ltd v. William Hill (Football) Ltd* (1964), it was said that this phrase was to be judged more in view of the quality of what was copied than with the quantity. So, where an advertiser photographed his wife and cut out her head, substituting that of the Princess of Wales, his subsequent use of the photograph for advertising purposes was held to infringe the copyright in the photograph of the Princess (*London Stereoscopic Society v. Kelly*, 1888). Section 48 (1) of the Act also states that reproduction also includes the conversion of an artistic work into a three-dimensional form or converting an artistic work from a three-dimensional to a two-dimensional form. But before an infringement can occur in the former case, it is necessary that non-experts should recognize the particular item as reproducing the original. Brooches, plaster dolls and toys can therefore infringe copyright in drawings and cartoons.

(i) Copying

Without copying, there can be no copyright infringement. If one person quite by himself produces an identical work to an existing copyright work, however unlikely that might be in practice, there is no infringement of copyright (*Macmillan & Co. Ltd v. Cooper*, 1923). It is generally accepted that an offence is committed as much by subconscious copying as it is by deliberate copying.

(ii) Innocent Copying

Where a work has been copied, subconsciously or deliberately, it may have been in ignorance of the original having copyright protection. However, this is as much an offence as copying a work known to possess copyright protection, though it can affect the injured party's remedies (*see* 5.18 and 5.18 (ii)).

5.14 Permitted Copying

Sections 6 and 9 of the Act permit what is called 'fair dealing' in literary, dramatic, musical and artistic works. No infringement occurs where copying is done for research and private purposes; nor is there any infringement when reproduction is for the purpose of criticism or review, although here there must be sufficient acknowledgment of the original.

Artistic works attract further exceptions. Works of artistic craftsmanship (which in this context includes sculptures and artistic works other than works of architecture, paintings, drawings, engravings and photographs) may be the subject of a painting, drawing, engraving, photograph or be included in a cinematograph film or television broadcast, provided that the particular work copied is permanently situated in a public place. The Act further provides that copyright is not infringed when a painting, drawing, engraving or photograph is made of a work of architecture, or the work is included in a cinematograph film or a television broadcast. In addition, the copyright in an artistic work is not infringed by the inclusion of the work in a cinematograph film or television broadcast if it is included only for background purposes or is otherwise incidental to the principal matters represented in the film or broadcast.

In relation to musical works, it is not an infringement to make a copy of a work if records of it have been previously been made or imported for sale, if they were made or imported by the copyright owner, and if the person making the record:

(i) Intends to sell the record by retail or supply it for sale by retail, or intends to use it to make other records for such sale or supply.

(ii) Notifies the copyright owner of his intention.

(iii) Pays a prescribed royalty, currently $6\frac{1}{4}$ per cent of the 'ordinary retail selling price'.

Example

In *Chappell and Co. Ltd v. The Nestlé Co. Ltd*, 1959, a manufacturer of records notified the copyright owners of his intention to make records of a musical work, subsequently selling the records to chocolate manufacturers for 4d. These manufacturers advertised the records as available for 1/6d plus three wrappers of their milk chocolate. By a bare majority, the House of Lords ruled that the cash with wrappers did not amount to an 'ordinary retail price'.

5.15 Ownership of Copyright

Section 4 (1) of the Act lays down the basic rule that the author of a copyright work is also the owner of the copyright. There are a number of qualifications to be made to this basic rule.

(i) Cinematograph Films, Television and Sound Broadcasts

In these cases, the Act says that 'the maker' owns the copyright, that is to say 'the person by whom the arrangements necessary for the making of the film are undertaken'. In the case of television and sound broadcasts, ownership of copyright is in the BBC or the IBA as appropriate. The Act was amended by the Cable and Broadcasting Act 1984 to give copyright in the appropriate case to the operator of a cable system.

(ii) Journalists

The Act states that where a journalist creates a copyright literary, musical or dramatic work as part of his contract of employment with a newspaper, magazine or similar periodical, the proprietor is entitled to the copyright so far as copyright relates to publication in the particular journal, but in all other respects the journalist holds the copyright. The parties can agree that the journalist holds copyright for all purposes.

(iii) Photographs, Portraits and Engravings

The Act provides that, except where the parties agree to the contrary, where a person commissions the taking of a photograph, the painting or drawing of a portrait, or the making of an engraving, and he agrees to pay in money or money's worth, the person commissioning the work owns the copyright.

(iv) Contracts of Service and Apprenticeship

Where a copyright work is produced by an employee in the course of his contract of service or apprenticeship, the employer is entitled to the copyright unless the parties have agreed to the contrary.

5.16 Assignment of Copyright

Assignment of copyright passes full ownership of the copyright from one person to another. Section 36 of the Act states that an assignment must be in writing and by or on behalf of the current owner of the copyright. Assignment can be partial in that it may: cover only a part of the remaining copyright period; be limited by country; or be limited to certain acts; or a combination of the foregoing. Where an assignment is made orally, it has effect in equity only. In such circumstances, the assignee can only sue for breach of the copyright assigned to him if he joins the legal owner as co-plaintiff. The assignor has to hold in trust any royalties received on behalf of the assignee. The legal title in the copyright remains in the assignor and any disposition by him of the legal title to an assignee who has no notice of the equitable assignment puts an end to that assignment. Section 37 allows for the assignment of future copyright, as where an author assigns copyright in a work yet to be written. The assignment must be in writing and signed by or on behalf of the assignor.

5.17 Licences

A licence is a permission to do an act in relation to a copyright work which would otherwise be infringement. The ownership of the copyright is unaffected by the existence of a licence which can be in any form, written, oral or implied. However, if the copyright owner is willing to grant an exclusive licence, this must be in writing and be signed by or on behalf of the copyright owner. Such a licence authorizes the licensee, to the exclusion of all others, to exercise those rights which, in the absence of the licence, would be the sole prerogative of the copyright owner. Broadly, an exclusive licensee is in the same position as an assignee (*see* 5.16). However, while the terms of a licence bind all subsequent owners of the copyright, they do not bind the owner who takes the copyright without notice of the licence, exclusive or otherwise.

5.18 Remedies for Infringement

Section 17 of the Act gives an injured party the right to relief 'by way of damages, injunction, accounts or otherwise'. An award of damages will reflect any loss suffered by the copyright owner through diminution of sales or the loss of the profit he would otherwise have made. If the infringement was flagrant, and if any benefit can be shown to have accrued to the defendant by reason of the infringement, and having regard to all other circumstances, the court can award such additional damages as it considers 'appropriate'. The Act prohibits awards of exemplary damages in s.17 which means that the additional damages which can be awarded 'go largely to compensation of the plaintiff's suffering from injured feelings and distress and strain' (*Beloff v. Pressdram Ltd*, 1973). Damages cannot be awarded against an innocent infringer, that is to say a person who neither knew nor had reasonable grounds to suspect that copyright subsisted in a particular work.

(i) Account of Profits

The plaintiff can ask either for damages or for an account of profits (an account is the only option where the infringement was innocent, *see* 5.18). By an account, the court, 'as the nearest approximation which it can make to justice, takes from the wrongdoer all the profits he has made by his piracy, and then gives them to the party who has been wronged' (*Colburn v. Simms*, 1843).

(ii) Infringing Copies

The injured party has full rights and remedies in respect of the conversion or detention of infringing copies, and plates to be used for producing such copies, as if he had been their owner since they were made. This gives him the right to delivery of the copies and plates as well as to damages for conversion. However, such damages cannot be awarded against the innocent infringer (*see* 5.18).

(iii) Injunction

In addition to compensation, a plaintiff may seek an injunction against repetition of the wrongful act. This will be granted where repetition is likely and there is a probability of damage.

5.19 Design Copyright

Under the Design Copyright Act 1956, the owner of an industrial design can enforce his own copyright against those who infringe it within fifteen years from the date when he first marketed the designed articles; after that period the design can be used without infringement. In order to bring an action for infringement, the following prerequisites are necessary:

(i) An example of the copyright articles in model or drawn form.

(ii) An article that has been either directly or indirectly copied from the copyright work.

(iii) A person must have copied it, or possess, or have possessed, the copy.

(iv) The copy must have been made within fifteen years after the article was first marketed.

5.20 Trade Marks

The law on trade marks is governed by the Trade Marks Act 1938. The Trade Marks Registry defines a trade mark as 'a symbol (whether word, device or a combination of the two) which a person uses in the course of trade in order that his goods may be readily distinguished by the purchasing public from similar goods of other traders'. The Act defines a trade mark as a

'mark used or proposed to be used in relation to goods for the purpose of indicating or so as to indicate a connection in the course of trade between the goods and some person having the right either as proprietor or as registered user to use the mark, whether with or without any indication of the identity of that person'.

5.21 Registration in Part A

A trade mark is only protected if it has been registered with the Trade Marks Registry, and it only receives protection in relation to the class of goods for which is has been registered. For example, a mark which is registered in relation to the class covering hand tools and instruments will not be protected in relation to its use under the class dealing with wines, spirits and liquors. There are 34 classes of goods in all. The register is furthermore divided into Part A and Part B. The significance of the distinction is dealt with in 5.23.

To be registered in Part A, the mark must display one of the following particulars:

(i) The name of the company, individual or firm represented in a special or particular manner.

(ii) The signature of the applicant for registration or some predecessor in business.

(iii) An invented word or words.

(iv) A word or words having no direct reference to the character or quality of the goods, and not being according to its ordinary specification a geographical name or surname.

(v) Any other distinctive mark.

A trade mark need not consist of, or contain, any words at all. Devices are registrable, if distinctive. In *Smith Kline and French Laboratories Ltd v. Sterling-Winthrop Group Ltd* (1975), registration was allowed of the design of a capsule, being half-coloured, half-transparent, the pellets inside the capsule being coloured. The Coca-Cola company, however, failed in its attempt to register its distinctive bottle as a trade mark since the function of the 1938 Act was to protect a distinctive mark and not the article marked (*Re Coca-Cola Co's Applications*, 1986).

5.22 Registration in Part B

Part B of the register is reserved for marks which are capable of distinguishing the goods, but which are not yet adapted to distinguish those goods. The point is that Part B is for marks which have not, at the date of application, become distinctive of the goods but which may thereafter become distinctive of them. A mark registered in Part B may, when substantial goodwill has been attached to it, later be registered in Part A. The same division of the register into 34 classes of goods as applies in relation to Part A (*see* 5.21) applies in relation to Part B, the classes themselves being identical.

5.23 Infringement

Registration gives the owner of the registered mark the exclusive right to use the mark in relation to the class of goods for which it is registered, and that right is also deemed to be infringed by any person who uses a mark which is identical to the registered mark or which so nearly resembles it as to be likely to deceive or cause confusion. Where the complaint is as to deceptive resemblance, the matter will have to be judged on the facts. For example, 'Margarita' was held to be an infringement of 'La Flor de Margaretta', 'Ca Radium' of 'Radium' and 'Muralol' of 'Mirabol'. On the other hand, 'Cocosoline' was not an infringement of 'Cottolene'; nor 'Robert Crawford' of the signature 'Daniel Crawford'; nor 'Ernalde' of 'Nilde'. Where the trade mark has been registered under Part B, the position is just the same except for the fact that no infringement occurs where the use complained of is not likely to deceive or cause confusion or to be taken as indicating a connection in the course of trade between the goods and the owner of the Part B mark.

5.24 Acts not Amounting to Infringement

The Trade Marks Act provides that certain apparent infringements are not to be treated as such.

(i) Where a trade mark is registered subject to conditions or limitations, no infringement may arise when an identical or similar mark is used in areas to which, by virtue of the condition or limitation, registration does not extend.

(ii) No offence arises where a trade mark is used in relation to goods connected in the course of trade with the owner of the mark if the owner has applied it to goods and has not removed or obliterated it, or has at any time consented to its use expressly or by implication.

(iii) No infringement takes place where use of the mark is 'reasonably necessary' to indicate that the goods are adapted to form part of, or be accessory to, other goods in relation to which the trade mark has been, or might be, legitimately used. It would therefore be legitimate to call film 'film for use with Kodak cameras', even though the film was *not* made by Kodak. Such film could not, however, be called 'Kodak film' since this would indicate that it *had* been made by Kodak.

(iv) No infringement arises if a person can prove continuous use of the mark by himself, or by a predecessor in title, from a date earlier than both the date of registration of the mark and that of first use of the owner of the registered mark or his predecessor in title.

(v) Where two or more identical or similar marks are both on the register, the use of one is not an infringement of the other.

(vi) The Act permits the *bone fide* use by a person of his own name or the name of his place of business or of the name of any of his predecessors in business. 'Bona fide use' is 'the honest use by the person of his own name without any intention to deceive anybody or without any intention to make use of the goodwill which has been acquired by another trader' (*Baume and Co. Ltd v. Moore Ltd*, 1957).

(vii) The use of a bona fide description of the character or quality of goods does not infringe a registered trade mark, provided that the description in no way refers to anyone who has the right to use the trade mark or to goods with which such person is connected in the course of trade.

5.25 Defensive Trade Marks

While it is a general rule that a trade mark can only be registered in relation where there is a present intention to use it, the Act allows for registration where an invented word or words is so well known in relation to the particular goods that its use in relation to other goods would be taken to indicate a connection between those other goods and the owner of the mark.

5.26 Certification Trade Marks

A certification trade mark is a mark which is adapted to distinguish in the course of trade goods certified by any person in respect of origin, material, mode of manufacture, quality, accuracy or other characteristic from goods not so certified. The symbol of the International Wool Secretariat is one such example. Such marks may only be registered in Part A, and may be registered only by those who do not carry on trade in goods of the kind to be certified.

5.27 Service Marks

As from October 1986, under an amending Act passed in 1984, service marks became registrable in exactly the same way, and with the same consequences, as trade marks in relation to goods. A service mark is a

'mark (including a device, name, signature, word, letter, numeral or any combination thereof) used or proposed to be used in relation to services for the purpose of indicating, or so as to indicate, that a particular person is connected, in the course of a business, with the provision of those services, whether with or without any indication of the identity of that person.'

5.28 Assignment

Section 22 of the Act states that a registered trade mark can be assigned provided that the assignment is entered on the register. Section 28 provides for registered users. A person other than the registered owner may be registered as a registered user. Subject to any agreement to the contrary, a registered user can call upon the owner to take action in the event of an infringement: if the owner fails to do so, the user may institute proceedings in his own name. However, registration may be refused if it would 'tend to facilitate trafficking' in a trade or service mark.

Example

A company wished to extend the character merchandizing aspect of its business by licensing traders to use the name of a popular fictional character of their own invention in relation to their goods. These were goods in which the company did not itself trade. The company, however, sought to register the mark in relation to the relevant class of goods and accompanied the application with a further application for those traders to be registered users.
Held (by the House of Lords): The registrar was right to refuse the application because it would 'tend to facilitate trafficking' since there was no real trade connection between the company and the potential registered users (re Holly Hobbie Trade Mark 1984).

5.29 Duration

Registration is in the first place for seven years, but can be renewed indefinitely for further periods of fourteen years. In the event of no bona fide use of the mark for five years, an application can be made for the mark to be removed from the register.

5.30 Remedies for Infringement

The successful plaintiff has three possible remedies. He may seek an injunction where a further infringement is threatened or likely to occur. He may seek delivery up, for destruction or the erasure of the marks, of any goods already marked with the infringing goods and in the possession or control of the defendant. He may also seek damages or an account of profits.

5.31 Registered Designs

Under the Registered Designs Act 1949, the owner of a new or original design may register it on application to the Patent Office. Once registered, protection lasts for five years, and this may be extended for two further periods of five years. A design which may be registered is a reference to

> 'features of shape, configuration, pattern or ornament applied to an article by any industrial process or means, being features which in the finished article appeal to and are judged solely by the eye, but does not include a method or principle of construction or features of shape or configuration which are dictated solely by the function which the article to be made in that shape or configuration has to perform'.

5.32 Passing off

Passing off is a common law offence and is in no way statutory. The essence of passing off is that: 'One man has no right to put off his goods for sale as the goods of a rival trader; and he cannot, therefore, be allowed to use names, marks, letters or other indicia by which he may induce purchasers to believe that the goods which he is selling are the manufacture of another person' (*Johnston v. Orr-Ewing*, 1882). The same principle applies to services. It does not matter that the defendant had no intention to deceive. It is only necessary that some name, mark or method of packing has become associated in the mind of the public with the plaintiff, and that there is a probability of confusion between his goods or services and those of the defendant.

Examples

In *White Hudson and Co. Ltd v. Asian Organization Ltd* (1964), sweets had been sold in Singapore in red cellophane wrappers bearing the word 'Hacks'. The majority of buyers could not read English and eventually acquired the habit of asking for the 'red wrapper cough sweets'. The defendants then proceeded to sell sweets in similar wrappers marked 'Pecto'. The court held that injunction would be granted to prevent the defendants from selling sweets in the Pecto wrapper without clearly distinguishing them from those of the plaintiffs. In *Parker-Knoll Ltd v. Knoll International Ltd* (1962) both parties manufactured furniture. The plaintiffs were well established in the United Kingdom. The defendants were recent arrivals from the United States. The House of Lords granted an injunction to restrain the defendants from continuing to use their own name without distinguishing its goods from those of the plaintiff.

It has also been held that a passing-off action can be brought by a plaintiff when he is only one of a number of people who are affected by the defendant's actions. In *J. Bollinger v. Costa Brava Wine Co.* (1960), an injunction restrained the use of the description 'Spanish Champagne' which did not come from the Champagne district of France. The injunction was permissible even though 'champagne' was not associated with the plaintiff's goods.

The courts have also held that the plaintiff cannot succeed in an action for passing off unless he is in a common field of activity with the defendant. In

McCulloch v. May (1947), a well-known broadcaster was held unable to stop his name being used in relation to a breakfast cereal because he was not in the same field of activity as the defendant. In *Wombles v. Wombles Skips* (1975), the creator of the mythical characters, the Wombles, was held, for the same reason, to be unable to prevent a builders' skip hire firm from using the name of those characters in their business.

5.33 Dishonest Trading and the Development of Passing Off

In recent years, the offence of passing off has been subject to considerable development to the point where it is claimed that it can be regarded as a general legal remedy against dishonest trading and unfair competition generally. Passing off is 'no longer anchored, as in its early nineteenth century formulation, to the name or trade mark of a product or business' (*Cadbury Schweppes v. Pub Squash*, 1980). A major case in the development of passing off was the decision of the House of Lords in *Erven Warnink BV v. J. Townend & Sons (Hull) Ltd* (1979). The plaintiffs manufactured and distributed an alcoholic drink known as 'advocaat', made out of a mixture of eggs and spirits. Advocaat was a distinct and recognizable drink made almost exclusively in Holland by a number of manufacturers as well as the plaintiffs. It had been sold in England for over 50 years and had become a popular drink through advertising and the name 'advocaat' had acquired a substantial reputation and goodwill. The plaintiffs had 75 per cent of the market, the rest being held by various Dutch manufacturers. The defendants manufactured an alcoholic drink in England out of dried eggs and Cyprus sherry, properly called 'Egg Flip', which they marketed as 'Old English Advocaat'. The defendants had not passed off their product as that of the plaintiffs and it was unlikely that any purchaser would suppose the defendants' drink to be the plaintiffs' product. However, the plaintiffs applied for an injunction restraining the defendants from selling or distributing under the name 'advocaat' any product which was not made out of eggs and spirits without the addition of wine. Lord Diplock said that the facts of the case revealed a case of 'unfair, not to say dishonest, trading for which a rational system of law ought to provide a remedy to other traders whose business or goodwill is injured by it'. He went on to say that there would certainly be passing off in any case where the following five elements were present:

1. Misrepresentation.
2. Made in the course of a trade.
3. To prospective customers of the defendant or ultimate consumers of goods or services supplied by him.
4. Which is likely to injure the business or goodwill of another trader.
5. Which causes actual damage to the business or goodwill of another trader, or which will probably do so.

He left open the question whether there would be passing off if not all those elements were present. In the instant case, he found that all five elements were present and an injunction was granted.

5.34 Remedies

An action for passing off lies even though no damage is proved; probability of damage is enough. The plaintiff may seek an injunction. It is in the discretion of the court whether to grant it, and the actual terms of the injunction are often among the most contested points in this class of litigation. With regard to compensation, the plaintiff can recover damages for his loss of profit and he may also recover for loss of business reputation and goodwill. The alternative to damages is for an account of profits actually made by the defendant in consequence of the passing off. It is not clear if an account can be requested if the defendant acted innocently; nor is it clear if more than nominal damages may be awarded if the defendant neither knew nor ought to have known that he was passing off.

5.35 Breach of Confidence

The law has recently been developing to protect those who are victims of a breach of confidence. The principle is that a plaintiff suing for breach of confidence must show three things:

1. That the information has the necessary quality of confidence.
2. That it was imparted in circumstances importing an obligation of confidence.
3. That there was an unauthorized use of that confidence (*Coco v. Clark*, 1969).

Examples

In *Seager v. Copydex Ltd* (1967), the plaintiffs had told the defendants about a new type of carpet grip. Without conscious plagiarism the defendants developed this idea which had been given to them in confidence. The plaintiff was awarded damages to compensate him for their having used his idea without paying for it. In *Fraser v. Thames TV* (1982), three actresses had given to a television company the idea of a soap opera relating the adventures of an all-girl rock band. They contemplated that they would take the main roles, but the defendants made use of the idea without using the girls who had suggested it and were required to pay damages for their breach. The remedies available for a breach of confidence comprise injunctions, and damages or an account of profits. In some cases, damages will be awarded, but not an injunction, as in *Seager v. Copydex* where the information had become publicly known at the time of the court action.

6 Bills of exchange and other negotiable instruments

6.1 The Meaning of Negotiability

A negotiable instrument is one which passes from hand to hand by delivery so as to give a holder who takes it in good faith a good title to that instrument, even though the person who transferred it had a defective title. The characteristics of a negotiable instrument are as follows:

(i) The title in it passes by mere delivery, or, where necessary, by delivery and endorsement.

(ii) No notice of such transfer needs to be given to the person who is liable on the instrument.

(iii) The holder of the instrument can sue in his own name.

(iv) The holder takes the instrument free of any prior defects providing he took in good faith.

6.2 Examples of Negotiable Instruments

A document will be a negotiable instrument either because it has become negotiable by Act of Parliament or because the courts have recognized a custom to that effect. Instruments made negotiable by Act of Parliament include Bills of Exchange (*see* 6.4) and Promissory Notes (*see* 6.26), the relevant legislation being the Bills of Exchange Act 1882. Instruments negotiable through custom include bank notes, share warrants, bearer debentures and treasury bills.

(i) Bank Notes

These are promissory notes made payable to bearer. When he presents a note for payment, it is not necessary for the bearer to explain how he came by it. However, if there is something in the circumstances to arouse suspicion, a bank would be entitled to refuse payment until satisfied of the bearer's good faith. If the bearer sued the bank for its refusal, the bank would have the burden of proving that the bearer was in bad faith.

(ii) Share Warrants

Share warrants are issued under the common seal of a company, stating that the bearer is entitled to the stocks and shares specified. These are to be distinguished from share certificates which are issued under the seal of a company which certify that the named party is entitled to a certain number of shares. Share certificates are not negotiable instruments because they are not transferable by delivery, or by delivery with endorsement. A form of transfer is needed to evidence the change of ownership and notification of the transfer has to be given to the company by sending the transfer for registration.

(iii) Bearer Debentures

Bearer debentures, also called bearer bonds, are negotiable when issued by an English company and are made payable to bearer. Foreign government bonds are negotiable if they are customarily negotiable in this country and the country of origin.

(iv) Treasury Bills

Treasury bills are receipts for cash lent to the government. They incorporate a promise to repay the loan, usually in 91 days. Each week the Bank of England acting for the Treasury invites offers of cash, much of which will be used to repay bills maturing that week.

6.3 Instruments resembling Negotiable Instruments

Certain instruments have some of the qualities of a negotiable instrument, but not all of them.

(i) Bills of Lading

A bill of lading is a document of title to goods which are freely transferable by delivery, with endorsement, like a negotiable instrument. It is, however, not a negotiable instrument because the person who obtains a bill takes subject to any defects in the transferor's title.

(ii) Dock Warrants

Dock warrants are issued by dock authorities certifying that the goods specified are held in a dock warehouse on behalf of the person in whose favour the warrant is drawn. The warrants are assignable by delivery plus endorsement, but since the transferee takes subject to any defects in title they are not negotiable instruments.

(iii) IOUs

An IOU is merely a written admission of the existence of a debt (with the implied promise to pay at some future date). They are not negotiable, however, because they do not contain an *express* promise to pay.

6.4 Bills of Exchange

The Bills of Exchange Act 1882 codified the law relating to cheques and bills of exchange, the most important kinds of negotiable instrument. Section 3 (1) of the Act defines a bill of exchange as an 'unconditional order in writing, addressed by one person to another, signed by the person giving it, requiring the person to whom it is addressed to pay on demand, or at a fixed or determined future time, a sum certain in money to or to the order of a specified person or to bearer'. The person issuing the order is called the drawer, and the person to whom it is addressed is the drawee. If the bill is made payable to a named person, or to his order, it is an Order Bill and he is the payee. An Order Bill requires to be endorsed by the payee before it can be transferred, while a bill made payable to bearer does not have to be endorsed. Section 3 (4) states that a bill is not invalid by reason of its not being dated. There are several aspects of this definition which require attention.

(i) Unconditional Orders

The order must be a positive order to pay and not a mere request or authorization. The common form of wording is: 'Pay X . . .', though: 'Please pay X . . .' is also regarded as unconditional. An order is not unconditional if: it gives the drawee a discretion as to whether he should pay or not (for example, 'Pay X if satisfied with goods consigned'); if it requires the drawee to do something more than to pay money (for example, 'Pay X and then notify me in writing'): or if it orders payment from a particular fund (for example, 'Pay X out of my current account'). In this last case, however, an unconditional order to pay coupled with a mention of a particular fund, for the guidance of the drawee, would be regarded as unconditional under the provisions of s.3 (3) of the Act. For example, it was held in *Guaranty Trust Co. of New York v. Hannay* (1918) that a direction to charge the amount of the bill to certain specified bales of cotton merely indicated the account to be debited with the amount and did not make the bill conditional.

(ii) Identifying Drawee

The drawee must be identified with reasonable certainty. A bill addressed to alternative drawees, such as 'Pay X or Y' would not be sufficient. It has also been held in *Orbit Mining and Trading Co. Ltd v. Westminster Bank Ltd* (1963) that an instrument made payable to 'cash' is not payable to 'the order of a specified person or to bearer' and therefore is not a bill of exchange.

(iii) The Sum Payable

A bill must order the payment of a 'sum certain in money', that is, not goods or services. Section 9 of the Act states that the requirements of the Act are satisfied even though the sum is required to be paid: with interest; or by stated instalments; or by stated instalments with a provision that on default the whole amount becomes due; or according to an indicated rate of exchange or according to a rate of exchange to be ascertained as directed in the bill. Section 9 (2) of the Act further states that where the sum payable is expressed in words and also in figures, and there is a discrepancy between the two, the sum denoted by the words is the amount payable.

6.5 Capacity and Consideration

Section 27 of the Act states the parties to a bill must have the ordinary capacity to make a contract (*see* Chapter 2). If, though, an infant does sign a bill, that constitutes a perfectly valid signature and allows enforcement of the bill. However, if the bill is dishonoured that infant could not be sued.

A bill also, like a contract, requires to be supported by consideration. Section 27 (1) of the Act provides that valuable consideration for a bill may be constituted by any consideration 'sufficient to support a simple contract'. In two ways, however, the Act alters the normal contractual position. First, s.27 (1) further provides that past consideration, that is to say any antecedent debt or liability, will suffice. This would mean that if a bill is drawn on 31 May for goods delivered at the beginning of the month, sufficient consideration has been provided. The other way in which the ordinary law of contract has been altered by the Act relates to the burden of proof. In normal contracts, the party seeking to enforce the contract must prove that he has given consideration. Section 30 of the Act reverses this in relation to bills of exchange by stipulating that it is for the defendant to show that no consideration has been given.

6.6 Inchoate Instruments

An inchoate bill is one lacking some material particular, such as the amount omitted or the payee's name omitted. Section 20 (1) of the Act states that the person in possession is presumed until the contrary is proved to have the authority to make good the omissions in any way he thinks fit. The section also provides that where a person signs a blank piece of paper and delivers it to another, intending it to be converted into a bill, that signature operates as authority to fill it up as a complete bill for any amount. In all the cases just mentioned, however, the Act adds that the bill can only be enforced if it is filled up within a reasonable time and if it is completed strictly within the limits of the authority given. After completion the bill is fully enforceable in the usual way. For example, suppose that A signs an inchoate instrument and delivers it to B with authority to complete it for not more than £100. If B fills it up for £1000, he cannot force A to accept liability for that amount. If, however, B negotiates the bill to C, who takes in good faith and without notice of the limit, C, as holder in due course can enforce the bill for the full £1000 against A.

6.7 Overdue Bills

A bill which is payable on demand is, according to s.36 (3), overdue when it has been in circulation for an 'unreasonable length of time'. This is a question of fact which depends on all the circumstances of the case. Other bills are overdue when the date fixed for payment has passed without the bill being presented. If a bill is overdue, it can still be negotiated, but s.36 (2) of the Act states that the transferee can get no better title to it than his transferor had.

6.8 Lost Bills

If a bill is lost before it becomes overdue, s.69 of the Act says that the holder can compel the drawer to issue a replacement. Where this happens the drawer can demand security from the holder to indemnify him against all persons should the bill be found. Section 70 of the Act further provides that in any action or proceeding on a lost bill, its loss shall not be set up as a defence, but an indemnity must be given against any other claims on the instrument in question.

6.9 Negotiation of Bills

Section 31 of the Act provides that a bill is negotiated by delivery in the case of a bill payable to bearer, but a bill payable to order is negotiated by delivery together with endorsement. Bearer bills and order bills are defined in 6.4. Section 32 of the Act states that for an endorsement to be valid, it must: be written on the bill itself and be signed by the endorser; relate to the full value of the bill; be endorsed by all payees if more than one; correspond exactly with the drawing; be on an additional piece of paper (an 'allonge') where there is no space for the endorsement. By the provisions of s.35 of the Act, a bill may be given a restrictive endorsement, prohibiting further transfer, so that it is no longer negotiable. The Act gives the following examples of a restrictive endorsement: 'Pay D only'; 'Pay D for the account of X'; 'Pay D or order for collection'. Since the bill becomes not negotiable as soon as it is restrictively endorsed, the endorsee receives a title which depends entirely on that of his transferor, and should the latter have no title or one subject to certain defects then the endorsee will suffer likewise.

6.10 Liability of Parties

(i) Necessity of Signature

Section 23 of the Act states that signature is essential to liability on a bill. Where a person signs a bill in a trade or assumed name, he is liable on the bill as if he had signed it in his own name. Furthermore, the signature of the name of a partnership, for example, 'Smith & Co.', is equivalent to the signature by the person so signing of the names of all persons liable as partners in the partnership. Section 26 of the Act further states that any agent signing a bill incurs full personal liability unless he makes it clear that he signs merely on behalf of someone else, as by signing 'per pro' or 'for and on behalf of' his principal. Thus, a company director who signs a cheque merely as 'manager' or 'director' will be personally liable on the cheque. To avoid this state of affairs, he should sign: 'J. Smith, director, for and on behalf of X Co.'.

Example

The directors of a company signed a bill on which the '&' was omitted from the name 'X & Co. Ltd'.

Held: The company was not properly named and the directors were personally liable on the bill.

(Hendon v. Adelman, 1973)

In the case of a signature being forged, s.24 of the Act provides that the forged signature is 'wholly inoperative'. The section applies the same rules to an unauthorized signature. Furthermore, the bill will be wholly void since it fails to meet the definition of bill in s.3 as being an order 'addressed by one person to another, signed by the person giving it'. If the bill is an order bill (*see* 6.4), endorsement is necessary to effect transfer. If that endorsement is a forgery, that will operate to nullify any transfer.

(ii) Liability of Acceptor

In the first instance, the bill is addressed to the drawee as the person on whom the bill is drawn. He is under no liability on the bill unless and until he accepts it, after which he assumes primary liability (and is called the acceptor). He is under no liability to the holders of the bill until he accepts liability. Section 17 of the Act specifies that acceptance is signified by the drawee signing across the face of the bill, with or without the addition of the date or such words as 'accepted'. Any indication that the drawee will perform his promise by other than the payment of money will not constitute an acceptance. Acceptance may be either general, that is to say an unqualified acceptance of the bill as drawn, or it may be qualified. Section 44 (1) states that the holder of a bill may refuse to take a qualified acceptance and, if he does not obtain what he wants, he may treat the bill as dishonoured.

(iii) Liability of Drawer and Endorser

Section 55 of the Act states that the drawer of a bill guarantees that, when it is presented, it will be duly accepted and honoured. He further guarantees that if it is dishonoured, he will compensate the holder or any endorser who is compelled to pay, provided that the requisite proceedings on dishonour are taken. The endorser of the bill gives the same guarantee as the drawer as to bill being accepted on presentation, and he also guarentees that if it is dishonoured, he will compensate the holder or any subsequent endorser who is compelled to pay. The drawer or any endorser can negate or limit his liability by clear words accompanying the signature.

6.11 Rights of the Holder

Section 2 of the Act defines a holder as 'the payee or endorsee of the bill who is in possession of it, or the person in possession of a bill which is payable to bearer'. Section 38 states that he can sue on the instrument in his own name. He does, however, take subject to all rights available against previous parties, including immediate parties, that is to say parties with whom he has entered into a contract in relation to the instrument.

6.12 Rights of the Holder for Value

A holder for value is defined in s.27 of the Act as the holder of a bill in relation to which value has been given at any time. Such a holder is said to be a holder for value in relation to the acceptor (*see* 6.10 (ii)) and all parties who were parties to the bill prior to value being given. The holder for value can enforce the bill against all such persons.

6.13 Rights of the Holder in Due Course

Section 29 of the Act defines a holder in due course as a person who: takes a bill which is complete and regular on its face; became the holder of the bill before it became overdue and without notice of the fact that it had been dishonoured (if in fact it has been dishonoured); and who took the bill in good faith, for value and without notice of any defects in the title of the transferor at the time of negotiation. Whether or not a bill is complete and regular on its face is a question of fact.

Examples

In *Arab Bank Ltd v. Ross* (1952), the Court of Appeal held that a negotiable instrument which had been incorrectly endorsed, in that 'company' had been omitted from the name of the indorsing company was not held by a holder as a holder in due course. A holder acts in good faith if he acts honestly, so that merely being negligent will not amount to a lack of good faith. If he wilfully or fraudulently abstains from inquiry or deliberately ignores the truth, this will amount to bad faith. It is important to realize that by s.30 (2) of the Act a holder (*see* 6.11) is presumed to be a holder in due course. There is an exception: if a bill is shown to be tainted by fraud or illegality, the holder is presumed not to be a holder in due course. However, the presumption that he is a holder in due course revives if the holder shows that, subsequent to the fraud or illegality, value has been given in good faith. Where a holder is a holder in due course, s.38 provides him with the following rights: he may sue on the bill in his own name; and he holds the bill free from any defect in title of any prior parties as well as from personal defences available to prior parties amongst themselves. Any holder can sue in his own name, but it is only the holder in due course who takes free of defects in title and from any defences available to prior parties amongst themselves.

In *Mackenzie Mills v. Buono* (1986), the defendants imported some furniture. After discussion with the suppliers, it was agreed that payment would be made by postdated cheques in exchange for a promise that the defective items would be replaced. A number of the cheques were dishonoured. A further cheque was endorsed by the suppliers and handed over to the plaintiffs who were a firm of solicitors acting for the suppliers. That cheque was also dishonoured. The defendants argued that the plaintiffs were not holders in due course since they had not given any value for it. The Court of Appeal ruled that the cheque having been given in payment of the furniture in anticipation of the defective items being replaced, it was clear that as between the suppliers and defendants value had been given, even though the defendants could argue in any action against the suppliers that the goods being defective, the consideration had wholly failed. It therefore followed that the plaintiffs were deemed by operation of the Act to be holders for value (*see* 6.12) and were also holders in due course by the operation of s.29. The plaintiffs were therefore entitled to judgment for the full amount of the cheque. The Consumer Credit Act 1974 has imposed certain restrictions on the holder in due course in relation to negotiable instruments taken under regulated agreements. These are explained in 6.27.

6.14 Duty to Present for Payment

Section 45 of the Act states that a bill which is payable on demand must be presented within a reasonable time of issue in order to render the drawer liable and within a reasonable time of any endorsement to render the endorser liable. The section provides that where a bill is not payable on demand, it must be presented on the day on which it falls due or the next business day if it is not a business day. Section 45 also says that presentment must be at a reasonable hour on a business day and at a proper place. Section 46 of the Act provides that delay in presentment for payment is excused if it is caused by circumstances beyond the control of the holder and is not imputable to his default, misconduct or negligence. When the delay ceases to operate, presentment must be made with reasonable diligence. The section further provides that presentment is altogether dispensed with if: it cannot be effected despite the holder's reasonable diligence (but the mere fact that the holder has reason to believe that the bill will be dishonoured does not do away with the necessity for presentment); the drawee is a fictitious person; presentment is waived, expressly or by implication.

6.15 Dishonour

A bill may be dishonoured by non-acceptance or non-payment. Section 43 of the Act states that a bill is dishonoured by non-acceptance when the prescribed form of acceptance is refused or cannot be obtained (*see* 6.10 (ii)), or when presentment for acceptance is excused and the bill is not accepted. Section 41 further states that presentment for acceptance is excused, and a bill is to be treated as dishonoured by non-acceptance, when: the drawee is dead or bankrupt; is a fictitious person or a person having no capacity to contract by bill; after the exercise of reasonable diligence, presentment cannot be effected; presentment has been irregular, but acceptance has been refused on some other ground. Section 47 states that a bill is dishonoured by reason of non-payment when it is presented for payment and payment is refused or cannot be obtained, or when presentment is excused and the bill is overdue and unpaid. For the circumstances when presentment is excused, see the preceding paragraph.

(i) Procedure on Dishonour

Sections 43 and 47 each provide that, on dishonour, an immediate right of recourse against the drawer and endorsers accrues to the holder. However, this right depends on the holder giving a valid notice to prior parties. Any drawer and endorser to whom notice is not given is discharged, except that where dishonour is by non-acceptance and notice of dishonour is not given, the rights of a holder in due course subsequent to the omission are unaffected. There is no prescribed form of notice, and any notice will do so long as the words are sufficient to identify the bill and clearly state that the bill has been dishonoured by the drawee or acceptor. In addition, s.49 lays down these rules.

(*a*) Notice must be given by or on behalf of the holder of the indorser who is himself liable on the bill.

(*b*) Notice may be given by an agent in his own name, or of the party entitled to give notice, whether the party is his principal or not.

(*c*) Where notice is given by or on behalf of the holder, that notice operates for the benefit of all subsequent holders and all prior endorsers who have a right of recourse against the party to whom it is given.

(*d*) Where notice is given by or on behalf of an endorser who is himself liable on the bill, such notice operates for the benefit of the holder and all endorsers subsequent to the party to whom notice is given.

(*e*) Notice may be given in writing or personal communication, and may be given in terms sufficient to identify the bill, and which also intimate that the bill has been dishonoured by non-acceptance or non-payment.

(*f*) The return of a dishonoured bill to the drawer or an endorser is deemed to be a sufficient notice of dishonour.

(*g*) A written notice need not be signed, and an insufficient written notice may be supplemented and validated by verbal communication. A misdescription of the bill shall not invalidate a notice unless the recipient is actually misled.

(*h*) Where notice is required to be given to a person, it can be given to him or an agent.

(*i*) Where the party giving the notice knows that the drawer or endorser is dead, the notice is to be given to a personal representative, if there is one and if he can be found with the exercise of reasonable diligence.

(*j*) Where the drawer or endorser is bankrupt, notice can instead be given to the trustee.

k) Where there are two or more drawers and endorsers who are not partners, notice is to be given to each one, unless one has the authority to receive notice on behalf of the others.

(*l*) Notice must be given within a reasonable time after dishonour. There is a statutory presumption, where the person giving and the person receiving the notice live in different places, that the notice has not been given in a reasonable time unless the notice is sent off by the next available post from the day after dishonour. If they reside in the same place, the notice must reach the relevant party the next day.

(*m*) Where a bill when dishonoured is in the hands of an agent, he may either notify the parties liable on the bill, or notify his principal. If the latter, the agent must give such notice within the same time as if he were the holder, and the principal, on receipt of the notice, has himself the same time for giving notice as if the agent had been an independent holder.

(*n*) Where a party to a bill receives notice of dishonour, he has after receipt the same period of time for giving notice to antecedent parties that the holder has after the dishonour.

(*o*) Where a notice of dishonour is duly addressed and posted, the sender is deemed to have given due notice of dishonour, notwithstanding any miscarriage by the Post Office.

Section 50 gives those circumstances where delay in, or failure to provide, notice of dishonour is excused. Delay in giving notice is excused where it is caused by circumstances outside the particular party's control, and is not imputable to his default, misconduct or negligence. The Act provides that when the cause of delay ceases to operate, the notice must then be given with reasonable diligence. Notice of dishonour is dispensed with: where, after the exercise of reasonable diligence, it cannot be given or does not reach the relevant party, as where a particular address cannot be found; where, the person entitled to notice, expressly or by implication waives his rights; as regards the drawer, where the drawer and drawee are the same person, where the drawee is a fictitious person or lacks capacity, where the drawer is the person to whom presentment for payment was made, or where the drawee was under no obligation to the drawer to accept the bill, or where the drawer has countermanded payment; as regards the endorser, where the drawee is a fictitious person or has no capacity and the endorser was aware of this when he endorsed, where the endorser is the person to whom the presentment was made, or where the bill was accepted or made only for the endorser's accommodation. (an accommodation party is a person who has signed the bill without receiving value, and for the purpose of lending his name to some other person).

(ii) Measure of Damages

Section 57 provides that where a bill is dishonoured, the measure of damages shall be the amount of the bill, interest from the time of presentment for payment where the bill was payable on demand, and in other cases from the maturity of the bill; the expense of noting, or when protest is necessary, and the protest has been extended, the expenses of protest (noting and protest are essentially relevant to foreign bills). These amounts can be recovered by the holder from any party liable on the bill; by the drawer who has been compelled to pay the bill from the acceptor; and by an endorser who has been compelled to pay the bill from the acceptor, from the drawer or a prior endorser.

6.16 Discharge of Bills

Sections 59, 63, and 64 provide that a bill is discharged when all rights of action on it are extinguished. Such discharge can be: by payment in due course; by cancellation; or in some cases by material alteration. Any alteration as to date, amount, time of payment and place of payment is material, but this list is not exhaustive. In addition, a bill is discharged under s.61 when the acceptor becomes the holder of a bill at or after maturity, and under s.62 where the holder in writing renounces his rights against the acceptor absolutely and unconditionally at or after maturity.

6.17 Cheques

The Act (s.73) defines a cheque as a bill of exchange drawn on a banker and payable on demand. It is not necessary that the words 'on demand' should appear on the cheque since the Act says that all bills are treated as payable on demand where no time is specified for payment. It follows that a postdated cheque is not really a cheque since it is not payable on demand. However, a banker is entitled to pay a postdated cheque when it falls due. If he pays before that date he cannot debit the customer's account, and must bear the loss if the customer stops the cheque before its due date. Cheques are also subject to the provisions of the Cheques Act 1957. The rules considered below apply to cheques only and, except where stated, not to other bills.

6.18 Crossings

Section 77 of the Act provides that a cheque may be crossed by the drawer or the holder. Crossing is said by s.78 to be a material part of a cheque, so that it is not lawful for any person to obliterate it, or, except where authorized by the Act, to add to or alter the crossing. Thus, an unauthorized alteration is a material alteration which renders the cheque unenforceable against prior parties who have not consented to the alteration. Section 76 of the Act provides for 'general' crossing and for 'special crossing'. The former arises when two transverse lines are drawn across the face of the cheque, thus //, with or without the addition of the words 'and company' (or some abbreviation), or 'not negotiable'. A cheque is subject to a special crossing when it indicates the name of a particular banker with or without the addition of the transverse lines. The effect of a general crossing is to make the cheque payable only to a collecting banker; in other words, it precludes the paying banker from paying cash for the cheque across the counter. The effect of a special crossing is that the paying banker must pay the cheque only to the collecting banker named on the crossing, and no other. Section 79 of the Act provides that the banker is liable for any loss occasioned where: he pays a cheque which is crossed specially to more than one banker (unless the additional special crossing merely indicates that one of the bankers named is to collect merely as agent for the other); he pays a cheque crossed generally otherwise than to a bank, that is, he treats it as an open cheque; or he pays a cheque crossed specially otherwise than to the banker named in the crossing or his agent.

When a cheque is crossed 'not negotiable', this is a crossing which, according to s.81 of the Act, deprives the cheque of its negotiability so that a person to whom it is negotiated obtains no better title than was possessed by the transferor.

Example

A clerk took a bank cheque from his employer which was already crossed 'not negotiable' and fraudulently made it payable to P.

Held: The employer could recover the value from P, who had obtained cash, since the clerk had no title to the cheque and P could get no better title than the clerk. A crossing 'account payee', or 'account payee only' is not a statutory crossing but is still one which is recognized by banking custom. A collecting bank which collects for some person other than the payee may therefore be liable in negligence.

(Wilson and Meeson v. Pickering, 1946)

6.19 Protection of Paying Banker

The bank on which a cheque is drawn is protected against liability if it pays in the following circumstances:

(i) Cheques with forged endorsements

Section 60 of the Act protects the bank if it pays in good faith and in the ordinary course of business. This applies to bills generally and not just cheques.

(ii) Crossed cheques

The bank is protected by the provisions of s.80 of the Act if it pays a crossed cheque drawn on it in accordance with the crossing, in good faith and without negligence.

(iii) Cheques not endorsed or irregularly endorsed

Section 1 of the Cheques Act 1957 protects the banker provided the cheque is drawn on the bank and is paid in good faith in the ordinary course of business.

6.20 Protection of Collecting Banker

The banker is an agent for the customer for collecting payment of cheques drawn on other banks and paid in by the customer to his own account. The banker must honour cheques where the customer has sufficient funds to meet the cheque, and if he dishonours it where there are sufficient funds there will be a breach of contract and the banker may be liable for damages in defamation proceedings if a defamatory remark is made on the cheque, such as 'no funds' (*Davidson v. Barclays Bank*, 1940). In an action for breach of contract for failing to honour a cheque, the customer has no right to claim damages for vexation and disappointment (*Rae v. Yorkshire Bank plc*, 1987). The collecting banker is protected from liability under the terms of s.4 of the Cheques Act where he receives payment for a customer who had no, or a defective title, provided he does so in good faith and without negligence. The following have been held to amount to negligence:

(i) Opening an account for someone without making adequate enquiries (*Hampstead Guardians v. Barclays Bank*, 1923).

(ii) Collecting payment for a customer of a cheque made out to the customer's employer without making adequate enquiries about him (*Underwood Ltd v. Martins Bank*, 1924).

(iii) Paying into a private account a cheque payable in an official capacity (*Ross v. London County Bank*, 1919).

(iv) Receiving payment for a customer of cheques clearly indicating that they are payable to him only as agent for someone else (*Bute v. Barclays Bank*, 1955).

(v) Where a bank uses a computer to identify the branch on which a cheque is drawn and a customer with accounts at two branches alters a cheque from branch A to draw it on branch B and the computer fails to recognize the change, if the customer stops the cheque by notice to branch B and the computer directs the cheque to branch A which pays the cheque, the bank may be liable for negligence (*Burnett v. Westminster Bank Ltd*, 1966).

Where a collecting bank is negligent, it may be sued for damages for the tort of conversion by the true owner of the cheque. Where the customer's own negligence in drawing cheques contributes to the loss, the amount recoverable from the banker is reduced under the provisions of the Law Reform (Contributory Negligence) Act 1945 (*Lumsden & Co. v. London Trustee Savings Bank*, 1971).

6.21 Endorsement of Cheques

Section 1 of the Cheques Act dispenses with the need for an endorsement where the apparent payee or endorsee of a cheque is paying it into his own account. The Committee of London Clearing Bankers, however, have decided that endorsement will still be required in these situations:

(i) If the payee, or his transferee, presents his cheque to the drawee bank for payment over the counter. A banker disregarding this would not be acting in the ordinary course of business as required by s.1 and would therefore be outside its protection. No endorsement is required where the customer presents his own cheque for payment.

(ii) With order cheques which are to be paid into an account other than that of the original payee, that is, order cheques which have been negotiated.

(iii) If the payee combines cheques and receipt forms marked 'R'.

6.22 Stale or Overdue Cheques

Section 36 of the Act, which applies to all bills including cheques, states that an overdue bill is one that has been in circulation for an unreasonable time, and a person who takes an overdue bill cannot be a holder in due course (*see* 6.13). The bill can still be negotiated but the transferee gets no better title to it than that held by the transferor. A stale cheque is one that has been in circulation for a considerable period of time. Banks generally refuse to honour a cheque which is more than six months old.

6.23 Termination of Banker's Authority

By virtue of s.75 of the Act, a banker's authority to pay a cheque drawn by his customer is terminated in the following circumstances.

(i) Countermand of payment: written or oral instructions not to pay will suffice, though in practice oral instructions have to be confirmed in writing.

(ii) Notice of death: this terminates the banker's authority; death alone does not.

In addition, a banker's authority is also terminated by:

(i) Mental incapacity: notice of the customer's incapacity terminates the banker's authority (*The Imperial Loan Co. Ltd v. Stone*, 1899).

(ii) The making of a receiving order in bankruptcy against the customer, or, in the case of a company, on the presentation of a petition for winding up.

(iii) On service of a garnishee order for the balance of the account (that is, a court order addressed to a debtor ordering him not to pay his stated debts to a creditor but to hold the money pending further orders from the court.

(iv) Notice of a defect in the presenter's title: this must obviously entail refusal to pay since a banker must pay in good faith.

(v) Insufficient credit in the account, or where payment would increase the level of indebtedness above an agreed limit.

(vi) Notice of a breach of trust, as when it is reasonably certain that the cheque in question, drawn by a trustee, is a withdrawal of money to be used otherwise than for the purpose of the trust.

6.24 Duties of the Customer

It is the duty of the customer, in drawing a cheque, to take usual and reasonable precautions to prevent forgery and fraud.

Example

M's clerk was entrusted with the task of filling in M's cheques for signature. The clerk prepared a bearer cheque on which the sum payable was not mentioned in words and which bore the figures £2.0s.0d. M signed it. The clerk then added the words 'One hundred and twenty pounds' and placed a '1' and a '0' either side the '2' in the spaces which he had left. The clerk obtained payment of the cheque. *Held*: The bank could debit the client's account to the full amount of the cheque, since the loss was caused by M's failure to ensure that the cheque could not be altered in the way it was.

(*London Joint Stock Bank v. Macmillan and Arthur*, 1918)

It has been held by the Privy Council (*see* Chapter 1) that a customer is under no duty to check the accuracy of his bank account.

Example

In *Tai Hing Cotton Mill Ltd v. Liu Chong Hing Bank Ltd* (1985) a dishonest employee forged cheques on his employer's account for over six years, taking around HK$5.5 million. The company did not check thoroughly its monthly statements and did not detect the loss. The Privy Council required the bank to make good the loss, ruling that the company was not required to check its bank statements nor to operate a system of control which would aid the bank in detecting fraud. A bank could impose such a duty, but it would have to do so expressly in the terms of its contract with the customer.

If a bank has credited the customer's account with more than it should have done, the customer is not generally entitled to retain the extra sum. However, if the customer had relied on the misleading statement and altered his position in reliance on it, the bank cannot reclaim the money.

Example

In *United Overseas Bank v. Jiwani* (1977), the bank was able to reclaim the money, even though part had been used to buy a hotel, since it was established that the customer would have made the purchase anyway and did not rely on the bank.

6.25 Payment by Cheque

Payment by a bill is conditional only, so a creditor is entitled to refuse payment by cheque. In any case, payment by cheque is not effective until the cheque is honoured (*Bolt and Nut Co. (Tipton) Ltd v. Rowlands Nicholls & Co. Ltd*, 1964). If a cheque is sent through the post and is lost, the loss falls on the sender, unless the creditor requested this method of payment. Such a request must be express (*Pennington v. Crossley & Sons*, 1897). Under the provisions of s.3 of the Cheques Act, an unendorsed cheque which appears to have been paid by the banker on whom it was drawn is prima facie evidence of receipt by the payee of the sum stated on the cheque, even without the payee's endorsement. Where payment is by credit card (which is of course not a negotiable instrument) the card holder is deemed to have settled his debt to the retailer unconditionally (*Re Charge Card Services*, 1988).

6.26 Promissory Notes

Section 83 of the Bills of Exchange Act defines a promissory note as 'an unconditional promise in writing made by one person to another signed by the maker to pay on demand or at a fixed and determinable future time a sum certain in money to or to the order of a specified person or bearer'. The most common type of promissory note is a bank note, payable to bearer. A promissory note differs from a bill in the following ways:

(i) Acceptance of a note is never necessary, since there is no drawee.

(ii) The maker is the person liable to pay. In the case of a bill, the drawer is only liable until the drawee accepts.

(iii) A note must contain an unconditional promise to pay. The acceptor of a bill may make a conditional promise to pay.

(iv) A promissory note is a *promise* to pay. A bill is an *order* to pay.

6.27 Negotiable Instruments under the Consumer Credit Act 1974

Sections 123–125 impose the following restrictions on the use of negotiable instruments under regulated agreements (see generally Chapter 11). A creditor or owner will not be able to take a negotiable instrument in payment other than a bank note or cheque. Where a cheque is taken, it must be negotiated direct to a bank. The Act further stipulates that a negotiable instrument cannot be taken of whatever kind as a security under a regulated agreement. If any of the foregoing provisions is not complied with, the agreement under which the relevant sum is payable can be enforced only on a court order. Where a negotiable instrument is taken in contravention of the Act, the person taking it is not a holder in due course (*see* 6.13). If that person further negotiates the instrument, the holder can enforce the instrument but the creditor or owner under the regulated agreement must indemnify the consumer who gave him the instrument. If a cheque is taken, which it can be, but it is not negotiated as it should be directly to a bank, that constitutes a defect in title. This means that any subsequent holder who knew or ought to have known of the defect in the cheque cannot enforce it. If he neither knew nor ought to have known, and enforces the cheque, the consumer has the same right of indemnity as in the case of an improperly taken negotiable instrument.

7 Criminal liability in business

7.1 Role of Criminal Law in Business

All business activity in the United Kingdom operates within a framework of criminal law. This law has been passed by the State for the general protection of the public against misleading, unfair or fraudulent practices. In the remaining chapters of this book we discuss the impact of this law on business in some detail, but first we must establish some basic rules on the liability arising from unlawful business practice.

7.2 Growth of Criminal Law

The criminal law on business activity is not the outcome of a grand design imposed by a wise and consumer-conscious government. The comprehensive framework of law currently existing has developed piecemeal over more than eight centuries. As a problem has been perceived a remedy has eventually been provided by Parliament. One of the earliest examples of State regulation of business is the Magna Carta of 1215 in which King John decreed that 'there shall be one measure of ale throughout the Realm and the like for corn and cloth'. At that time there was such widespread malpractice in the use of weights and measures that it was to the benefit of both traders and public to have a controlled system of fair measurement. In later years the sale of adulterated food, the manufacture and distribution of dangerous substances and products, and the misdescription of goods and services were all subject to criminal legislation. Today, almost every aspect of business activity is subject to legal control to a greater or lesser extent.

7.3 Criminal Liability

In Chapter 1 we discuss the nature of law, the operation of the courts and the mechanism of prosecution. It is sufficient in this chapter to remind ourselves that a breach of the criminal law can result, if proven, in a fine or imprisonment. However, it is important to appreciate that criminal liability varies according to the type of business involved:

(i) A sole proprietor (a one-man or one-woman business) is wholly liable for all criminal acts committed in the course of his or her business and can be prosecuted, fined and/or imprisoned as a result thereof.

103

(ii) In a partnership all partners are equally liable to prosecution, but it is open to the prosecutor to bring proceedings against one or more partners only where there is evidence that they are responsible for the offence and the other partners were not involved.

(iii) A limited company is a legal entity in its own right and may be prosecuted in its registered name, the documents relating to the prosecution being served on the company secretary at its registered office. Obviously, a company cannot be sent to prison but it may be fined.

(iv) Where the commission of an offence by a company may be attributable to the act, default, consent or connivance of a director, manager or other senior servant of a company most trading law statutes provide that such a person may be prosecuted in addition to or instead of the company.

(v) Where a person, partner or company is liable to prosecution for an offence and it can be shown that the offence was committed due to the act or default of another person, that person may be prosecuted instead of or in addition to the principal offender subject to the principal offender being able to prove that he or she had exercised all due diligence and had taken all reasonable precautions to avoid commission of the offence (*see* 7.5). In this context 'another person' can be an employee, a supplier, or an agent.

(vi) Where a person has wilfully assisted in the commission of an offence he or she may be prosecuted for aiding, abetting, counselling or procuring the commission of the offence in addition to or instead of the principal offender.

7.4 Guilty Knowledge and Strict Liability

Except in cases of fraud or culpably reckless conduct, most offences against trading legislation are of strict liability. This means that it is not necessary for the prosecutor to prove that the accused intended to commit the unlawful act or, indeed, that he even knew it was being committed. The commission of the unlawful act itself is sufficient for conviction.

This potentially harsh doctrine is necessary in the interests of enforcement. If it were not so a dairyman, for example, facing a well-justified charge of selling watered milk would merely have to tell the court that he was unaware of the water in his milk to escape conviction. The proper protection of the public against trading offences would be near impossible. Conscious of the fact that the untempered operation of this doctrine would be contrary to natural justice, Parliament has provided a series of statutory defences which, if proved to the satisfaction of the court, can earn an acquittal for the accused.

7.5 Statutory Defences

In all statutory defences the usual burden of proof is reversed. To prove his case the prosecutor must prove that the accused is guilty 'beyond all reasonable doubt'. To show that he is entitled to be acquitted the accused must prove that he has satisfied the provisions of the defence 'on the balance of probability'. This is a less onerous burden of proof than that on the prosecutor because the objective of the defences is to ensure that no person becomes criminally liable for an event which cannot reasonably be avoided. It is an exercise in natural justice.

Over the years statutory defences have evolved. Certain of the earliest ones, still in operation today, are of little practical value. Section 100 of the Food Act 1984 (this Act was merely a consolidating measure and did not change the law) which is substantially unchanged from 1875, requires the accused to prove:

(i) that the commission of the offence was due to the act or default of another person; *and*

(ii) that he had exercised all due diligence and had taken all reasonable precautions to secure that the provisions in question were complied with; *and*

(iii) he must bring proceedings against the 'other person' himself.

This 'three-limbed' type of defence is difficult to prove and burdensome bearing in mind that the 'other person' is most likely to be an employee of the accused company or trader.

Section 24 of the Trade Descriptions Act 1968 is an improvement in that it has only two limbs. The accused must prove:

(i) that the commission of the offence was due to a mistake or to reliance on information supplied to him or to the act or default of another person, an accident or some other cause beyond his control; *and*

(ii) that he took all reasonable precautions and exercised all due diligence to avoid the commission of such an offence by himself or any person under his control.

It remains difficult to establish a chain of evidence linking (i) and (ii).

Section 34 of the Weights and Measures Act 1985 is in the now standard form of defence for modern statutes. It has one limb only and requires the accused to prove only that he took all reasonable precautions and exercised all due diligence to avoid the commission of the offence.

7.6 Reasonable Precautions and Due Diligence

The single-limbed defence of 'all reasonable precautions and all due diligence' appears in all new trading law statutes (other than consolidating measures) dating from 1978 and may be expected to be applied to all future legislation which incorporates offences of strict liability. There are variations in the wording in different statutes and additional provisions extend or restrict the application of the defence in special circumstances. The basic principle of law is that where offences are of strict liability no trader should be liable to conviction when he has done all that could reasonably be expected of him to avoid the commission of the offence.

The defence is no easy way out of criminal liability. The terms 'all reasonable precautions' and 'all due diligence' have been the subject of much judicial interpretation (*see* page 107) and we now have a reasonably clear picture as to what must be done by a business to establish a good defensible position. The essential requirement is that there must be a viable control system which must be approved by the company at board level, recorded and operated in a coordinated manner. The extent of the control system will vary with the size and resources of the business, the nature of its product or service and the perceived risk arising from the law to which it is subject. What is required for a large national company may not be necessary for a smaller business. The test is, what is *reasonable* bearing in mind all the circumstances of the case.

7.7 A Due Diligence System

The following summary sets out the basic principles of a good due diligence system:

(i) Those operating the business must be competent to a reasonable standard and must be capable of anticipating and preventing faults and errors which commonly beset that type of business.

(ii) The control system must be approved by those responsible for the business (the board), be written down and form part of the 'standing orders' of the business.

(iii) The responsibilities of each person in the system should be identified, written into the job specification and acknowledged by the employee.

(iv) The operation of the system must be recorded in a manner which identifies faults and indicates their rectification.

(v) The system must be supervised by departmental managers, area supervisors or similar people and their checks should be recorded.

(vi) The employer should ensure that training is given to all those who operate the system to a standard which ensures that the requirements are fully understood.

(vii) Product specifications and quality control systems should be recorded and form a part of the system.

(viii) Records of ingredient or component supplies together with warranties (*see* 7.8) relating thereto should be entered into the system.

The above notes are merely a brief summary of what is required. It must be stressed that there can be no blueprint system. The standard of diligence required varies from a simple entry in a daybook that all is well by a small one-person business to a comprehensive system for a large manufacturer or retailer. Most well-managed businesses do all that is required as a matter of routine. It is often the case, however, that the system is not recorded and thus the necessary standard of proof is lacking.

Example

A 'flash offer' was made in a supermarket offering money off washing powders. The manager of the store failed to supervise or check on an assistant who put on display only packs indicating the full price. The company had a due diligence system of visits by supervisors and instructions to managers.

Held: After conviction in the magistrates court the company appealed unsuccessfully to the High Court and then to the House of Lords where it was held that the manager was 'another person' and the company had exercised all reasonable precautions and all due diligence as required in s.24 of the Trade Descriptions Act 1968.

(*Tesco Supermarkets Ltd v. Nattrass* [1972] AC 153; [1971] 2 All ER 127 (HL))

Example

A watch was advertised as being 'waterproof' but filled with water when immersed in a bucket. The company pleaded that they had taken all reasonable precautions and had exercised all due diligence.

Held: They had taken no precautions since the elementary precaution of dipping the watch in a bowl of water would have revealed the problem.

(*Sherratt v. Geralds the American Jewellers* (1970) 114 Sol Jo 147 (DC))

Example

A dog was sold as a 'Sheltie' when in fact it was a crossbreed. The defendants were not dog breeders and knew nothing of the business concerned. They had relied on a unsigned pedigree certificate given to them by the person from whom they had bought the dog. They pleaded that they had relied on information given to them and had made out the due diligence etc. defence.

Held: The need for all reasonable precautions and all due diligence was the greater because they were not experts and they had failed to establish the defence.

(*Sutton London Borough v. Perry Sanger & Co. Ltd* (1971) 135 JP Jo 239)

Example

Pencils were sold with a higher lead-chromium content than permitted by safety regulations (*see* 9.3 (xx)). The company had assurances from its overseas suppliers that the pencils complied with United Kingdom legislation but they had not had any analytical checks carried out in the United Kingdom.

Held: Such analysis was an obvious precaution which could have been taken and the company had failed to make out the defence.

(*Garret v. Boots Chemists Ltd*, 1980)

Example

Meat was wrongly described as 'rump steak'. The butchers concerned had employed an expert to advise them and he had failed to notice that the meat was other than as described because it was frozen and difficult to identify.

Held: The company could not rely on the defence because they had failed to make enquiries of their suppliers which was an essential step when the meat could not be indentified.

(*Amos v. Melcom (Frozen Foods) Ltd*, 1985) 149 JP 712 (DC))

7.8 Warranty

A warranty is a guarantee from a supplier that the goods he is selling conform to description and are lawful for sale in the United Kingdom. Warranties have an important role in the civil law relating to the sale of goods (*see* Chapter 3) but in criminal law they offer a defence to a charge that goods have been offered for sale or sold contrary to the law.

In the Food Act 1984 and the Weights and Measures Act 1985 a complete defence is offered where it can be shown that the defendant was in possession of a valid warranty and had no reason to doubt that the products were other than as warranted. In other trading law statutes (for example, s.24 of the Trade Descriptions Act, 1968) there is no specific defence of warranty but a defence of 'relying on information provided' is offered. It amounts to much the same thing save for the fact that it is directly linked to the onerous test of all reasonable precautions and all due diligence.

Under the Food Act 1984 and the Weights and Measures Act 1985 a warranty need be no more than a name on an invoice. No specific guarantee that the product conforms to legal requirements is required.

Warranties are most important for retailers and, to a lesser extent, to importers. All businesses in these fields should insist on warranties as a matter of course and ensure that they are recorded as part of the due diligence system discussed in 7.7 above.

7.9 Dealing with Investigating Officials

It is an offence to obstruct an investigating public official under acting on powers conferred by a statute and he is empowered to seek certain information to assist him in the proper exercise of his duties. Such officials may be trading standards officers or environmental health officers employed by local authorities, an official of the Office of Fair Trading or the Department of Trade and Industry, Customs and Excise officials, certain marketing board officials and a number of others.

All investigating officials are required by law to produce credentials when requested to do so. Those credentials should specify the Acts of Parliament which the officer is empowered to enforce and give confirmation that he is a properly appointed officer of a specified public authority. No person posing as an official should be admitted to business premises unless he is able to produce authentic credentials.

7.10 Admissions of Guilt

In nearly all trading law statutes the powers of officials to require information are tempered by a requirement that no person should be required to give any information which might incriminate. The dividing line between information to which the official is entitled and that which might incriminate is often obscure.

However, the Police and Criminal Evidence Act 1984 requires that when an investigating officer (whether he be a police officer or a civilian) reaches a point in his investigation where he believes that an offence has been committed he must caution the person being interviewed before proceeding further. As a general rule, businessmen should never answer questions after the caution has been given without first seeking legal advice.

8 Product descriptions and advertising

8.1 Introduction

The truthful description of goods offered for sale in business transactions has long been a matter of concern. If a product is misdescribed there may be a breach of one of the implied terms of contract under the Sale of Goods Act 1979 (*see* Chapter 3). That is a matter of civil law and the rules now incorporated in the Act of 1979 were established more than a century ago to enable the courts to settle disputes between persons doing business together. At about the same time, however, Parliament concluded that it was against the general public interest for goods to be falsely described and the Merchandise Marks Act 1887 was passed to forbid the use of false trade descriptions in the sale of goods. That was a matter of criminal law and it is the modern criminal laws on product misdescriptions that are discussed in this chapter.

The law on misdescriptions of services has been slow to develop. Until 1982 breaches of contract as a result of failure to fulfil a contract of service was a matter for the common law. In that year, however, the Supply of Goods and Services Act (*see* Chapter 3) was passed to bring the civil law on services into line with that for goods. The first criminal law on reckless statements about the provision of services was contained in the Trade Descriptions Act 1968. This too will be considered in this chapter.

During the last 25 years the criminal law on false or misleading descriptions has been extended to cover an ever wider range of goods and services. In addition to the general provisions of the Trade Descriptions Act 1968 special laws relating to food, medicines, consumer credit, consumer safety, animal feeding stuffs, prices, and many other matters have been made. The purpose of this chapter and those which follow is to acquaint the student of marketing law with the principles involved.

8.2 Business Transactions

Generally speaking, the criminal law relating to the description of goods and services applies only to people acting in the course of trade or business. It is not an offence for a private individual to describe falsely something he or she may wish to sell; although it has been held to be an offence if such falsehood leads a trader into commiting an offence.

Example

If a private motorist trades in his used car against another car and falsely declares to the trader that its odometer reading is genuine the trader would commit an offence against s.1 of the Trade Descriptions Act 1968 if he resold the car without making it clear that the odometer reading was incorrect.

Held: The motorist could be held to be responsible for the commission of the offence by the dealer under s.23 of the Act.

(Olgeirsson v. Kitching, 1985)

8.3 In the Course of Trade or Business

It is often difficult to decide whether or not a transaction is carried out in the course of trade or business and is thus subject to the criminal law. The sale of goods which are ancillary to the principal business concerned, such as the sale of used equipment, is in the course of business and it is not necessary that the person concerned should be in full-time occupation relating to the transaction.

Example

A shoe repairer sold electric fires from his own home in his shop.

Held: This was a sale in the course of business even though it was not the principal business of the defendant.

(Southwark London Borough v. Charlesworth, 1983, 147 JP 89, DC)

8.4 Trade Descriptions

In 1887 the Merchandise Marks Act of that year prohibited the application of false trade descriptions to goods. It was the first time that Parliament had sought to control falsehood in trade and it remained the only criminal law on the misdescription of goods generally for the next 91 years. The Act was not very successful because no public authority was required to enforce it. Although some local authorities voluntarily used the Act for particular prosecutions the absence of any powers of entry, inspection and seizure put them in a very weak position.

In 1968 the Trade Descriptions Act was introduced and was heralded as being a very important step forward in consumer protection. In fact it was based on the principles of the 1887 Act and the principal offences concerning goods were almost unchanged. The 1968 Act has achieved a considerable improvement in the honesty of labels, advertisements and trading generally. It remains by far the most important criminal law statute for marketing executives and that is why it is dealt with in some detail in this chapter.

A trade description can be about any of the following matters:

(i) The quality, size or gauge of goods—this would cover incorrect declarations of quantity on packs or at the point of sale, false statements about the thickness of material used in manufacture and incorrect sizes for garments. A false statement of quantity would also be an offence against the Weights and Measures Act 1985.

(ii) The method of manufacture, production, processing or reconditioning—this could include the processing of food such as pasteurization, the treatment of metals such as galvanizing, and the fitting of replacement new parts in domestic equipment or cars. A false statement about such matters in respect of food may also be an offence against the Food Act 1984 and one in respect of medicines against the Medicines Act 1968.

(iii) The composition—a misleading list of ingredients in a food product, or a false statement about the materials used in a product generally are all examples of possible offences under this provision. Again the Food Act 1984 and the Medicines Act 1968 may also apply to offences where appropriate. The Agriculture Act 1970 may apply to offences in respect of the composition of fertilizers or animal feeding stuffs.

(iv) The fitness for purpose, strength, performance, behaviour or accuracy—the volume of sound produced by a hi-fi system, the time taken to boil by an electric kettle, the suitability of a shackle in the rigging of a yacht, the power produced by an internal combustion engine, and the timekeeping of a clock are all examples of this provision.

(v) Any physical characteristics not included above—this is what legal draftsmen call a 'bucket provision'. If anything has been overlooked in the foregoing provisions then it is caught by this general subparagraph.

(vi) Testing by any person or the results thereof—a false claim that a product had been tested by a well-known authority on such goods would breach this requirement.

(vii) Approval by any person or conformity with a type approved by any person—this covers false claims about all recognized approval systems such as the BSI Kite Mark, the MOT tests on vehicles etc.

(viii) Place or date of manufacture, production, processing, or reconditioning—false statements about the country of origin of imported goods, the year of manufacture of a car, or the date when a painting was completed by the artist are examples of this subparagraph's application.

(ix) The person by whom manufactured, produced, processed or reconditioned—this provision is often used to deal with the problem of counterfeited goods where it is implied that the product is made by or reconditioned by a reputable manufacturer. It has had a wide impact on the problem of counterfeited video tapes.

(x) Other history, including previous ownership or use—false statements about the authenticity of paintings or antiques or the number of previous owners of a used car are examples of this subparagraph's application.

8.5 Trade Descriptions Act 1968

Section 2 (1)

This section makes it an offence to (i) apply a false trade description to goods and (ii) to supply or offer to supply goods to which a false trade description has been applied. The very wide terms of these provisions have encouraged enforcement authorities to attempt to extend the Act to matters which do not immediately appear to be covered.

Example

The words 'extra value' are not a trade description (*Cadbury Ltd v. Halliday*, 1975, 2 All ER 226, 1975, 1 WLR 649).

Certain matters are excluded by the Act itself, such as information required to be applied to goods by other legislation, for example, grade marks on eggs and indications of fibre content of textiles.

8.6 False trade descriptions

For any description on any of the matters above to be false it must be 'false to a material degree'. This is a manifestation of the doctrine of *de minimis* which decrees that the law 'is not concerned with trifles'. Its purpose is to prevent trivial prosecutions for matters such as the 'whiter than white' claims of detergent manufacturers. We reached the ultimate in whiteness years ago. Such claims are advertisers' puffery and are not to be taken seriously.

The doctrine of *de minimis* is to be found in most criminal statutes. For example, for there to be an offence against s.2 of the Food Act 1984 the food delivered must be 'to the prejudice of the purchaser'. This means that its defect must be of significant importance to the buyer. In weights and measures law tolerances for weighing and measuring equipment and goods packed to the 'average quantity system' are prescribed.

8.7 Section 3: Application of trade descriptions

A trade description can be applied directly to goods by way of a label, packaging or other document; it can be derived from anything in, on or with which the goods are placed to which a trade description has been affixed or annexed; it can be applied orally; or it can be established by a request from a buyer which includes a description even though the supplier may say nothing.

The terms of the Act in respect of the application of trade descriptions are so wide that it is wise to assume that anything said about a product, and however that information is conveyed to the buyer, is in fact the application of a trade description. In practice it is very difficult to prove that an oral trade description has been applied in the absence of corroborating evidence from a witness for the prosecution.

8.8 Section 4: Trade descriptions used in advertisements

Where a trade description is used in an advertisement there is a presumption that it refers to all goods of the class described whether or not they are in existence at the time the advertisement is published. In determining whether goods are of a class described in an advertisement it is necessary to consider the form and content of the advertisement but also the time, place, manner and frequency of its publication and all other matters which might cause a person to whom goods are supplied to think that they belong to the class described in an advertisement.

However, statements published in newspapers, books or periodicals or in any film or sound or television broadcast are not trade descriptions unless they are a part of an advertisement.

Thus, a description of a car in a published road test report in a motoring magazine is not a trade description but it would become one if the manufacturer used the report in full or in part in an advertisement.

8.9 Unlawful use of trade descriptions

The Act creates two offences where false trade descriptions are applied to goods in the course of a trade or business;

(*a*) It is an offence to apply a false trade description to goods.

(*b*) It is an offence to supply, or offer to supply, goods to which a false trade description is applied.

The first offence would be committed by any person or company who actually applied a false trade description to goods. Thus a manufacturer could commit an offence in applying labels to his own products or by advertising them. An advertising or sales promotion agency who originate descriptions for clients' goods might commit an offence unless they could show that they were acting under instructions from a client and could prove a defence (*see* Chapter 7). A retailer could commit the offence in respect of any trade descriptions originated by him for use in his stores or by way of advertisements.

The second offence can be committed by a person or company who supplies goods to which a false trade description has been applied either by himself or by some other person. This offence is usually committed by retailers who sell goods already labelled or advertised by their suppliers but such a retailer may be able to plead a defence if he can show that he had relied on the information supplied to him and had no reasonable cause to doubt that it was accurate (*see* Chapter 7).

The following examples indicate how the courts view false trade descriptions. Regard must always be had to the context in which the description was used.

Example

Imitation jewellery was marked '9ct', '18ct' and 'PLAT'.
Held: These marks implied that they were 9ct and 18ct gold and platinum respectively and were therefore false trade description.

(Ealing London Borough Council v. Warren, 1981)

Example

The term 'cold cast bronze' was used for statuettes made from fibreglass which was then sprayed with a fine outer skin of 90 per cent copper and 10 per cent tin.
Held: This was a false trade description.

(London Borough of Southwark v. Elderson Industries Ltd, 1981)

Example

The term 'rolled gold' has been held not to be a false trade description when used in respect of cuff-links on the grounds that it was a trade custom to use the term in that context and the items were very cheap. The description could not, therefore, have been false or misleading.

(*F. W. Woolworth & Co. Ltd. v. Kingston on Thames Royal London Borough*, 1968, 1 QB 802, 1968 1 All ER 401)

Example

The words 'extra value' when applied to bars of chocolate do not refer to any of the matters defined as being a trade description by section 2 of the Act and are not, therefore, an offence.

(Cadbury Ltd v. Halliday, 1975, 2 All ER 226)

Example

A mileage figure on an MOT Certificate for a car is not a trade description because it merely records the mileage at the time of the test.

(Corfield v. Sevenways Garage Ltd, 1984)

Example

Furniture which was advertised by photographs showing it in ready assembled form when in fact it was only available in kit form was held to be in breach of the Act.

(Queensway Discount Warehouse Ltd v. Burke, 1985)

Examples

The word 'beautiful' applied to a car which was superficially attractive but which was unroadworthy was a false trade description.

(Robertson v. Dicicco, 1972, RTR 431)

Similarly the words 'immaculate condition' constituted an offence when applied to a car in bad mechanical condition.

(Kensington and Chelsea (Royal) London Borough Council v. Riley, 1972, RTR 122)

In similar circumstances the words 'mechanically superb', 'excellent condition throughout', and 'showroom condition' have been held to be a breach of the Act.

Example

The word 'waterproof' when applied to a watch which was not so was in breach of the Act.

(Sherratt v. Geralds the American Jewellers, 1970, 114 Sol Jo 147)

Example

An electric torch for use in lighting a gas cooker which had been described in an advertisement as being suitable for this purpose but which in fact would not function with the cooker concerned was held to constitute an offence.

(British Gas Corporation v. Lubbock, 1974, 1 WLR 37)

8.10 Disclaimers

The above cases, and many more like them, indicate the wide application of the Trade Descriptions Act 1968. The question arises as to whether it is possible to use words in advertisements, other documents, labels and the like which will disclaim responsibility for any falseness in a description. In *Norman v. Bennett*, 1974, 3 All ER 351, 1974, 1 WLR 1229, which has become the leading case on the use of disclaimers, it was held that for a disclaimer to be effective it must be as bold, precise and compelling as the description it seeks to qualify. In that case there was a small notice in a car showroom which stated that odometer readings on cars on display were not necessarily correct. The court was not impressed with it and decided that it did not affect the falseness of the odometer readings.

Whether or not a disclaimer is effective is a question of fact to be decided in each case. Faced with such a decision the businessman should put himself in the position of a ordinary consumer and ask himself whether he would be misled by the description with or without the disclaimer. It should always be borne in mind, however, that truthful descriptions do not require disclaimers.

8.11 Origin Marking

There is nothing in the Trade Descriptions Act 1968 which requires goods to be marked with an indication or origin. The Act merely makes it an offence to give a *false* indication of origin. However, there are other statutory requirements on origin marking as follows.

The Trade Descriptions (Place of Production) (Marking) Order 1988 replaced earlier legislation on compulsory origin marking because those requirements were not based on community law and created a barrier to the free exchange of goods. This order requires that where the presentation of goods suggests that they were manufactured or produced elsewhere than is the case they shall be marked with or accompanied by a clear, legible and conspicuous statement as to the place where they were manufactured or produced. The order applies to all products (other than food, medicines, fertilizers and feeding stuffs).

The Food Labelling Regulations 1984 (regulation 6) require that where the absence of an indication of the *place* of origin could mislead a buyer as to the actual place of origin then the food shall be marked with such an indication. Thus a product marked 'Norfolk Crab Paste' which was in fact made in Bristol would have to be marked 'Made in Bristol (or Avon)'.

EEC regulations on the grading of horticultural produce require that packages of most types of fruit and vegetables shall bear an indication of the geographical region from which the produce originates.

8.12 False Claims as to Royal Approval or Award

It is an offence to give any false indication in the course of trade or business that any goods or services supplied or any methods adopted are of a kind approved of or supplied to Her Majesty the Queen or any member of the royal family. Similarly, any unapproved use of the symbols or emblems of the Queen's Award to Industry which is likely to deceive is an offence.

8.13 False claims as to persons supplied

Any false indication in the course of trade or business that goods or services are of a kind supplied to any person is an offence. This prevents the false use of well-known personalities (other than the royal family) as having bought goods or services being advertised or offered for supply.

8.14 False or Misleading Statements as to Services

The Trade Descriptions Act 1968 provided for the first time criminal sanctions against the making of false or reckless statements about the provision of services. It prohibits the making of a statement in the course of trade or business which *is known to be false* or to *recklessly* make a statement which is false as to the provision of services, accommodation or facilities; the nature of services, accommodation or facilities or the time or manner in which such services etc. are provided. Statements about the examination, approval or evaluation by any person of services etc. and the location or amenities of any accommodation are also caught by the offences.

The first offence requires proof that the person charged knew that the statement he made was false. Proof of guilty knowledge is always difficult and generally speaking requires some admission by the defendant or documentary evidence of prior knowledge on his part.

The second offence covers statements which are made regardless of whether they are true or false.

These offences have had a significant impact on the package holiday business but a lesser one on the provision of other services. Because of its apparently wide application enforcement authorities have been encouraged to bring proceedings in a variety of circumstances where the Act, on a strict interpretation of its provisions, was never intended to apply. The following examples show how the courts have reacted to such cases:

Example

A guarantee on a used car was not honoured even though the sellers knew that there were faults in the vehicle which ought to be corrected.
Held: That an offence had been committed.
                    (*Bambury v. Hounslow London Borough Council*, 1971, RTR 1 DC)

Example

An offer to 'turnerize' a roof by a jobbing builder who used a different and inferior process was an offence.
                    (*Parsons v. Barnes*, 1973, Crim LR 537)

Example

A false oral statement to the purchaser of a bungalow that it was covered by the National House Builders Registration Council ten-year guarantee is an offence.
                    (*Breed v. Cluett*, 1970, 1 QB 459; 1970, 2 All ER 662)

Example

An unfulfilled statement of intention is not an offence. A builder promised to complete a garage within ten days and to a particular design but failed to do so. *Held*: This was not contrary to this Act.

(*Beckett v. Cohen*, 19731, 1 All ER 120; 1972, 1 WLR 1593)

Example

The offer of free hire of 20 video films with a video recorder when only six were available and without mention that postage and packaging was payable is an offence.

(*Cowburn v. Focus Television Rentals Ltd*, 1983, 147 JP 201, DC)

Example

The offer of accommodation described as being airconditioned when in fact it is not an offence.

(*Wings v. Ellis*, 1984, 1 All ER 1046, 148 JP 183)

Example

Overbooking of airline seats and the failure to honour a ticket as a result is not an offence.

(*British Airways Board v. Taylor*, 1976, 1 All ER 65, 1976, 1 WLR 13)

The apparently contradictory nature of these judgments and many more like them arise from the difficulty of proving either that the statements concerned were made with guilty knowledge or that they were recklessly made. In each case the courts consider the evidence and decide whether the necessary burden of proof has been discharged by the prosecution.

Proposals to make offences in respect of services of strict liability (as they are in respect of goods under s.2 of the Act) were originally contained in a review of the Act issued by the Director General of Fair Trading in 1976 (Cmnd 6628). Similar proposals have been made since that date by the Consumers Association and other consumer interests. The difficulty is that if this were done it would become a criminal offence to simply be inefficient—a concept fraught with difficulties.

8.15 Orders made under the Trade Descriptions Act 1968

The Secretary of State for Trade and Industry is empowered to make Orders requiring that goods must be marked with or accompanied by information. The only Order currently in operation is the *Trade Descriptions (Sealskin Goods) (Information) Order 1980* which requires that goods containing sealskin must be clearly marked as such and also state the country from which the seals were taken.

8.16 Information Orders

Certain Orders have been made under the European Communities Act 1972 requiring product information to be given in accordance with EEC requirements. They are:

(a) The Crystal Glass (Descriptions) Regulations 1973

This implements Council Directive No 69/493/EEC and requires that where descriptions generally used for crystal glass are used the product must conform to compositional standards.

(b) The Textile Products (Indications of Fibre Content) Regulations 1973

These implement Council Directive No 71/307/EEC and require that with certain exceptions textile products shall be marked with an indication of the percentage of various fibres used in them.

8.17 The Hallmarking Act 1973

This Act provides for the assaying, hallmarking and description of articles made from precious metals. Under the Act it is an offence to apply to any article a description which indicates that it is wholly or partly made from gold, silver or platinum unless it bears a hallmark. This prohibition does not apply if the word 'gold' is qualified by the words 'plated' or 'rolled'; if the word 'silver' is qualified by the word 'plated' or if the word 'platinum' is qualified by the word 'plated' (s.1 and schedule 1).

8.18 Food

By virtue of its importance to every citizen the sale and supply of food is controlled by a most complex and extensive body of legislation. The Food Act 1984 prohibits the sale to the prejudice of the purchaser of food which is not of the nature, substance or quality demanded (s.2); food which is unfit for human consumption (s.8); and the adulteration of milk and cream (s.36 and 38). There are strict controls to prevent food poisoning and specific controls on meat and shell fish. Standards of hygiene in the preparation and storage of food are enforced by the Act and regulations made under it. In this book we are concerned only with the descriptions used for food and s.6 of the Act is directly relevant.

(i) False or misleading labels and advertisements for food

It is unlawful to give a label with any food offered for sale or to publish an advertisement which falsely describes the food or which is likely to be misleading as to the nature, substance or quality of the food. These two offences can be distinguished by the fact that 'false', in law, means wholly untrue; whereas 'misleading' is a lesser term which, although not wholly untrue, can mislead as to the essential characteristics of the food.

(ii) Nature, substance and quality

These are most important terms which appear throughout food legislation and also in the law relating to medicines and animal feeding stuffs. To a certain extent the terms are overlapping but judicial interpretation of them and commonsense enables the following broad definitions to be established.

Nature mean kind, sort of species. Giant prunes described as plums, cod sold as haddock, battery-produced eggs sold as free range eggs etc. are examples of 'nature'.

Substance means that there is something in the food which ought not to be there. Foreign bodies such as a piece of metal in a meat pie; mouldy food which is not so bad as to be unfit for human consumption; residues of pesticides in food generally or antibiotics in milk are examples of substance.

Quality means that the product falls below a compositional standard which is generally acceptable to the ordinary consumer or is imposed by law.

(iii) Food Labelling

Council Directive 79/112/EEC as amended is the European Community framework for food labelling. It has been implemented in the United Kingdom by the Food Labelling Regulations 1984.

Food which is ready for delivery to the ultimate consumer or a catering establishment must be labelled with the following information, subject to numerous exemptions for specific foods and particular labelling requirements imposed by other regulations:

(a) There must be a name for the food which is either required by law, or if there is no name required by law a customary name, or if there is no customary name or a customary name is not used the name must be sufficiently specific to indicate the true nature of the food and to enable it to be distinguished from other foods with which it might be confused.

(b) There must be a list of ingredients in descending order by weight.

(c) Any special storage conditions or conditions of use must be given.

(d) There must be an indication of minimum durability for foods with a shelf-life of less than eighteen months in the form of a 'best before' date (a 'sell by' date may be used optionally for short shelf-life foods).

(e) The name and address or registered office of the manufacturer or packer, or of a seller established with the EEC must be shown.

(f) Particulars of the place of origin must be given if failure to give such particulars might mislead a purchaser to a material degree as to the true origin of the food.

(g) Instructions for use must be given if it would be difficult to make appropriate use of the food in the absence of such instructions.

Food which is not prepacked or which is ready for immediate consumption need only bear a product name and the categories of additives which have been used in its preparation. Certain meat and spreadable fish products must also show added ingredients and/or a statement of the minimum meat or fish content or, if added water is present, a statement of the amount added.

(iv) Claims about food products

Claims that foods have been specially prepared for particular nutritional requirements, that they are a source of energy, suitable for diabetics, have slimming benefits, are a source of protein, vitamins or minerals, are low in polyunsaturated fatty acids or cholesterol etc. are strictly controlled by the regulations and, if such claims may be lawfully made, additional information must be given.

8.19 Medicinal Products

The labelling and advertising of medicinal products is strictly controlled in a similar manner to that of food save for the fact that most medicinal products may not be sold unless there is a valid product licence in existence for them. This licence often prescribes what must appear on the product label in addition to the minimum labelling requirements applicable to all medicinal products and it may also indicate what may be said about the product in advertising.

They are offences in the Medicines Act 1968 about false or misleading advertisements and labels and medicines which are not of the nature, substance or quality demanded by the purchaser.

8.20 Animal Feedstuffs

Feedstuffs for farm animals and pet cats and dogs are controlled by the Agriculture Act 1970 and regulations made thereunder in pursuance of Community requirements. It is an offence to sell animal feedstuffs containing deleterious materials which are unwholesome and the regulations require that they be labelled with certain information about ingredients (*The Agriculture Act 1970, s.73 and 73A; the Feeding Stuffs Regulations 1982*).

8.21 Weights and Measures

There is a complex system of law applicable to the sale of goods by weight, measure or number. The following is a summary of the principal requirements:

(a) Sale by quality

The law requires that certain goods *must* be sold by weight, measure or number and the manner in which they must be sold is prescribed. It is an offence to sell goods so prescribed in any other manner even if the correct quantity is given.

All other goods may be sold by weight, measure or number if the seller so chooses, but if they are so sold then certain rules about the marking of the quantity must be obeyed.

(b) Prescribed quantities

Many foods and some other goods may only be prepacked in certain prescribed quantities (pack sizes). It is an offence to sell them in any other quantity. Under EEC requirements we can expect to see an extension of the 'prescribed quantity' concept to other goods during the next few years.

(c) Quantity marking

All goods which are required to be sold by weight, measure or number, whether in a prescribed quantity or not *must* be marked with a statement of that quantity and the manner in which that statement is made is laid down. Goods which are voluntarily sold by quantity must also be marked with a statement of quantity in the approved manner when prepacked.

(d) Short weight, measure or number

It is an offence to sell short weight, measure or number in respect of all goods whether or not they are required to be sold by quantity. It is also an offence to sell a lesser quantity than corresponds to the price charged; for example, if a unit price of '85p per kg' is given and 85p is charged for a quantity of less than 1 kg the offence is committed even if no mention is made of weight by the buyer or seller.

(e) Net or gross weight

Most goods are required to be sold by net weight and even if there is no mention of net weight that is the weight which must be sold. Certain foods, however, are allowed to be sold by gross weight provided that the wrapper/container weights do not exceed prescribed maximum amounts.

(f) Minimum and average weight or measure

The average weight and measure system was introduced into the United Kingdom in 1980 (1978 for wines). This system permits all prepacked goods, subject to certain exemptions, to be packed above or below the declared quantity within strict limits. All goods may, however, continue to be packed to the minimum system; in other words all quantities are at or above the declared quantity, because compliance with the minimum system automatically results in compliance with the average system.

8.22 Fair Trading

The Fair Trading Act 1973 established the Office of Fair Trading under its Director-General. The Director-General of Fair Trading enjoys extensive powers to deal with unfair and restrictive trade practices and is under a duty to draw the attention of the Secretary of State to matters which might justify legislative intervention.

Part III of the Act empowers the Director-General to seek assurances from persons (companies) carrying on a course of conduct which is detrimental to consumers that they will refrain from continuing that conduct. If the Director-General is unable to obtain an assurance, or if one is given and not honoured, the Director-General of Fair Trading is empowered to bring proceedings against the alleged transgressor before the Restrictive Practices Court. That court may enforce an undertaking by injunction (an order of the court to refrain from a certain practice) or may accept a further assurance if the evidence warrants a more lenient course of action.

Example

The Director-General of Fair Trading sought an injunction to ensure that a company would refrain from a course of conduct which resulted in 46 offences against the Food and Drugs Act 1955 through the court. The court accepted an assurance from the company instead of issuing an injunction.

(*Director-General of Fair Trading v. Smiths Bakeries (Westfield) Ltd*, 1978)

Action under Part III of the Act may be taken by the Director-General in respect of any of the matters in this chapter and those which follow.

As a result of a number of recommendations by the Director-General of Fair Trading to the Secretary of State a number of Orders have been made under powers conferred by the Fair Trading Act 1973. They are as follows:

(i) Mail Order Transactions (Information) Order 1976

This Order requires that all advertisements (other than those by television, radio or film) which invite the payment of money before delivery of the goods to include the full name and address of the person (company) carrying on the business.

(ii) Consumer Transactions (Restrictions on Statements) Order 1976

This Order prohibits the use of notices or statements which are void under the Unfair Contract Terms Act 1977 (*see* Chapter 3) or which are inconsistent with the warranty implied by the Trading Stamps Act 1964. This is intended to prevent consumers from being misled about their statutory rights by disclaimers. Where any mention of the buyer's rights is made in documents or notices relating to a contract then it is necessary to state that the buyer's right are not affected.

Example

A notice stating 'sold as seen and inspected' by a used car dealer was contrary to the Order.

(*Hughes v. Hall*, 1981 RTR 430)

(iii) Business Advertisements (Disclosure) Order 1977

This Order requires that where an advertisement by a trader does not make it clear that the offer is made in the course of business there shall be a statement to

that effect in the advertisement. The form of the ~
it is generally accepted that the word 'Trade' is su~.
 The Order seeks to prevent traders from masquer~
selling their own property thus depriving a buyer from hi~
Sale of Goods Act 1979.

8.23 Unsolicited Goods and Services

The Unsolicited Goods and Services Act 1971, as amended, provi~
unsolicited goods are sent or delivered for sale or hire they become the p~
of the recipient as a gift provided he gives notice to the sender within 30 da~
receiving the goods and they are not retrieved by the sender. The same result w~
occur if the sender does not collect the goods within six months. The offence does
not arise if the recipient reasonably believes that the goods were not unsolicited or
if the goods were sent for use in the course of a trade or business.
 It is an offence to send out demands for payment for unsolicited goods.

Example

Copies of the *Readers' Digest* magazine continued to be sent to a former buyer
who had cancelled his subscription and demands for payment were sent. The
company knew that the subscription had been cancelled but due to an error this
had not been communicated to the computer and the demands had been sent out.
Held: The goods were not unsolicited and the demands for payment were
consequently not unlawful.

(Readers' Digest Association Ltd v. Pirie, 1973, SLT 170)

 It is an offence against the Act to demand payment for unsolicited entries in
trade directories, and also to send to persons books, magazines or leaflets which
describe human sexual techniques.

8.24 Misleading Advertising

Although the Trade Descriptions Act 1968 and the other statutes discussed in
this chapter apply to advertising, the main organ of control of advertising in the
United Kingdom has always been the industry's own self-regulation system (*see*
Chapter 14). From the moment of the United Kingdom's accession to the Treaty
of Rome in 1973 there was pressure for a legal system of control to replace the
voluntary system. After a prolonged period of negotiation a compromise was
reached which allows the United Kingdom to keept its voluntary system
provided it is backed by legal sanctions. Council Directive 84/450/EEC of 10
September 1984 relating to the approximation of the laws of member states
concerning misleading advertising required that all member states should have
ensured that adequate and effective means exist for the control of misleading
advertising in the interests of consumers as well as competitors and the general
public. Such means included the power to take legal action against such
advertising. At one time it was believed that the system of statutory control
exercised by the Independent Broadcasting Authority (IBA), the system of self-
regulation operated by the Advertising Standards Authority and the Trade

iptions Act 1968 were together sufficient to meet the requirements of the ctive (for a review of the IBA and ASA control systems see Chapter 14). wever, it was concluded that some additional legal back-up was required ere the voluntary system failed to achieve the necessary degree of control. Accordingly, the Control of Misleading Advertising Regulations 1988 (*see* 14.8 (v)) empowers the Director-General of Fair Trading to obtain injunctions where an advertisement is deemed to be misleading within the meaning of the Directive.

In determining whether advertising is misleading the Directive requires that account shall be taken of all its features and in particular any information it contains concerning:

(i) The characteristics of goods and services, such as their availability, nature, execution, composition, method and date of manufacture or provision, fitness for purpose, uses, quantity, specification, geographical or commercial origin or the results to be expected from their use, or the results and material features of tests or checks carried out on the goods or services.

(ii) The price or the manner in which the price is calculated, and the conditions on which the goods are supplied or the services provided.

(iii) The nature, attributes and rights of the advertiser, such as his identity and assets, his qualifications and ownership of industrial, commercial or intellectual property rights or his awards or distinctions.

The Directive requires that laws and administrative arrangements shall be such as to require the publisher of a misleading advertisement to cease publication or, if the advertisement has not actually been published, to withdraw it.

The effectiveness of the 1988 regulations and the Directive have yet to be seen. It was no secret during the consultation leading to the regulations that the new powers conferred on the Director-General were to be very much a last resort and the bulk of control was to remain with the IBA and the ASA.

9 *Product safety*

9.1 Civil and Criminal Liability

The sale of dangerous products can have consequences in both civil and criminal law. Under the laws of the United Kingdom a person who is injured by a defective product has remedies in contract, in tort (or delict in Scotland) and of strict product liability. In order to adequately protect the population in general criminal legislation provides for standards of construction and manufacture for goods offered for sale or supply to consumers with penalties where goods are found to be unsafe.

9.2 Civil Remedies

Under the law operating before the Consumer Protection Act 1987 came into operation, a contractual remedy for injury by dangerous goods was normally only available against the person who supplied the goods (the retailer) and not against the manufacturer or importer. Further, if the person who was injured was not the purchaser of the product he or she generally had no remedy in contract. In such cases action would have had to be in tort and the injured party would have faced the need to prove that the manufacturer, or someone else in the chain of supply, had been negligent. Such proof was always difficult to achieve although in recent years the courts have tended to take a more sympathetic view of the degree of proof required and there has been a gradual move towards an implied general duty to sell safe goods to consumers.

Remedies in contract and tort remain available but following a review of product safety law by the Law Commission (Cmnd 6831, June 1977) and the Royal Commission on Civil Liability and Compensation for Personal Injury (The Pearson Commission; Cmnd 7054, March 1978) the United Kingdom government agreed that the existing law was unsatisfactory and accepted that a system of strict liability should be introduced. However, action was deferred pending agreement on an EEC Directive on Product Liability. This Directive was adopted on 25 July 1985 (85/374/EEC) and implemented in the United Kingdom from 1 March 1988 by Part I of the Consumer Protection Act 1987.

(i) The Directive on Product Liability

The Directive requires Member States to introduce laws imposing strict liability on producers of defective products that cause damage. If a claimant suffers damage (death, personal injury of damage to goods for private use) as a result of a defective product he will no longer have to prove negligence, although he will have to prove that the product was defective and that his damage was a result of the defect in the product.

Products include all movables (not buildings) with the exception of primary agricultural products which have not undergone an initial industrial process and game.

The producer on whom strict liability falls is generally the manufacturer or importer into the Community of the finished product or of the defective raw material or component. In order to give the claimant a clear route of action, strict liability is also attached to anyone who presents himself as a producer (for example, retailers' own brand products) and, where the producer cannot be identified, someone further up the chain of supply. The Directive imposes joint and several liability, without prejudice to rights of contribution and recourse provided in national laws.

A product is deemed to be defective when it does not provide the safety which a person is entitled to expect taking into account all the circumstances. These include the presentation of the product (for example, instructions for use), reasonable expected use and the time when the product was put into circulation.

There are defences in certain circumstances, including cases where the producer proves that the state of scientific and technical knowledge when he put the product into circulation was not such as to enable the existence of the defect to be discovered. This is the much discussed and controversial 'development risks' defence.

The new laws of strict liability do not affect the law of contract or of tort but there is a limitation period of three years from discovery of the damage, the defect and the identity of the producer, for the bringing of proceedings, and a long-stop period of ten years from the date when the product was put into circulation for the extinction of all rights.

It is possible for manufacturers to insure against product liability risks. Premiums naturally vary from industry to industry depending on the nature of the product concerned and its potential risks. In the period leading to the adoption of the Directive in the United Kingdom there has been much concern about some of the enormous awards of damages in the United States where a similar system operates. Sensational awards of damages in the United States are more attributable to the American legal system than to the merits of the cases.

The Directive provides a Community-wide system of protection for consumers which requires that redress should be available irrespective of national boundaries. Arrangements are being made to enable citizens of one member state to bring proceedings in the courts of another and for the mutual enforcement of judgments between member states.

9.3 Criminal Liability

The first products to be controlled by criminal law were foodstuffs because of their potential for injury to the population in general. Today, all protection in respect of the safety of food emanates from the Food Act 1984 and the Food and Environment Protection Act 1985. It is an offence to sell food which is not of the nature, substance or quality demanded by the buyer (thus convering such matters as foreign bodies in food, contamination, by mould or pesticides residues and the like; *see also* Chapters 8) or food which is unfit for human consumption. Provision is also made for minimum standards of hygiene in premises where food is manufactured, packed or sold. The latter Act empowers the Secretary of State to ban the sale of all or certain specified foods in geographical areas in response to a major emergency (for example, the radiation hazards caused by the Chernobyl accident) and to control the manufacture, importation, sale and use of pesticides.

The safety of certain products and practices is ensured by special legislation. For example, the storage and sale of poisons is controlled by the Poisons Act 1972; medicinal products are very strictly controlled by the Medicines Act 1968; the manufacture, storage and use of explosives is covered by the Explosives Substances Act 1883 and the Explosives Act 1875; the storage of petroleum products is dealt with by the Petroleum Consolidation Act 1929; and the use, conveyance and storage of dangerous and toxic substances is controlled by regulations made under the European Communities Act 1972. These latter controls are based on EEC requirements and are the same throughout all member states. The laws of member states on explosives and poisons, for example, have not yet been harmonized. The construction and safety of motor vehicles is controlled by the Road Traffic Acts 1960 and 1972 and the Road Traffic Regulation Act 1984. Safety in merchant shipping is achieved through the Merchant Shipping Acts 1894 to 1984, and the Merchant Shipping (Load Lines) Act 1967; and that in civil aircraft through the Civil Aviation Act 1982.

The safety of all other consumer goods is ensured by the Consumer Safety Act 1978, which empowers the Secretary of State to prohibit the sale of dangerous products, and, more importantly, Part II of the Consumer Protection Act 1987. That Act introduced into the United Kingdom for the first time the concept of a general statutory duty to sell safe goods to consumers.

Under the Consumer Protection Act 1987, it is an offence to sell goods which fall below the general safety requirement. That requirement is that the goods must be reasonably safe bearing in mind the manner in which and the purposes for which they are marketed; any instructions or warnings given with them as to their use or storage; any published standards of safety (for example, BSI specifications) or regulations made under the Consumer Safety Act 1978; and the existence of any means by which it would have been reasonable, bearing in mind the cost, likelihood and extent of any improvement, for the goods to have been made safer. The general safety requirement applies to all consumer goods except, growing crops, water, food, feedstuffs or fertilizer, gas supplied through pipes, aircraft (other than hang-gliders), motor vehicles, controlled drugs or licensed medicinal products and tobacco.

Many classes of consumer goods are directly controlled as to their safety by regulations made under the Consumer Safety Act 1978 or the Consumer Protection Act 1987. They are as follows (in alphabetical order).

(i) Aerosols

The Aerosol Dispensers (EEC Requirements) Regulations 1977/1140 require that the EEC mark (the reversed epsilon) shall only be marked on an aerosol container if that container complies with Council Directive No 75/324/EEC. That Directive makes provisions as to the dimensions, strength and impeller of aerosol containers.

There is no statutory requirement that aerosol containers must comply with the Directive. The position is that if the EEC mark is used then the requirements of the Directive are invoked.

(ii) Babies' Dummies

The Babies' Dummies (Safety) Regulations 1978/836 require that dummies must comply with BS 5239:1975 as to materials, strength, design and construction. The dummies must be made entirely of rubber, or plastics, or a combination of components made entirely of rubber and components made entirely of plastics. A notice must be enclosed in containers of babies' dummies or the container itself must be marked with clear and legible instructions for the safe use of the dummies; instructions shall be given as to the washing before and after use, the storing in a dry covered container, and the dismantling and testing before use. These particular instructions should be distinguished from other words by use of the words 'Caution' or 'Warning'.

(iii) Carrycot Stands

The Stands for Carrycots (Safety) Regulations 1966/1610 require that cot stands shall have stoutly affixed to them a durable label stating in legible and durable characters the maximum length and width of carrycot which the stand is designed to accommodate. The base of a cot stand, when set upon a flat surface, shall be wider than the width and at least as long as three-quarters of the length specified in the label. The carrycot must be effectively retained in position on the stand by a guard rail or rigid steps operating upon the corners of the carrycot at a point not less than 7.5 cm (3 inches) above the underside of the bottom of the carrycot and the underside of the bottom of the carrycot must be not more than 42.5 cm (17 inches) above floor level. There are particular requirements as to the strength and weight-carrying capacity of cot stands.

(iv) Cooking Utensils

The Cooking Utensils (Safety) Regulations 1972/1957 require that kitchen utensils for cooking food must not be coated on any surface designed to come into contact with food with a tin or other metallic coating which contains any lead or lead compound so that the proportion by weight of lead calculated as the element (Pb) exceeds 20 parts in 10,000 parts of that coating.

(iv) Cosmetic Products

The Cosmetic Products Regulations 1978 require that cosmetics shall not contain certain substances and that other substances may only be contained up to maximum limits. The substances concerned are listed in the Schedule to the Regulations.

The Regulations also require that the container or the outer packaging in which a cosmetic product is sold must bear a label containing the following particulars:

(a) The name or trade name and address or registered office of the manufacturer of the product or a seller thereof being a manufacturer or seller established within the EEC.

(b) In the case of cosmetic products which are liable to deteriorate to a state where they can cause damage to human health within thirty months an expiry date must be shown.

(c) Certain substances when used in cosmetic products are required to be accompanied by certain information.

(d) Where a cosmetic product contains lanolin the words 'contains lanolin' must appear.

(e) Where there are prescribed precautions as to use they must appear on the label.

(f) An identifying number or mark for the batch of cosmetics must appear.

The particulars required must be visible, indelible and easily legible.

The 1978 Regulations are going to be progressively amended and revoked by the Cosmetic Products (Safety) Regulations 1984. The new Regulations will impose new requirements as to the use of preservatives in cosmetic products, the use of ultraviolet (UV) filters and for the marking of particulars about preservatives and filters. An important change in the law which came into effect on 1 January 1986, is that the Secretary of State has power to authorize the use of any substance in a cosmetic product subject to certain conditions.

(v) Dangerous Substances

The Dangerous Substances and Preparations (Safety) Regulations 1980/136 prohibit the sale of any ornamental object intended to produce light or colour effects by means of different phases in which any liquid substance which is listed in the Schedule to the Regulations is used.

The Notification of New Substances Regulations 1982/1496 require that any manufacturer or importer of a new substance, that being a chemical element or chemical compound as it occurs in the natural state or as produced by industry, excluding any additive shall be notified to the Health and Safety Executive before being incorporated into products.

The Classification, Packaging and Labelling of Dangerous Substances Regulations 1984/1244 impose extensive requirements as to classification and labelling of dangerous substances. Substances are designated as dangerous by virtue of various classifications. Each classification, which is based on technical data, invokes requirements as to a symbol indicating the nature of the danger, and the use of warnings on packaging. Examples of classifications are: explosive, oxidizing, extremely flammable, highly flammable, flammable, very toxic, toxic, harmful, corrosive and irritant. For the purposes of labelling the rules are based upon classifications of products as pesticides, solvents, paints, varnishes, printing inks, adhesives and similar products.

The principal responsibility for compliance with these Regulations rests, of course, with manufacturers and importers. In respect of own brand labels, however, it should be borne in mind that provision is made for the defence of due diligence and reasonable precautions.

(vi) Detergents

The Detergents (Composition) Regulations 1978/564 prohibit the sale of detergents containing certain substances and prescribe tests for ascertaining whether these substances are present in detergents. Standards are prescribed for certain permitted substances and other substances are exempted from the prohibition when used in particular detergents or in particular quantities.

(vii) Electrical Appliances

The Electrical Appliances (Colour Code) Regulations 1969/310 require that appliances operating on a supply of 100 volts or more and fitted with a flexible cord or cable must have the leads in specified colours and there must be a label attached to the lead with the following words set out in legible characters:

'IMPORTANT—the wires in this mains lead are coloured in accordance with the following code:
Green and yellow: earth
blue: neutral
brown: live'.

(viii) Electric Blankets

The Electric Blanket (Safety) Regulations 1971/1961 require that electric blankets must be made in accordance with BS 3456: Section A4 1971. Where a blanket is individually packed in a box or other container there must be a marked statement informing the buyer whether the blanket is for use as an overblanket or underblanket and if it is an underblanket, there must also be a statement as to whether the blanket is of a type which may be left switched on when the bed is occupied.

Each electric blanket must be marked with the following information:

(*a*) The rated voltage or voltage range in volts.
(*b*) The rated input of volts.
(*c*) A warning against using the blanket when folded, rucked or creased.
(*d*) A warning against laundering or dry cleaning, or against both laundering and dry cleaning, as the case may require.

In the case of a blanket to be connected only to an AC electricity supply or only to a DC electricity supply the type of current (AC or DC) to be used must be stated.

The following additional information must be marked:

(a) In the case of an overblanket

A warning against using the blanket other than as an overblanket.
A warning against switching on the blanket when it is wet.

(b) In the case of an underblanket for heating a bed when it is occupied

A warning against using the blanket other than as an underblanket.

(c) In the case of an underblanket for heating a bed only when unoccupied

A warning against using the blanket other than as an underblanket.
A warning against switching on the blanket when it is wet.
A warning either that the blanket must be disconnected from the electricity supply before the user gets into bed or that the blanket must be switched off before the user gets into bed.

(ix) Electrical Equipment

The Electrical Equipment (Safety) Regulations 1975/1366 requires that various items of electrical equipment shall comply with appropriate British Standards. They are as follows:

Type of equipment	BS Number
Shavers, hair clippers and similar appliances	BS 3456: Section 2.5: 1970, as amended.
Clocks	BS 3456: Section 2.6: 1971
Hand-held massage appliances with an input of 0.5 amperes or less at full load	BS 3456: Section 2.18: 1970
Hand-held appliances for skin and hair treatment which have an input of 3 amperes or less at full load	BS 3456: Section 2.21: 1973
Hand-held appliances in respect of which no particular requirements in BS 3456 were published before 1975 and which have an input of 0.5 amperes or less at full load	BS 6500
Electric heaters for baby feeding bottles	BS 3456: Section 2.15: 1970
Massage appliances not intended to be hand-held	BS 3456: Section 2.18: 1970
Ventilating fans	BS 3456: Section 2.29: 1971
Appliances for skin and hair treatment not intended to be hand-held and having an input of 3 amperes or less at full load	BS 3456: Section 2.31:
Lighting fittings	BS 6500

There are also specific requirements as to the safety and design of lampholders and certain switches, electrical plugs and terminals, and electric heaters.

The Regulations, generally speaking, require that electrical equipment shall be made according to reasonable standards of manufacturing practice.

(x) Explosives

Certain products such as fireworks, guncaps, and cartridges may only be sold by retailers who are registered with the local authority. There are requirements as to the safe storage of such products and their labelling. In all cases guidance should be obtained from the local authority explosives inspector.

(xi) Food Imitations

The Food Imitations (Safety) Regulations 1985/99 prohibit the supply of certain products which look like food or smell like food or like flowers or taste like food. The products covered are toys and the following items which are designated as 'regulated products': Erasers, writing, drawing and painting implements and materials, pentops, pencil tops, pencil sharpeners, scissors, paper fasteners, pins, and any product designed for use as a container, holder or dispenser of adhesive, string, tape, ink or other writing, drawing or painting fluid.

The prohibitions do not apply if the product will not fit inside a truncated cylinder, which is defined in the Regulations, or if, when placed inside the cylinder, the product protrudes beyond the open end of the cylinder. Neither does the prohibition apply if the product merely has food depicted on it and neither smells like food nor like flowers nor tastes like food. The Regulations do not apply to products which look like food by chance or coincidence, provided that those products do not also smell like food or like flowers or taste like food.

The Regulations do apply to parts of products covered by the Regulations which are designed to be detachable, without the use of tools, from those products or which can be severed from them by applying certain prescribed tests.

(xii) Gas Catalytic Heaters

The Gas Catalytic Heaters (Safety) Regulations 1984/1802 prohibit the sale or supply of liquid petroleum gas heaters which incorporate a catalytic unit containing unbonded asbestos and catalytic units containing unbonded asbestos for use in such heaters.

(xiii) Glazed Ceramic Ware

The Glazed Ceramic Ware (Safety) Regulations 1975/1241 require that ceramic ware above a certain minimum size designed for use with food or drink for human consumption must be within the permissible limits for release of lead and cadium as laid down in BS 4860: 1972. There are exemptions for certain collectors' pieces or items more than 100 years old.

(xiv) Heating Appliances

The Heating Appliances (Fireguards) Regulations 1973/2106 require that all gas and electric fires and oil heaters must be fitted with a guard in accordance with BS 145: 1971.

(xv) Hood Cords

The Childrens' Clothing (Hood Cords) Regulations 1976/2 prohibit the use of a cord drawn through the material to secure the hoods of childrens' outer garments.

(xvi) Materials and Articles in Contact with Food

The Materials and Articles in Contact with Food Regulations 1987/1523 require that materials and articles which are intended to come into contact with food must be made in accordance with good manufacturing practice and must not pass onto the food concerned properties which might be injurious to health or bring about the deterioration of the organoleptic quality of the food.

As a result of recent EEC Directives these Regulations will be substantially extended in the fairly near future.

(xvii) Nightdresses

The Nightdresses (Safety) Regulations 1967/839 require that fabrics from which childrens' nightdresses and infant gowns are made must be of a type which satisfies the performance requirements of BS 3121: 1959 and be able to pass the flammability test in BS 2963: 1958. Other nightdresses must either conform to the same requirements or bear the following words in legible and durable characters:
'Warning—keep away from fire.'

(xviii) Oil Heaters

The Oil Heaters (Safety) Regulations 1977/167 impose detailed requirements as to the stability, design, safety devices, guards, emissions, warning notices and temperature of oil heaters for domestic use which burn kerosene (paraffin).

(xix) Oil Lamps

The Oil Lamps (Safety) Regulations 1979/1125 require that oil lamps for indoor domestic use must conform to BS 2049:1976. The regulations control the design and safety of such lamps and the warnings which must accompany them.

(xx) Pencils and Graphic Instruments

The Pencil and Graphic Instruments (Safety) Regulations 1974/226 control the maximum amounts of arsenic, cadmium, chromium, mercury, antimony, lead, barium, and derivatives thereof which may exist in any pencil, pen, brush, crayon, chalk, and other similar articles.

(xxi) Perambulators and Pushchairs

The Perambulators and Pushchairs (Safety) Regulations 1978/1372 require that perambulators when manufactured shall conform to BS 4139:1967 and pushchairs shall conform to BS 4792:1972. There are specific requirements as to the construction of perambulators and pushchairs and the braking devices to be used with them.

(xxii) Poisons

The Poisons Act 1972 and Orders made under that Act control the sale of poisons which are divided into two parts. Part 1 poisons may only be sold by registered pharmacists, and part 2 poisons may be sold by other traders provided they are on an official list of sellers kept by the local authority. The following are the basic labelling requirements for part 2 poisons:

(*a*) Where the poison appears in the poisons list the name used in that list must appear on the label. Where the poison is not on the list then the accepted scientific name for the poison must be used or a name descriptive of the true nature and origin of the poison will suffice.

(*b*) The proportion of poison named which is in the product must be stated.

(*c*) The word 'Poison' must appear and/or in specified cases additional words such as 'caution—this substance is caustic', etc.

(*d*) Special precautions must appear in respect of specified poisons.

(*e*) The name and address of the seller must appear on the label.

(*f*) Particulars must be set out clearly and distinctly and must not be obscured or obliterated. In respect of certain poisons some of the above information must be given in a specific colour and/or given special prominence by underlining or being stated in a separate box or display.

The containers for poisons must be impervious to the poison and sufficiently stout to prevent leakage arising from ordinary risks of handling and transport. In the case of a liquid contained in a bottle of not more than 1.14 litres, the outer surface of the bottle must be fluted vertically with ribs or grooves recognizable by touch.

(xxiii) Toys

The Toys (Safety) Regulations 1974/1367 impose the following basic requirements in respect of the safety of toys.

(*a*) Cellulose nitrate may not be used in toys except in pingpong balls and the paint-on toys.

(*b*) Paint coatings on toys may not contain more than maximum prescribed amounts of lead, arsenic, soluble cadmium, soluble barium, soluble antimony or chromium and soluble mercury.

(*c*) The operating voltage of mains operated electric toys is controlled.

(*d*) Pile fabrics on toys must satisfy BS 4569:1970.

(*e*) Where fabrics are used in the manufacture of toys, then there are requirements as to the washing and dry-cleaning of them.

(*f*) Thickness and sharpness of sheet metal used in the manufacture of toys is controlled.

(*g*) Pointed metal wire and chiming mechanisms are controlled as to use and manufacture.

(*h*) Toys with facial features must have any component parts made of wood, glass, metal, fabric, plastic etc. attached as prescribed.

(*i*) Plastic bags with openings (whether sealed or not) of 190 mm or more must be made of plastic 38 microns (μ) thick or more when used for individual packaging of toys.

Impending EEC requirements will soon impose much more extensive controls on toys.

(xxiv) Toy Watersnakes

The Toy Watersnakes (Safety) Order 1983/1366 prohibits the sale of any toy watersnake if the water in it contains any bacterium of the species *Escherichia coli* or if any sample of 100 ml or less of the water in it contains four or more coliform organisms.

(xxv) Children's Furniture

The Children's Furniture (Safety) Order 1982 prohibits the sale of any items of children's furniture which contain more than 200 g of polyurethane foam or expanded polystyrene.

(xxvi) Upholstered Furniture

The Furniture and Furnishings (Fire) (Safety) Regulations 1988/1324 impose extensive new requirements as to the flammability of foam-based furniture and coverings. The requirements are being phased in from July 1988 to March 1993.

10 *Prices*

10.1 Introduction

With the exception of welfare milk and certain agricultural products subject to EEC intervention price policy there is no control on retail prices in the United Kingdom. Although the power to control prices in certain circumstances was exercised as recently as 1978 by the government of the day by virtue of powers contained in the Prices Act 1974 those powers were repealed in 1980. At the same time the Prices Commission, whose role was to monitor retail prices and advise the Secretary of State as to government action thereon, was abolished.

In 1988 there is no formal legal machinery for the control of retail prices. All legislation on prices is concerned with the form in which information about prices is given to consumers and whether or not that information is misleading. Legislation on prices may, therefore, be divided into two groups:

(*a*) requirements that actual selling prices and/or unit prices shall be given;
(*b*) prohibitions on the indication of misleading prices.

10.2 Compulsory Price Information

A number of Orders were made by the Secretary of State under the Prices Act 1974 during the years 1975 to 1979. They required that the actual selling price and/or the unit price should be given where meat, fish, cheese, fruit and vegetables and prepacked milk in vending machines was offered for sale. The Orders were still in operation in 1988 but may be replaced when the proposed EEC Directive on Unit Pricing (*see* 10.3) is adopted.

Other Orders have been made under the Prices Act 1974 and are concerned with the giving of prices generally for food and drink and sleeping accommodation. They require that, subject to numerous exemptions, a price list should be exhibited where food, drink and sleeping accommodation is offered.

All of these Orders were made at a time when it was thought that the giving of price information would assist in the fight against inflation. They remain on the statute book because it is now thought that they do no harm and may on occasion be useful.

10.3 Unit Pricing

Unit pricing means the giving of a price per unit quantity on the pack or on display material at retail level. The EEC Commission is keen to see a much wider use of unit pricing as a measure of consumer protection. It is proposed that the concept should be applied to nearly all foods together with a wide range of other products. Other categories of product proposed for inclusion in a general requirement for unit pricing are cosmetics, paints, varnishes and similar products, soaps and detergents, toiletries and a variety of hardware products. Together with the proposed unit pricing directive there is a proposal for a greater use of prescribed pack sizes.

The negotiations on these two directives have been long and hard with the United Kingdom almost isolated in its opposition to unit pricing. The principal objection to unit pricing is that it takes no account of quality. A product may appear to be more expensive than a rival based on the unit price, but if the quality is taken into account it may be the cheaper of the two.

A report of a Select Committee of the House of Lords (1984) supported the British government's resistance to unit pricing and recommended that it should be used only where there was no prescribed pack size for the product concerned. It is now certain that the two Directives will be adopted and unit pricing will be applied to a wider range of goods than currently controlled by the Orders made under the Prices Act 1974. When the Directives are adopted the Orders will be revoked and replaced by new ones.

10.4 False Indications of Price

In the late 1960s there was much concern about the use of false indications of price by retailers. There was ample evidence to show that many reductions in price were bogus and the practice of suggesting that a product could be bought for a lower price than was actually charged was widespread. Accordingly, the government introduced a clause to the Trade Descriptions Bill at a late stage in an attempt to deal with the problem. Section 11 of the Trade Descriptions Act 1968, as that clause was to become, has proved to be a useful measure which has had considerable success in banning some of the more blatant misrepresentations of price.

Section 11 of the Trade Descriptions Act 1968 made it an offence to give false indications of price as follows:

(*a*) where it was claimed that a price was the same as or less than a previous selling price;
(*b*) where it was claimed that a price was the same as or less than a recommended price.

The Act created two important presumptions. First, where a price was indicated as having been reduced from a previous price it was assumed, unless the contrary was stated, that the higher price had been on offer for a continuous period of not less than 28 days in the preceding six months. This was intended to ensure that reductions were genuine. Secondly, it was assumed, unless the contrary was stated, that a recommended price was that of the manufacturer or supplier and applicable generally for supply by retail in the area where the goods were offered. The 28-day rule was easily circumvented by the use of disclaimers and rendered almost meaningless by judicial precedent. For example, the Divisional Court ruled that the 28-day period need not be the most recent 28 days in the preceding six months but could be any 28-day period within that time. The presumption on recommended prices was also easily avoided by the use of letters or words which suggested that the price was not recommended by the manufacturer or supplier.

The most successful provison of s.11 has been the ban on indications that goods are being offered at a price less than that at which they are in fact being offered. It has rendered the practice of 'buncing' (the indication of a lower price on the shelf edge than appears on the pack or is charged at the checkout) in self-service stores almost a thing of the past. It has also been used to prevent the concealment of ancillary charges such as VAT or postage and packing.

Section 11 of the Trade Descriptions Act 1968 applied only to goods and did not extend to services.

10.5 Bargain Offers

After a few years' experience of the Trade Descriptions Act 1968 it was clear that misleading prices were still a problem although, with hindsight, it may not have been as serious as it seemed at the time. The Director General of Fair Trading began consultations with consumer and trade bodies and produced recommendations, backed by consumer surveys, to prohibit all price comparisons and worth or value claims unless they were done in an approved manner. The most serious matter appeared to be the abuse of recommended prices. It was common for certain manufacturers to recommend a price which was two, three or four times the expected retail markup and then for the retailer to discount that recommended price thus creating the illusion of a bargain.

The government accepted the recommendations of the Director General and made an Order under the Prices Act 1974. It proved to be the most unpopular and controversial piece of consumer legislation ever enacted. Its principal defect lay in its attempt to classify those price indications which were acceptable and those which were not. It sought to prohibit all price comparisons for goods and services but then to exempt certain pricing comparisons which were deemed to be acceptable. Such an approach was certain to fail for it presented no bar to the dishonest trader who quickly invented new ways to evade its restrictions but its convoluted language was a major burden to reputable businesses who could not understand what was required of them.

10.6 Part III of the Consumer Protection Act 1987

This Act repealed s.11 of the Trade Descriptions Act 1968 and the Secretary of State then revoked the 1979 Order. Both were replaced by a general statutory duty not to use price indications which were misleading.

It is an offence to give by any means whatever a misleading indication as to the price at which goods, services, accommodation or facilities are available. The offence is very wide for it includes not only price indications which are misleading at the time they are given but also those which later become misleading through changed circumstances. The offence can be committed not only by the person or company offering the goods or services to the public but also by agents, advertisers or publishers. There are, however, special defences where it can be shown that all due diligence and all reasonable precautions have been exercised and in respect of the innocent publication of advertisements.

The term 'misleading' includes circumstances where:

(*a*) it is suggested that a price is less than it in fact is;

(*b*) it is misleadingly suggested that a price depends on certain facts or circumstances;

(*c*) it is suggested that certain ancillary charges are included which are not in fact included;

(*d*) it is misleadingly suggested that prices will increase, decrease, or remain the same; and

(*e*) consumers are encouraged to rely on the validity of the price indication by facts or circumstances which do not apply.

Unlike the former provisions of the Trade Descriptions Act 1968 this Act extends the control on misleading indications of price to all services including:

(*a*) the provision of credit or of banking or insurance services and the provision of facilities incidental to the provision of such services;

(*b*) the purchase or sale of foreign currency;

(*c*) the supply of electricity;

(*d*) the provision of a place, other than on the highway, for the parking of motor vehicles;

(*e*) the parking of non-residential caravans.

Contracts of employment and investment business are not deemed to be services for the purposes of this Act.

10.7 Regulations

The Act empowers the Secretary of State to make regulations as to the control of price indications and the enforcement of the Act and such regulations as may be made. Initially regulations will be confined to the establishment of the general rule that comparisons with previous prices should only be made if the higher price has been on offer for a period of not less than 28 days in the preceding 6 months; and that recommended prices should only be those of the manufacturer or supplier and should approximate to current retail price for the goods concerned.

10.8 Codes of Practice

The Act makes provision for the Secretary of State to approve codes of practice after appropriate consultation for the purpose of giving guidance with respect to good price marking. Such codes are given a unique status in law. Although it is not an offence to contravene an approved code of practice the codes may nevertheless be relied on in any proceedings to establish the guilt or innocence of the accused and for establishing or negating any defence.

10.9 The Code of Practice on Price Indications

As befits their purpose, codes of practice are regularly changed and amended. Certain basic principles of pricing practice may, however, be established from earlier legislation and the draft code which was under discussion in late 1988. They may be summarized as follows.

(i) General Price Comparisons

A 'price comparison' is defined as being an indication that the price at which something is offered for sale or hire (whether it be goods or services) is less than some other price. The Code applies however the indication of price is made including TV or press advertisements, catalogues, leaflets, notices, price tickets or shelf edge marking. It also applies to oral statements of price.

All price comparisons should be clear as to their meaning, and it is assumed that words such as 'regular price' or 'reduced from' refer to the trader's own previous price. Words such as 'usual price' or 'normal price' should not be used unless it is made clear whose prices are being referred to.

(ii) Introductory Prices, 'After-Sale Prices', or Warnings That Prices are Going Up

Introductory offers may be made without giving the price which will be charged after the offer is over. If the price to be charged after the offer is quoted then it should be charged after the end of the introductory period for at least 28 days during the following three months. 'Special promotions' where it is stated that prices will be held while stocks last, are also acceptable if only limited amounts of stock are available.

Abbreviations such as 'ASP' and 'APP' should not be used to indicate 'After Sale Price' or 'After Promotion Price'. Such terms should be given in full.

(iii) Comparisons with Other Traders' Prices

Such comparisons are only permitted if the other trader is named in the offer and his price is quoted. Statements such as 'if you can buy these goods cheaper elsewhere we will refund the difference' should only be made if it is the intention to honour them.

(iv) Comparisons Relating to Different Circumstances

It is permitted to quote different prices for different quantities of the same goods, shop soiled and perfect goods; different states of goods, for example, in kit form or ready assembled; and different classes of people such as new and existing customers, general customers and pensioners, etc. In all such cases the basis of the comparison should be clear and sufficient goods should be stocked to ensure that advantage can be taken of the alternatives.

(v) Comparisons with Recommended Prices

The sectoral bans on comparisons with recommended prices imposed by the 1979 Order and applicable to beds, electrically-powered domestic appliances, consumer electronic goods, carpets and furniture are unlikely to be continued in operation but there will be a general requirement that recommended prices should reflect current retail prices. This idea is unpopular with the Office of Fair Trading and enforcement authorities who believe that all comparisons with recommended prices should be banned.

For the time being recommended prices used for comparison prices should be genuine ones by the manufacturer or supplier applicable generally to the goods or services concerned. Initials should only be used for 'RRP' (recommended retail price). In all other cases the type of recommended price should be written in full, for example, manufacturer's recommended price.

(vi) References to Value or Worth

Such references are permitted provided their meaning is made clear. It is necessary to be able to substantiate such statements and general unsubstantiated claims such as 'worth £25—our price £20' are likely to be misleading.

(vii) Sales and Special Events

Indications that goods are being offered in a sale or some other special event should include the original price or basis of comparison and, of course, all such offers should be genuine and honoured.

(viii) Rules for Reduced Prices

The 28-day rule for reduced prices has been retained from the Trade Descriptions Act 1968 (*see* paragraph 10.4) but it can no longer be 'disclaimed' and it must be the most recent 28-day period during the past 6 months. The rule does not apply to food and drink nor to other goods with a shelf life of less than 28 days. Where prices are stage reduced to clear stocks the 28-day rule applies only to the first price.

(ix) Free offers

If any value is ascribed to 'free goods' then it should be the trader's own previous price, a recommended price, another named trader's price and so on. Where any goods or services are offered as being 'free' then they should be *genuinely* so and there should be no hidden charges.

(x) Extra Quantity in the Pack

There are two considerations for such offers. First, in respect of the price, the new added value packs should be sold at the same price as the standard pack immediately preceding it. Second, in respect of the quantity, the new higher quantity must be marked on the pack. Where the goods are required to be packed in prescribed pack sizes under weights and measure law it is not possible to offer additional quantity in the pack unless the new pack size is one of the higher prescribed sizes or the additional quantity is a separate pack of one of the smaller prescribed sizes or is below the lower limit of the range of pack sizes.

(xi) Ancillary Charges

Postage and packing charges should either be included in one inclusive price or clearly shown separately. VAT-inclusive prices should be given. Similarly, service charges, cover and minimum charges should be clearly indicated and, where possible, shown as an inclusive price.

(xii) Other Provisions of the Code

The code makes special provision for holiday and travel charges, bureau de change rates and the sale of new homes. Generally speaking the requirements are that all such charges should be clearly indicated with the original price or charge statement.

10.10 Redeemable Vouchers and Coupons

The very popular sales promotion device of offering vouchers or coupons which should be surrendered against cash or used to obtain a reduction from the price of future purchases were entirely free from control under former legislation. They are subject to special rules in the British Code of Sales Promotion Practice and the British Code of Advertising Practice.

However, by virtue of the very wide terms of s.20 of the Consumer Protection Act 1987, a voucher or coupon promotion which is misleading as to the price which must be paid for goods or services, or the discount which may be obtained thereon, may constitute an offence.

It should also be borne in mind that where the offer of vouchers or coupons is a term of contract for the sale of goods or the supply of services, a breach of that contract may be actionable.

10.11 Prize Draws, and Competitions

A popular sales promotion technique is to offer prize draws and competitions. Such devices are yet another way of offering additional value or incentives as an alternative to reduced prices. All such operations are subject to the Lotteries and Amusements Act 1976. Only a local authority or a registered charity is permitted to hold a lottery and it therefore follows that every such promotion must be framed in a manner which ensures that it is not a lottery. The test is whether there is a 'consideration'. If any charge, direct or indirect, is made for entry to a prize draw or similar device then it is an unlawful lottery. It is therefore unlawful to require the customer to make a purchase before he or she can enter the prize draw. It must be open to everyone irrespective of whether they buy goods or services.

    (*Imperial Tobacco v. Attorney-General*, 1981, AC 718, 1980, 2 WLR 466)

In order to ensure that a competition is not an unlawful lottery it is necessary to ensure that the degree of skill required is greater than the degree of chance.

The British Code of Sales Promotion Practice has certain rules about prize draws and competitions to ensure that the terms being offered are clear to consumers.

11 *Consumer credit*

11.1 Objects of Consumer Credit Control

The control of credit trading is a relatively recent phenomenon when compared with other aspects of consumer protection. Parliament first sought to control money lending towards the end of the nineteenth century when it became conscious of the socially and economically disruptive results of extortionate lending. The Pawnbrokers Act 1872 and the Moneylenders Act 1900 were passed in an attempt to curb the worst excesses of unscrupulous moneylenders and the criminal fraternity in which they operated. During the years which followed more statutes were passed culminating in the Hire Purchase Act 1965 and the Advertisements (Hire Purchase) Act of 1964.

During the 1960s the government embarked on a long-term review of credit law and the Crowther Committee on Consumer Credit was charged with the responsibility of producing a comprehensive report and recommendations. The Committee finally reported in 1971 (Cmnd 4596) and most of its recommendations were enacted in the Consumer Credit Act 1974. That Act proved to be one of the most complex statutes ever to be enacted. Indeed, there are practitioners who would claim that it is near incomprehensible in parts. There have been many calls for further reform and simplification of the law but the truth is that the subject is so indigestible that further reform is very unlikely.

Although the Act received the Royal Assent in 1974 it took a further eleven years before all its provisions were brought into operation. This long delay was due in part to the fact that some of the Orders and regulations made in the early years of its life were badly drafted and caused much concern in the credit industry. Many of these regulations and Orders are still in operation today although the Director General of Fair Trading, who is responsible for the administration of the Act, has announced a review of certain of them.

The final batch of regulations to be made were all concerned with the 'truth in lending' provisions of the Act. They all came into operation on 19 May 1985 and, by general consent, are much better drafted than the earlier ones. The Act is now fully in operation and all former statutes concerned with pawnbroking, money-lending and hire purchase have been repealed.

11.2 Objects of the Consumer Credit Act 1974

The central objective of the Act is to give uniform protection to individuals (including sole traders and partnerships but not corporations) who incur debts

144

of up to £15,000. There are numerous exemptions but overall the Act seeks to treat all debtors in the same way and does not differentiate, as former legislation did, between different types of credit.

To achieve this objective the Act attempts to ensure that only honourable people are engaged in the offering, negotiating and granting of credit through a system of licensing. It also controls the manner in which credit business is sought and prescribes the form in which agreements shall be recorded and regulated. Essentially this Act is a hybrid one in that it contains criminal provisions for the punishment of people who trade while unlicensed or break any of the rules for the general protection of the public, and civil provisions under which individuals and credit businesses can seek redress.

11.3 What is Credit?

A credit agreement is an agreement between an individual (the debtor) and any other person (the creditor) by which the creditor provides the debtor with credit of any amount. Consumer credit agreements are limited to those where the maximum amount of credit does not exceed £15,000*. All such agreements are categorized as 'regulated agreements' (those to which the law in its entirety applies) and 'exempt agreements' (those which enjoy partial or total exemption from the Act) (s.8 of the Consumer Credit Act 1974).

'Credit' is defined by the Act as including a cash loan and any other form of financial accommodation. The Act also covers consumer hire agreements which are defined as not being hire-purchase agreements (because such agreements are credit agreements) but agreements for hire which are capable of subsisting for more than three months and do not require the hirer to make payments exceeding £15,000* (ss.9 and 15 of the Consumer Credit Act 1974).

11.4 Credit Businesses Controlled by the Act

In addition to creditors generally the Act specifically brings the following ancillary business within its ambit.

(i) Credit Brokers

Any business which effects introductions of individuals desiring loans or other credit, or goods on hire, to traders offering such facilities is a 'credit broker' and subject to trading control. This covers the professional broker but includes, for example, retailers who do not offer credit from their own resources but arrange it for their customers with finance houses. Most motor dealers, for example, are credit brokers because few of them provide credit from their own funds.

*This upper limit is adjusted from time to time. The figure of £15,000 was set by the Consumer Credit (Increase in Monetary Limits) Order 1983/1878.

(ii) Debt Counsellors and Debt Adjusters

Generally speaking, any person who advises or acts on behalf of a consumer in respect of a consumer credit or hire agreement is a debt counsellor or adjuster. There are, however, many exemptions which include lawyers (solicitors and barristers in England and Wales; an advocate in Scotland). Housewives who run a mail order catalogue from their own homes are also exempted as are Citizens Advice Bureaux and certain charities such as Age Concern.

(iii) Debt Collectors

Control is extended to such people because of the oppressive methods employed by them in the past. A debt collector is any person who takes *any steps* to procure payment. The same persons as for counselling and adjusting are exempted.

(iv) Credit Reference Agencies

These organizations (sometimes called credit reference bureaux) are brought within the scope of the Act mainly to ensure that consumers have a right of access and correction to information held about them (*see also* Chapter 13 on data protection).

11.5 The Licensing System

The Act requires that all persons (unless specifically exempted) engaged in consumer credit or hire business or any of the ancillary businesses discussed above must hold a licence issued by the Director General of Fair Trading. There are six licence categories:

    Category A: consumer credit business
    Category B: consumer hire business
    Category C: credit brokerage
    Category D: debt adjusting and debt counselling
    Category E: debt collecting
    Category F: credit reference agency

Licences are further divided into 'standard licences' and 'group licences'. The latter are for issue to certain professional bodies, such as the Law Society, or service organizations, such as Citizens Advice Bureaux, so that a single licence covers all accredited members and it is not necessary for each member to apply for a standard licence in his own right. The former is the normal type of licence granted to individual traders.

All licences are issued by the Director General of Fair Trading for a maximum period of 15 years. The Director General must be satisfied that the applicant is a 'fit person' to carry on the business to which the licence refers. He must also be satisfied that the trading name is not misleading. Acts indicating 'unfitness' include fraud, other dishonesty, violence, contravention of consumer protection legislation, sex or race discrimination and any deceitful, oppressive, unfair or improper business practices. It is not necessary that the acts be unlawful, nor is it necessary that there have been convictions or judgments entered against the person concerned. The object of the Director General's assessment is one of character in the widest sense because of the links between credit trading and the criminal community in former years.

The Director General may vary, suspend or terminate a consumer credit licence. Such action is sometimes taken against traders who have been convicted of offences against consumer protection legislation. This is particularly so in respect of used car dealers who have been convicted under the Trade Descriptions Act 1968 for 'clocking' (winding back the odometer readings) of used vehicles (Part III of the Consumer Credit Act 1974).

11.6 Sanctions for Credit Trading while Unlicensed

To trade without a licence or beyond the scope of a licence is an offence attracting a maxmimum penalty in a magistrates' court of a fine of £2,000 or an unlimited fine or imprisonment for up to two years on conviction in the Crown Court. There are numerous other offences in the Act in respect of licences including failure to notify changes in the licensed particulars and carrying on a business under a name not specified in a licence.

Perhaps a more powerful sanction than those at criminal law is the fact that any agreement entered into by an unlicensed trader is unenforceable in the courts. Any regulated agreement or agreement for the services of a credit broker, debt collector, debt counsellor, debt adjuster or credit reference agency cannot be enforced unless the Director General wishes to issue a Validating Order. In considering whether to issue a Validating Order the Director General has regard to how far the consumer has been prejudiced by the failure to obtain a licence. Such an order would not be made where the trader is of bad character or would for any other reason be refused a licence (ss. 39 and 40 of the Consumer Credit Act 1974).

Example

A person who lends money occasionally from his own resources to provide a source of income is not running a consumer credit business. There is a fundamental difference between lending money and carrying on a money lending business.

(*Wills v. Wood*, 1983)

Example

A motor trader had lost his consumer credit licence and could only sell cars for cash. He set up a separate credit broking business in part of his premises to which he referred customers requiring credit. The customers did not know that they were dealing with anyone other than the motor trader.
Held: He was running an unlawful credit broker business by referring customers to a finance company.

(*Hicks v. Walker*, 1984)

11.7 Appeals Against Refusal etc. of a Consumer Credit Licence

Where the Director General of Fair Trading refuses a licence, grants one in different terms from those sought, varies or suspends a licence the applicant has a right of appeal to the Secretary of State and/or, if a point of law is concerned, to the courts. There are set procedures for such appeals (ss. 41 and 42 of the Consumer Credit Act 1974).

Example

An applicant for a consumer credit licence was refused by the Director General of Fair Trading because he had been convicted of fraud against the Inland Revenue. After appealing unsuccessfully to the Secretary of State he appealed to the High Court.
Held: The granting of a licence is a privilege not a right which is to be granted only to those whom the Director General, on proper evidence, believes to be a fit and proper person.

(*North Wales Motor Auctions v. Secretary of State for Trade*, 1981)

11.8 Seeking Business: General Controls

The following general controls are exercised on canvassing and advertising for credit business. For specific controls on advertising see 11.9 below.

(i) False or Misleading Advertisements

It is an offence for an advertiser to use an advertisement which conveys information which in a material respect is false or misleading. Furthermore, it is an offence to state or imply an intention on the advertiser's part which he has not got. This provision equates to s.1 of the Trade Descriptions Act 1968 (*see* Chapter 8) (s.46 of the Consumer Credit Act 1974).

(ii) Advertisements where Goods are Not Sold for Cash

It is an offence for a person offering credit agreements for the supply of specific goods or services to advertise that intention if, at the time concerned, he is not also prepared to sell the goods or provide the services for cash. This offence enacts the view of the Crowther Committee that it is undesirable to allow the sale or supply of goods or services on credit alone where a cash payment will not be accepted (s.45 of the Consumer Credit Act 1974).

(iii) Canvassing off Trade Premises

It is an offence to canvass agreements between a debtor and creditor off trade premises. It is also an offence to solicit the entry of an individual as a debtor into an agreement during a visit made in response to a request unless that request has been made in writing. This offence is intended to prevent the enticement of vulnerable householders into signing credit agreements in their own homes. The theory is that if they have taken the trouble to travel to business premises or to write and invite the salesmen into their homes they will be more prepared to consider the full impact of the agreement (s.49 of the Consumer Credit Act 1974).

(iv) Circulars to Minors

It is an offence to send a circular to a minor (a person under the age of 18 years) inviting him or her to borrow money, obtain goods on credit or hire, obtain services on credit or apply for information or advice on borrowing money or otherwise obtaining credit or hiring goods. It is a defence for a person charged with this offence to prove that he did not know that the recipient was a minor but if the circular is sent to a person at a school or other educational establishment for minors the sender is assumed to have known that the person is a minor (s.50 of the Consumer Credit Act 1974).

(v) Unsolicited Credit Tokens

It is an offence to give a person a credit token (a redeemable card, check, voucher, coupon, stamp, form, booklet or other document or item) which invites him or her to borrow money, obtain goods on credit or hire, obtain services on credit or apply for information or advice on borrowing money etc. (s.50 of the Consumer Credit Act 1974).

Example

A firm of shoe retailers sent out to all former customers a cardboard replica of a credit card with an invitation to present it at the shop whereupon credit was given to anyone with a bank account.
Held: Such a replica is an unsolicited credit token and unlawful.
(*Elliot v. Director General of Fair Trading*, 1980, 1 WLR 977)

11.9 Advertising

Regulations have been made which strictly control the form and content of all advertising. The term 'advertising' is very widely drawn for it includes every form of advertising whether in a publication, by television or radio, by display of notices, signs, labels, showcards or goods, by distribution of samples, circulars, catalogues, price lists or other material, or by exhibition of pictures, models or films, or in any other way. It therefore follows that any means of communication between a person offering credit or credit services and consumers is 'advertising' for the purpose of the Act and regulations.

The regulations divide all credit advertisements into three classes: simple, intermediate and, full credit (or hire) advertisements. The regulations are complex and controversial but, for the purposes of the following summary, the mandatory, optional and prohibited information which may appear in each class of advertisement is given.

(i) Simple Credit (Hire) Advertisements

(a) Mandatory information

None.

(b) Optional information

1. The name of the advertiser.
2. The advertiser's occupation.
3. Information not of a credit nature.

Prohibited information

1. Any price.
2. Any other information about credit.

The purpose of simple credit advertisements is merely to call attention to the existence of a credit business, for example, 'A. Bloggs, Moneylender'. It is commonly used on posters and hoardings at exhibitions and sporting events but has little other practical value.

The inclusion of any other information, such as a cash price, could render a simple credit advertisement unlawful. The test is whether the advertisement indicates a willingness to provide credit.

Example

The use of a sticker on a car windscreen stating 'Lombard North Central' together with the company's logo and a cash price for the car was held not to be an indication of willingness to provide credit but rather to draw the attention of consumers to the company name and logo.

(*Jenkins v. Lombard North Central plc*, 1984, 1 All ER 828; 1984, 1 WLR 307)

(ii) Intermediate Credit (Hire) Advertisements

(a) Mandatory information

1. A name.
2. An address or phone number or both for written quotations.
3. An indication that a written quotation about credit terms can be obtained on request.
4. Any need for security.
5. Any need to take out an insurance policy etc.
6. Any need to pay money on account as a condition of the loan.
7. The cash price if there is one. There can be no cash price if the offer is for goods generally rather than for specific goods.
8. If the cash price is given, the annual percentage rate of interest (APR) must also be given.
9. Where the APR is given but may vary this must be stated and if the APR includes any life assurance premiums this too must be stated.

10. If there is no charge for credit this must be stated.

11. In the case of a store budget account (often known as revolving credit) two statements of APR must be given. The first should be calculated on the assumption that the customer has used all the credit available to him and the second on the assumption that he had used one third of the credit.

(b) Optional information

1. The occupation of the advertiser.
2. A statement that credit facilities are available.
3. The APR (if not already required).
4. If the offer is restricted to particular classes of persons, for example, only to people over the age of 21.
5. Any way in which cash buyers are treated differently from credit buyers.
6. The maximum or minimum amount of credit available or both.
7. Any statutory or similar requirements about minimum deposits and the duration of agreements (there were no such requirements in operation in 1988).
8. If the advertiser has included the APR for any reason *one* only of the following items may be included:

(i) amount of advance payment;
(ii) duration of the agreement;
(iii) frequency of payments;
(iv) total amount payable.

(c) Prohibited information

1. Any information not given above.
2. Intermediate credit (hire) advertisements are by far the most common in everyday advertising. In its most simple form an intermediate advertisement might read:

LOANS AVAILABLE
No advance payments: Typical **APR 35 per cent**
Contact:
A. BLOGGS LTD
85 Loan Street, Poundton, Devon
for written details of credit terms

3. Full Credit Advertisements
(a) Mandatory information

1. The name and address of the advertiser.
2. The APR.
3. A statement of any variation in the APR.
4. Any need for insurance.
5. Any security required.
6. Any restriction as to classes of persons to whom the offer is applicable.

7. Any way in which cash customers are treated differently from credit customers.

8. The amount of any advance payments, their number and frequency.

9. A statement of any uncertain payments which may have to be made.

10. The frequency of payments.

11. The amount of each repayment.

12. The cash price—if there is one.

13. The total number of payments.

14. The total amount payable.

There is no limit to the amount of additional information that may be given in a full credit or hire advertisement provided always that it is true and not misleading. Full credit advertisements usually appear in shops or in mail order or direct marketing advertisements where the customer fills in a coupon in order to establish a contract. An example of a typical full credit advertisement may be:

A. BLOGGS LTD
85 Loan Street, Poundton, Devon
for Loans £100 to £500:
Typical example—borrow £250 and pay back 12 monthly instalments of £25:
Total amount payable £300—**APR 41.3 per cent**
Not available to persons under 21

There are many exemptions and variations of the above rules. This is particularly the case for in-store advertising where it is not necessary that a name or address be given and there are relaxations of the rules as to cash prices and the form in which the advertising is done.

The foregoing notes are for guidance only, and in drafting any advertisement reference should be made to the regulations or to the Office of Fair Trading Guidance notes on them.

There are also rules about the form of advertisements of which the most important is that the APR must be given greater prominence than any other rate such as the annual flat rate or the monthly period rate, and it must be given no less prominence than any statement about period, the amount of any advance payment, or the amount, number or frequency of other payments or charges other than the cash price (the Consumer Credit (Advertisements) Regulations 1980, as amended SI 1980/54).

11.10 The Annual Percentage Rate (APR)

The Annual Percentage Rate (APR) must be calculated in accordance with regulations. The Office of Fair Trading has issued Guidance Notes entitled 'Consumer Credit Act 1974—Credit Charges—How to Calculate the Total Charge for Credit and the Annual Percentage Rate of Charge (Consumer Credit (Total Charge for Credit) Regulations 1980/51).

11.11 Quotations

A written quotation must be given to a customer if he or she requests written information about either credit of up to £15,000 (unless the proposed agreement would fall within one of the exemptions) or hire where the total payments do not exceed £15,000 (Consumer Credit (Quotations) Regulations 1980/55).

11.12 Credit Agreements

The following types of consumer credit agreement are regulated by the Consumer Credit Act 1974 and are collectively known as 'regulated agreements'.

(i) Hire Purchase Agreement

This is an agreement, other than a conditional sale agreement, under which the goods are bailed in return for periodical payments and the property in the goods passes at the conclusion of the agreement on the exercise of an option to purchase, or the doing of a specified act or the happening of some other specified event. In recent years hire purchase agreements have declined in number in favour of credit sales and revolving credit agreements under which property in the goods passes immediately on signing the agreement.

(ii) Conditional Sale Agreement

This is the sale of goods or land under which the purchase price is paid in instalments and the property in the goods or land remains with the seller, notwithstanding that the buyer is to have possession of the goods or the land until such conditions as may be specified in the agreements are fulfilled. This type of agreement is rare in consumer transactions and is usually used in business agreements. It is, in effect, a hire purchase agreement with special conditions and which may be extended to land.

(iii) Credit Sale Agreement

A credit sale agreement is one under which the price is payable by instalments not being a conditional sale agreement. Property passes to the buyer at once. This is by far the most common form of agreement in consumer transactions.

The Act regulates the foregoing types of agreement by categorizing them as follows.

(iv) Debtor–Creditor–Supplier Agreements

A debtor–creditor–supplier agreement is one where a transaction between a supplier and a debtor is financed by a creditor. Most hire purchase and credit sale agreements fall into this category where a retailer acts as an agent (broker) for a finance house to finance purchases from his business (s.11 of the Consumer Credit Act 1974).

(v) Debtor–Creditor Agreements

These are agreements where the debtor obtains credit from a bank, moneylender or insurance company for the purchase of goods or services from a third party to the agreement. In such agreements the supplier may be unaware that the transaction is being financed by credit (ss. 12 and 13 of the Consumer Credit Act 1974).

(vi) Credit Token Agreement

Under a credit token agreement credit is provided by way of cards, checks, vouchers, coupons, stamps, forms, booklets or other documents or things provided by a creditor who undertakes that on production of the token he will provide cash, goods or services on credit and that when the credit token is produced to a third party who supplies cash, goods or services to the holder of the token, he will reimburse the supplier in return for payment to him by the holder. This is the type of agreement concerned where credit cards are used (s.14 of the Consumer Credit Act 1974).

(vii) Linked Agreements

If a debtor is obliged or persuaded to enter into more than one regulated agreement at the same time or, as a condition of the first agreement, must so do at a later time then the second and subsequent agreements are 'linked agreements'. To qualify as a 'linked transaction' the agreement in question must have been: entered into in accordance with a term of the regulated agreement; financed by a debtor–creditor–supplier agreement; or initiated by the creditor or owner or his associates or a person representing both creditor or owner and seller. Linked agreements may be found in the financing of the purchase of a domestic freezer with an ancillary agreement for the supply of food or a second agreement to cover insurance of goods bought on a principal agreement (s.19 of the Consumer Credit Act 1974).

(viii) Small Agreements

A small agreement is a regulated agreement where the sum required for credit does not exceed £50, other than a hire purchase or conditional sale agreement (s.17 of the Consumer Credit Act 1974).

11.13 Exempt Agreements

The Act does not regulate credit agreements where the creditor is a building society or a local authority or where by an Order made by the Secretary of State exemption, is conferred on insurance companies, an employers' organization or trade union, a charity, a land improvement company or a body corporate named or specifically referred to in any Act of Parliament. So far such Orders have been made in respect of more than 200 such bodies (see the Consumer Credit (Exempt Agreements) (No. 2) Order 1985/757) (s.16 of the Consumer Credit Act 1974).

11.14 Regulation of Agreements

The Consumer Credit Act 1974 requires that all regulated agreements must be:

(*a*) in writing;
(*b*) comply in form and content with regulations made by the Secretary of State;
(*c*) contain all express terms in legible form;
(*d*) be signed by the debtor in person and by or on behalf of all other parties.
(s.61 of the Consumer Credit Act 1974).

The form of agreements is laid down in the Consumer Credit (Agreements) Regulations 1983/1553 with special provisions for the modification of existing agreements. The forms used for various types of agreement discussed above must comply in every detail with the specimens in the Schedules to the Regulations. Use of documents which do not conform to the regulations would render an agreement unenforceable.

11.15 Guarantees and Indemnities

The Act makes provision for the form and content of securities and guarantees used in connection with regulated agreements. Again, if such guarantees are not in the prescribed form any agreements to which they apply are unenforceable (s.105 of the Consumer Credit Act 1974 and the Consumer Credit (Guarantees and Indemnities) Regulations 1983/1556).

11.16 Cancellation of Agreements

Consumer credit (hire) agreements may be cancelled by either party subject to certain prescribed conditions and safeguards. The form in which this must be done is prescribed by regulations. Similarly, the rebate of charges on early settlement by the borrower is controlled by regulations (ss.57, 58 (1), 64 (1), 71 (3), 180 and 189 of the Consumer Credit Act 1974; the Consumer Credit (Cancellation Notices and Copies of Documents) Regulations 1983/1557; the Consumer Credit (Repayment of Credit on Cancellation) Regulations 1983/1559; and the Consumer Credit (Rebate on Early Settlement) Regulations 1983/1562).

11.17 Enforcement, Default and Termination

The notices and forms which must be sent to debtors in default of their agreements are prescribed by regulations. In general, a creditor is precluded from terminating an agreement or enforcing the provisions of an agreement unless he has served a notice complying with the provisions of the regulations (ss.76 (3) and (5), 87 (4), 88 (1) and (4), 98 (3) and (5), 182 (2) and 189 (2) and the

Consumer Credit (Enforcement, Default and Termination Notices) Regulations 1983/1561).

11.18 Extortionate Credit Bargains

All consumer credit agreements are subject to judicial review on application by the debtor. Particular provision is made to protect consumers from extortionate bargains. A regulated agreement is extortionate if it requires the debtor or a relative of his to make payments which are grossly exorbitant or otherwise grossly contravene ordinary principles of fair dealing (ss.137, 138 and 139 of the Consumer Credit Act 1974).

Example

Where an interest rate is high but at the normal rate current at the time it was not unfair to the borrower and not extortionate.

(*Woodstead Finance Ltd v. Petrov*, 1986)

Example

An application for reopening a credit transaction by a debtor cannot be upheld by a court if the applicant has been deceitful and has not disclosed all the circumstances of the case to his creditors nor to the court.

(*Ketley v. Scott*, 1981, ICR 241)

11.19 Joint Liability of Creditor and Supplier

A most important protection for debtors is that where there has been any misrepresentation or breach of contract by the supplier the supplier and creditor are jointly and severally liable to the debtor. This protection applies to all regulated agreements except those for a single item costing £10 or less or more than £30,000. Thus if a product was misdescribed by the supplier or, for example, it was not fit for the purpose intended for it, or was not of merchantable quality and the supplier was no longer in business the debtor would be able to claim against the creditor provided the credit agreement was still current (s.75 of the Consumer Credit Act 1974).

Example

A motorist bought a car by way of a regulated debtor–creditor–supplier contract. The car was seriously defective and the debtor rescinded the credit contract. *Held*: On being sued by the creditor he was not entitled to rescind the contract with the creditor but this decision was reversed on appeal.

(*United Dominions Trust v. Taylor*, 1980, SLT (Sh Ct) 28)

Example

The creditor is liable for misrepresentations by the supplier and the debtor was entitled to repudiate the credit contract where the supplier described a car to be used as a minicab as being 'in perfect mechanical condition' which was far from the truth.

(*Porter v. General Guarantee Corpn*, 1982)

12 Monopolies, mergers, restrictive trade practices and competition

12.1 Introduction

The potentially adverse effects of unrestrained monopolies and mergers have exercised the minds of governments for hundreds of years. It has always been, and remains, one of the most difficult economic problems facing any government for the power of governments to resist a proposed merger or to prevent a monopoly situation is limited. No matter what statutory powers may be available it is often the case that prevention of a merger or the breaking of a monopoly may result in unacceptable loss of business and employment. Until 1623 monopolies were created by and disapproved of by Royal Decree. Most active in this field was Queen Elizabeth I who exercised her prerogative to confer monopoly privileges on traders who introduced new businesses or products. By the end of the sixteenth century, however, Parliament had become alarmed by the undesirable practices arising from these monopolies and the Queen was persuaded to abolish all monopolies which were found to be injurious by fair trial at law. The first statute to control monopolies was assented to by James I in 1623. Section 1 of the Statute of Monopolies rendered all monopolies for the sole buying, selling, making, working or using of any thing within the Realm 'utterlie void and of none effecte'. During the next 350 years many different forms of control were introduced culminating in the Monopolies and Restrictive Practices (Inquiry and Control) Act 1948.

Control of restrictive trade practices is of more recent origin, although of course a monopoly situation is the ultimate in restrictive practice. Essentially, a restrictive trade practice is an agreement between two or more businesses as to the prices to be charged for goods or services, the terms and conditions of supply and related matters. Practices outside a monopoly situation were originally controlled by the 1948 Act but are now subject to the Fair Trading Act 1973 and the Restrictive Trade Practices Act 1976.

Anticompetitive practices were not recognized as being a problem distinct from restrictive practices until the late 1970s. The principal concern was that certain trade practices, some of which were new but others were of long standing, could distort, restrict or prevent competition. This concern resulted in the highly innovative Competition Act 1980 which seeks to prevent price discrimination between distinct and separate groups of customers, predatory pricing and vertical price squeezing.

12.2 Monopolies

(i) The Monopolies and Mergers Commission

The Fair Trading Act 1973 extended the functions of the former Monopolies Commission and renamed it the Monopolies and Mergers Commission. The Competition Act 1980 added yet more functions. Its function is to report on any question referred to it under the Acts in relation to:

(*a*) the existence or possible existence of a monopoly situation;

(*b*) a transfer of a newspaper or of newspaper assets under the provisions of Part V of the Act intended to prevent undue concentration by reason of mergers in one newspaper proprietor;

(*c*) the creation, or possible creation, or a merger situation qualifying for investigation under Part V of the Act;

(*d*) the efficiency and costs of the service provided by, or the possible abuse of a monopoly by public bodies such as nationalized industries supplying goods or services by way of business, public bus service operators, statutory water undertakers etc.

In reporting on matters referred to it the Commission is required to take into account the desirability of:

(*a*) maintaining and promoting effective competition between UK suppliers of goods and services;

(*b*) promoting the interests of consumers, purchasers and other users of goods and services in the United Kingdom as regards price, quality and variety;

(*c*) promoting, through competition, the reduction of costs and the development of new techniques and new products, and of facilitating the entry of new competition into existing markets;

(*d*) maintaining and promoting the balanced distribution of industry and employment in the United Kingdom;

(*e*) maintaining and promoting competitive activity in export markets.

In recent years the Commission has been very active dealing with 20 or more referrals each year. Its reports are usually acted upon by the Secretary of State in exercise of his powers conferred by the Fair Trading Act 1973 and the Competition Act 1980.

(ii) A Monopoly Situation

The basic criterion for determining whether or not a monopoly situation exists is whether one-quarter of the supply of goods or services in the United Kingdom is in the hands of one person or one group. A monopoly situation may also exist where agreements are in operation preventing the supply of goods or services, although such a situation would be more likely to be seen as a restrictive trade practice under the Restrictive Trade Practices Act 1976 (*see* 12.8 below). A group is defined as being any two or more persons, not being part of an interconnected group of companies, who so conduct their affairs as to prevent, restrict or distort competition.

(ii) The EEC Dimension

Article 85 of the Treaty of Rome prohibits such agreements which affect trade between member states of the Common Market, and s.8 of the Fair Trading Act 1973 applies similar criteria to monopoly situations affecting the export of goods. Whether particular trading practices fall within national legislation or are subject to the Treaty of Rome is seldom clear for an activity intended for one purpose can indirectly affect another. The EEC Commission is very active and diligent in the investigation of alleged monopoly situations which have the potential to restrict trade between Member States for they strike at the very foundations of the Common Market.

(iv) Power to Control Monopolies

The Fair Trading Act 1973 makes the Director General of Fair Trading responsible for monopoly references but the Secretary of State may also make references directly to the Commission. The Director General has certain investigative powers to assist him in determining whether a monopoly situation exists with a view to a reference to the Commission. It is a criminal offence to wilfully neglect to furnish information required by notice or to supply false or misleading information.

Where the report of the Commission indicates that a monopoly situation exists and is contrary to the public (or EEC) interest then the Secretary of State may make an Order by Statutory Instrument prohibiting the carrying out of an agreement. Other, more drastic powers, include the transfer or vesting of property in other bodies and the creation, allotment, surrender or cancellation of shares. As an alternative to the exercise of these powers the Act empowers the Director General to seek an undertaking from the parties concerned for action to remedy the adverse effects identified in the report of the Commission. Such an undertaking may be enforced in the courts. In practice, most adverse reports from the Commission are settled in this way.

Example

(*a*) The British Airports Authority's commercial activities were carried out in a generally satisfactory manner but the Commission recommended that planning and sales targets should be updated and improved; tendering procedures should be linked to performance indicators; and a greater range of products should be available at retail outlets at airports (1986).

(*b*) The Commission concluded that the proposed merger of Great Universal Stores (GUS) plc and Empire Stores (Bradford) was against the public interest and it was undesirable for GUS to be in a position to materially influence the policies of Empire. It was recommended that the merger should not proceed and GUS should reduce its shareholding in Empire to below 10 per cent. Undertakings to this effect from GUS were accepted by the Secretary of State and, after the shareholding had been reduced to 12.7 per cent revised undertakings were accepted in 1986 (1983).

(*c*) The pricing policies and certain other practices of Pitney Bowes plc and Roneo Alcatel plc were operating against the public interest in respect of the supply, maintenance and repair of postal franking machines. The Post Office was found to be carrying out similar practices which were also commented upon by the Commission. The two companies were found to control 88 per cent of the market. Undertakings were given to the Director General of Fair Trading by the two companies and the Post Office introduced new procedures following the report.

12.3 Mergers

Control of Mergers

There was no statutory power to control mergers until the passing of the Monopolies and Mergers Act 1965. The provisions of that Act were replaced by the Fair Trading Act 1973 which empowers the Secretary of State to order that a proposed merger should not proceed. The objective or merger control is to ensure that monopoly situations do not arise by identifying and controlling a developing monopoly situation through mergers. The duty to keep situations under review is given to the Director General of Fair Trading under the 1973 Act. As a result of experience since the passing of the 1973 Act many companies seek prior advice from the Director General about mergers that they may have in mind.

It is open to the Director General of Fair Trading to recommend to the Secretary of State that a proposed merger be referred to the Monopolies and Mergers Commission for investigation. Of the 150 or so proposed mergers per annum in the years 1980 to 1986 only about five per cent were referred to the Commission and of these about half were prohibited or amended by exercise of statutory power by the Secretary of State.

The Director General is the Chairman of the Interdepartmental Mergers Panel which has been informally established to ensure that merger policy is generally in line with the policy of the government of the day. It is generally agreed that the existing mergers control machinery is sufficiently flexible to ensure that the public interest is safeguarded with a minimum of interference in business.

12.4 Restrictive Trade Practices

(i) Registration of Trade Practices

The Restrictive Trade Practices Act 1976, as amended by the 1977 Act of same title, makes the Director General of Fair Trading responsible for the control of restrictive practices in respect of goods and services. That control is achieved by a system of registration backed, where necessary by referrals to the Restrictive Trade Practices Court.

(ii) Registerable Agreements: Goods

An agreement in respect of goods must be registered if it is an agreement between two or more persons carrying on business in the United Kingdom which imposes restrictions in relation to:

(*a*) prices or charges;

(*b*) the terms or conditions on which people are to do business;

(*c*) the quantities or descriptions of goods to be produced, supplied or acquired;

(*d*) the manufacturing processes to be used, or the levels or amounts of goods to be manufactured;

(*e*) the persons with whom business is to be done;

(*f*) the areas or places of the business.

(iii) Registerable Agreements: Services

Agreements between two or more persons carrying on business in the United Kingdom for the supply of services are registerable if they restrict:

(*a*) charges;

(*b*) the terms or conditions on which people are to do business;

(*c*) the extent and scale on or to which services are made available, supplied or obtained;

(*d*) the form or manner of making available, supplying or obtaining services;

(*e*) the persons with whom business is to be done.

(iv) General Aspects of Agreements

In respect of both goods and services restrictions include negative obligations, whether stated or implied, qualified or unqualified. Such a negative obligation arises whenever a person agrees to limit the freedom he would otherwise have to enter into future transactions.

Restrictions also exist where an agreement does not specifically restrict the parties' action but gives privileges or benefits only if they comply with certain conditions or where an agreement imposes obligations on parties if they do not comply with certain conditions. Similarly, restrictions may exist where payments are calculated in such a way as to penalize the supply, production or acquisition of goods or the making available, supplying or obtaining of services in excess of agreed amounts.

(v) Exempt Agreements

Certain agreements are wholly or partly exempted from registration. They include:

(*a*) agreements authorized by statute;

(*b*) exclusive dealing agreements;

(*c*) trade mark agreements;

(*d*) patents and registered designs;

(*e*) knowhow agreements;

(*f*) copyright agreements;

(*g*) agreements with overseas operation;

(*h*) agreements which promote productivity or efficiency and are of importance to the national economy;

(*i*) agreements for holding down prices if approved by the Secretary of State or the Minister of Agriculture, Fisheries and Food;

(*j*) agreements in respect of particular occupations or businesses including:

1. coal and steel;
2. wholesale cooperative societies;
3. agriculture, forestry and fishing;
4. the Stock Exchange;
5. international shipping;
6. air transport;
7. road passenger transport;
8. insurance;
9. building societies;
10. unit trusts;
11. certain financial matters.

(*k*) professional services including:

1. barristers, advocates and solicitors;
2. medical professions;
3. dental professions;
4. veterinary professions;
5. nursing;
6. architecture;
7. certain accounting and auditing services;
8. patent agencies;
9. parliamentary agencies;
10. certain surveying services;
11. certain engineering services;
12. education;
13. ministers of religion.

Certain of these exemptions are controversial and in the eyes of some critics of the system, free from control some of the activities which are most in need of it. The professional exemptions, for example, are granted by Order (the Restrictive Trade Practices (Services) Order 1976), but it must be noted that despite the exemptions the Director General of Fair Trading has used his persuasive abilities to bring about more competition in the legal, architectural and surveying services.

(vi) Trade Associations

An agreement between members of an association which restricts their freedom to trade or imposes obligations on them may be a registerable agreement under the Act. It is commonplace for trade and professional bodies to produce 'Codes of Practice' or 'Guidance Notes' for their members on trading standards, manufacturing methods or a number of other matters (*see* Chapter 14). If such codes or notes refer to any of the matters listed on pp. 160–1, then registration may be necessary.

(vii) Criteria for Registration

Agreements submitted to the Office of Fair Trading are first considered and, if registerable, are placed on the Register of Restrictive Agreements. Copies of that register are kept in London, Edinburgh and Belfast. All registered agreements are referred to the Restrictive Practices Court unless the Director General of Fair Trading makes representations to the Secretary of State that the restrictions do not merit such proceedings and the Secretary of State concurs. The functions of the Restrictive Practices Court are to consider whether an agreement is contrary to the public interest and in so doing it must be satisfied that any one or more of a number of specified circumstances apply. These circumstances are often called 'gateways' and include the following:

(*a*) the restrictions are reasonably necessary, having regard to the character of the goods or services, to protect the public against injury in respect of their use;

(*b*) the removal of the restrictions would deny to the public as purchasers, consumers or users of other specific and substantial benefits or advantages;

(*c*) the restrictions are reasonably necessary to counteract measures taken by a person who is not a party to the agreement with a view to preventing or restricting competition;

(*d*) the restrictions are reasonably necessary to enable the parties to an agreement to negotiate fair terms of supply from persons not parties to the agreement who control a preponderant part of the trade or business concerned;

(*e*) the removal of the restrictions would be likely to have a serious and persistent effect on the general level of unemployment in conditions actually pertaining or reasonably foreseeable;

(*f*) in similar circumstances to (*e*) above the removal of the restrictions would be likely to cause a reduction in the volume of earnings or substantial export business;

(*g*) the restrictions are reasonably required for the maintenance of other restrictions not found by the Court to be contrary to the public interest;

(*h*) the restrictions do not directly or indirectly restrict or discourage competition to any material degree and are not likely to do so.

(viii) Failure to Register

Details of a registerable agreement must be sent to the Office of Fair Trading before the relevant restrictions come into operation and in any case within three months of the making of the agreement. These time limits apply even if the agreement is temporary or made to meet an emergency situation. It is possible that an agreement which is not initially registerable becomes so because of later amendments to it. Where a registered agreement is terminated immediate notification must be sent to the Office of Fair Trading.

It is often the case that companies or trade bodies seek the advice of the Office of Fair Trading while agreements are still under consideration. This is encouraged not only because it can avoid difficulties at a later stage but also because the Director General has no power to grant any dispensation from the time limits. He can, however, extend the time if application is made within the time limit specified for providing details.

If details are not submitted to the Office of Fair Trading within the time limits the restrictions in the agreement are void and it is unlawful for any party to the agreement to give effect to them or to seek to enforce them. Failure to submit details of an agreement is not a criminal offence but the Director General of Fair Trading can apply to the Restrictive Practices Court for an Order stopping any party from giving effect to the restrictions in the agreement or enforcing or purporting to enforce them and giving effect to, or purporting to enforce, the restrictions in any other registerable agreement, details of which have not been provided to the Office.

It the Director General of Fair Trading has reasonable cause to believe that an unregistered agreement exists he can issue a notice to the persons concerned requiring them to inform him whether there is an agreement and whether they are a party to it. Failure to respond to such a notice is a criminal offence.

Example

The interests of consumers are of great importance in deciding whether agreements fall within the gateways. In *Re Net Book Agreement*, 1962, 3 All ER 751 the publishers of books agreed that the majority of their titles were not to be sold to the public at less than their net price and were to be subject to standard conditions of sale. The Court found that while there was no valid argument that there would be a loss of export earnings there was a case for saying that the removal of the restrictions would deny to the public certain benefits such as a large number of booksellers maintaining a good stock of books ((b), p. 163 above). The Net Book Agreement was allowed to remain in operation.

Example

The Court places considerable importance on free competition. In *Re Yarn Spinners' Agreement* the agreement sought to maintain agreed prices and it was pleaded that abandonment would lead to the closure of mills and a substantial loss of employment.
Held: Although the loss of employment was a risk, the benefits of free competition outweighed this and other factors.

(*Re Yarn Spinners' Agreement*, 1959, 1 All ER 299)

Example

The application of the Act is restricted to trading agreements and rarely extends to leases and related matters. In *Ravenseft Properties Ltd v. Director General of Fair Trading*, 1977, 1 All ER 47; 1977, 2 WLR 432, it was held that certain underleases and licences granted by the applicant property company and containing restrictive covenants did not require registration under the Act. Only in most exceptional circumstances of collateral agreements or special conditions of sale and leaseback could restrictive convenants fall within the ambit of the Act.

Example

The term 'agreement' had a very broad meaning for if it were otherwise many agreements would escape control. The term includes all arrangements and understandings, however informal, including written and verbal agreements.

(Fisher v. Director General of Fair Trading, 1982, ICR 71)

Example

Groups of companies must comply with the rules in their trading with others within the same group. Where two companies agree to accept restrictions on the supply of goods to a third company which is a subsidiary of one of them, parent and subsidiary are not treated as one.

(Registrar v. Schweppes (No. 2), 1970–1971, LR 7 RP 336)

(ix) Competition

The provisions of the Competition Act 1980 are complementary to those of the Restrictive Trade Practices Act 1976. They are intended to deal with anticompetitive practices which, although not necessarily restrictive in the sense of the 1976 Act, are nevertheless contrary to the public interest.

The Act states that a person is engaged in an anticompetitive practice if he pursues a course of conduct, which of itself or when taken together with a course of conduct pursued by other persons associated with him, has or is intended to have or is likely to have the effect of restricting, distorting or preventing competition in connection with the production, supply or acquisition of goods in the United Kingdom or any part of it or for the supply or securing of services in the United Kingdom or any part of it.

Anticompetitive practices include:

(*a*) price discrimination between distinct and separate groups of customers according to their degree of sensitivity to price levels;

(*b*) predatory price—the practice of temporarily selling at prices below cost, with the intention of driving a competitor from the market so that future prices may be raised and profits enhanced;

(*c*) vertical price squeezing—where a vertically integrated firm controls the total supply of an input which is essential to the production requirements of its subsidiary and also its competitors, it is possible to manipulate the position so that the profits of competitors are squeezed;

(*d*) tie-in sales—the practice of stipulating that a buyer must purchase part or all of his requirements of a second product from the supplier of a first product;

(*e*) full line forcing—the practice which requires a buyer to purchase quantities of each item in a product range in order to be able to buy any of them;

(*f*) rental only contracts—contracts which restrict customers to rentals or leases only;

(*g*) exclusive supply—the situation where a seller supplies only one buyer in a given area thus limiting competition between that buyer and his competitors;

(*h*) selective distribution—restricting supplies only to those outlets which satisfy specific qualitative and quantitative criteria;

(*i*) exclusive purchase—a contract by a distributor to stock only the products of one manufacturer in return for an exclusive supply agreement.

(x) Exemptions

By virtue of the Anticompetitive Practices (Exclusion) Order 1980 certain sectors of trade and industry are exempted from the provisions of the Competition Act 1980. They include international shipping and aviation, small firms with a turnover of less than £5m and having less than a 25 per cent of a relevant market and not being a member of a group with turnover or share figures exceeding those sums and practices arising from agreements which are registerable under the Restrictive Trade Practices Act 1976. The logic of this latter exemption is that any anticompetitive practices would be taken into account by the Restrictive Practices Court when reviewing the agreement concerned.

(xi) Control of Anticompetitive Practices

The machinery of control is similar to that for restrictive trade practices discussed above. The Director General of Fair Trading may himself seek to control or eliminate such practices by negotiation and undertakings or he may refer the matter to the Monopolies and Mergers Commission for investigation.

Example

Attempts by local newspapers to prevent estate agents from advertising in other papers are anticompetitive. In 1986 the *Western Mail and Echo* gave undertakings to the Director General of Fair Trading that they would desist from this practice.

Example

Groups of advertisers who decided to boycott certain newspapers and intended to produce their own property advertising newspaper were advised by the Director General of Fair Trading that this was an anticompetitive practice.

(*Re Abingdon Newspaper Boycott*, 1985)

Example

Refusal to grant licences for the supply of replacement body parts for motor vehicles may be an anticompetitive practice. In 1984 the Director General of Fair Trading reported that the *Ford Motor Company Ltd* was pursuing a course of conduct which constituted an anticompetitive practice by refusing to grant licences for the supply of body parts to other manufacturers on the grounds that the parts were protected by copyright. The Director General had unsuccessfully sought undertakings from the company and therefore referred the matter for investigation by the Monopolies and Mergers Commission. The Commission reported that although the Company had a right at law to protect copyright in their products the practice of preventing other suppliers from providing parts, as they had done since 1960, would lead to a monopoly situation and as such would be anticompetitive.

Example

The practice of broadcasters in limiting the time during which advance programme schedules could be published by other publishers was not against the public interest. In *Re British Broadcasting Corporation and Independent Television Publications Ltd*, 1984, the Monopolies and Mergers Commission decided that the refusal to grant licences for such publication for periods in excess of those specified by the BBC and ITP was not anticompetitive.

12.5 Resale Price Maintenance

(i) Prohibition of Resale Price Maintenance

The practice of maintaining resale prices by agreement or pressure on retailers from manufacturers was originally abolished, with certain exemptions, by the Resale Prices Act 1964. That Act was intended to stimulate competition and reduce general price levels by preventing major manufacturers from maintaining artificially high retail prices. To some extent this objective was achieved but it was not appreciated at the time the extent to which the balance of power in the market place would move from manufacturers to major retailing groups during the next 10 to 15 years. Today, it is generally accepted that the power of major retailers to force uneconomic discounts from manufacturers through 'own branding' is more of a problem than the risk of resale price maintenance.

The current law on this subject is contained in the Resale Prices Act 1976 which consolidated the relevant provisions of the Resale Prices Act 1964 and the Restrictive Trade Practices Act 1956. The Act prohibits collective resale price maintenance. In particular the Act states that any term or condition of a contract for the sale of goods by a supplier to a dealer or any agreement between a supplier and a dealer is void in so far as it purports to establish or provide for the establishment of minimum prices to be charged. It is unlawful for a supplier of goods to include or require to be included or to notify dealers of such a term. If such practices are carried on it is not a criminal offence but would give rise to civil action by way of injunction or other appropriate relief on application by the Crown or any person adversely affected by the term.

(ii) Exemptions

The provisions of the Act are subject to the power of the Restrictive Practices Court to exempt any class of goods if certain 'gateways' can be satisfied. They are:

(*a*) the quality of variety of the goods would be substantially reduced; or

(*b*) the number of retail establishments selling the goods would be substantially reduced; or

(*c*) the retail prices at which the goods are sold would in general and in the long run be increased; or

(*d*) the goods would be sold by retail to the public under conditions likely to cause danger to health in consequence of misuse by the public; or

(*e*) the necessary services actually provided in connection with or after the sale of the goods by retail would cease or be substantially reduced.

(iii) The Net Book Agreement

The maintenance of resale prices for the sale of books is not unlawful–see example, p. 164 above.

(iv) Medicaments

In *Re Medicaments Reference (No. 2)*, 1971, 1 All ER 12, 1970, 1 WLR 1339 the Court found that medicaments and drugs should be granted exemption because in the absence of resale price maintenance, the availability of goods for sale and the necessary services accompanying sales would be substantially reduced because some distributors would tend to stock fast-moving lines only and cut prices on popular items thus making the more comprehensive service offered by pharmacists uneconomical.

(v) Recommended Prices

The Act does not prevent the practice of suppliers or others recommending retail prices, but see the controls on price comparisons in Chapter 10.

Example

No exemption would be granted in respect of sugar and chocolate confectionery because there was no evidence that supermarkets would squeeze out sales by small shops.
(*Re Chocolate and Sugar Confectionery Resale Price Reference*, 1967, 3 All ER 261)

13 *Data protection**

13.1 Introduction

The Data Protection Act 1984 is intended to serve two purposes. First, there was a need to control the use of computers which store personal data because of their potential for the invasion of the privacy of individuals. Second, there was evidence of damage to the United Kingdom's international trade because of our delay in ratifying the Council of Europe Convention for the Protection of Individuals with Regard to Automatic Processing of Personal Data. It had been said that the United Kingdom was becoming a dumping ground for poor quality data. The Act implements the Convention in almost every detail.

It is important to appreciate that the Act is only concerned with data which is processed automatically. Although the word 'computer' does not appear anywhere in the Act there is no doubt that manual and semi-mechanical data systems (for example, microfiche) are exempted from control.

The Act also applies only to 'personal data' which is defined as being information about a living individual, including expressions of opinion about him or her, but excluding any indication of the intentions of the data user in respect of that individual. Thus the Act does not apply, for example, to trading lists which merely bear the names and addresses of corporate bodies, but if the name of a person within a corporate body is entered then the Act does apply.

The effect of the Act on marketing activity, therefore, is likely to be in matters of staff records, customer lists, guarantee records, servicing schedules and sales targets.

13.2 Application of the Act

Liability under the Act arises for two classes of organizations or individuals. *Data users* are those who control the contents and use of a collection of personal data processed, or intended to be processed, automatically. A *computer bureau* is one who processes data for data users, or allows data users to process personal data on his/her equipment.

There are a number of points to note in respect of the business use of personal data:

*The author gratefully acknowledges the consent of the Data Protection Registrar to the use of extracts from his publications in this chapter.

169

(*a*) Data users who control the contents and use of data from within the United Kingdom are subject to the Act irrespective of where the processing of the data is carried out.

(*b*) The data need not be in current use; the holding of data with the intention to use it in the future is sufficient to invoke the provisions of the Act.

(*c*) The sale, leasing, buying or storing of trading lists may mean that a data user is also a computer bureau and therefore attracts additional liability under the Act.

(*d*) Registered companies are legal entities in their own right and it may be that a number of companies within a group of companies may be individually liable to the Act. If one company in the group stores and processes data for others it may be a computer bureau.

13.3 Legal Rights for Data Subjects

The Act creates legal rights for data subjects, that is, individuals to whom personal data relates. A data subject may:

(*a*) seek compensation for damage and any associated distress caused by the loss, destruction or unauthorized disclosure of data or by inaccurate data;

(*b*) apply to the courts for the rectification or erasure of inaccurate data;

(*c*) obtain access to data of which he or she is the subject.

13.4 Data Protection Principles

The entire rationale of the Act is based on the data protection principles derived from the European Convention. They may be summarized as follows. Personal data shall:

(*a*) be collected and processed fairly and lawfully;

(*b*) only be held for specified, lawful and registered purposes;

(*c*) only be used for registered purposes or disclosed to registered recipients;

(*d*) be adequate and relevant to the purpose for which they are held;

(*e*) be accurate and, where necessary, kept up to date;

(*f*) be held no longer than is necessary for the stated purpose;

(*g*) have appropriate security surrounding them.

The principles also incorporate the entitlement of data subjects to have access to data discussed above.

13.5 Considerations Arising from the Data Protection Principles

The data protection principles have a considerable impact on the business use of data. Some examples are given below.

(i) Unauthorized Copying of Data

The unauthorized copying of trading lists is quite common. Although it is uncertain whether trading lists are protected by copyright (the point has never been tested in the courts) there is no doubt that it is theft contrary to s.15 of the Theft Act 1968. There have been a number of successful private prosecutions by list owners for such offences. It therefore follows that copied data has been obtained unfairly and unlawfully.

(ii) Registered Purposes

The purpose for which data is held must be registered (see below for registration generally). It is therefore necessary to register all the purposes for which data may be used in the future. For example, is a list of credit customers now being used for mailed advertising being used for the same registered purpose?

(a) May only be disclosed to registered recipients

It it necessary to ensure that no data is leased or sold to another party unless there is proof that they are registered as required by the Act.

(b) Be accurate and up to date

It is virtually impossible to keep trading lists accurate and up to date because data subjects move to a different address, marry and die. Note, however, the Mailing Preference Service discussed below.

(c) Be held no longer than is necessary

Trading lists tend to have a long life being used again and again for related purposes. Due to adverse public reaction to 'junk mail' (mailed advertising based on lists) it is necessary to consider whether there ought to be a maximum lifespan for such lists. Such would also be compatible with the need to keep lists accurate and up to date.

13.6 The Data Protection Registrar

The Registrar is the key figure in the operation of the Act and he enjoys wide powers of enforcement, licensing and control to ensure compliance with the Act. The duties of the Registrar are:

(a) to compile and maintain the register of data users and computer bureau and to provide facilities for members of the public to examine the register;
(b) to promote observance of the data protection principles;
(c) to consider complaints from data subjects;
(d) to disseminate information to the public about the Act and his functions under it;
(e) to encourage, where appropriate, the production of codes of practice, by trade associations and other bodies, to guide data users in complying with data protection principles;

(*f*) to cooperate with other parties to the Council of Europe Convention and act as United Kingdom authority for the purposes of the Convention;

(*g*) to report annually to Parliament on the performance of his functions under the Act.

13.7 Registration

All existing data users and computer bureaux should have been registered with the Data Protection Registrar by 11 May 1986. Persons or organizations becoming such after that date must register before they begin to use data. The purpose of the registration is to permit the Data Protection Registrar to know by whom personal data is held so that he may exercise his statutory functions in ensuring compliance with the data protection principles. Application for registration must be made on prescribed forms details of which are obtainable from the Registrar.

The details required for the register are:

(*a*) the category of registration, for example, data user or computer bureau;

(*b*) the name and address of the applicant; if the applicant is a registered company its number on the register of Companies under the Companies Act 1985 must be given;

(*c*) a description of the personal data to be held, the purpose for which it is to be held or used;

(*d*) a description of the sources from which data or the information contained in the data is obtained;

(*e*) a description of the person or persons to whom data may be disclosed;

(*f*) the names or a description of any countries or territories outside the United Kingdom to which data may be directly or indirectly transferred;

(*g*) one or more addresses for the receipt of requests from data subjects for access to data.

Once application is made the applicant is deemed to be registered until the registrar indicates to the contrary. A registration is valid for a period of up to 3 years unless a shorter period is requested or required by the registrar.

13.8 Powers of the Registrar

The registrar may refuse an application for registration; he may attach conditions to such registration as he thinks fit; or he may revoke a registration if he has evidence of breaches of the Act by the registered person or organization. In addition to these powers relating directly to registration he enjoys the power to issue three types of 'notice'. They are as follows:

(i) Enforcement Notices

This notice contains a statement of the principle or principles which the registrar is satisfied have been or are being contravened by the registered person on whom the notice is served, with an explanation of the reasons for so believing. The steps to be taken to rectify the alleged breaches are specified and a date by which those steps must be taken is stated. The right of appeal against such a notice (see below) must be explained in the notice.

(ii) Transfer Prohibition Notice

This notice may be served to prevent the overseas transfer of data where the registrar is satisfied that a contravention of any of the principles may result from the transfer. Where the state to which the transfer is intended is bound by the European Convention the registrar may not prohibit the transfer unless he is satisfied that the details are to be transferred on to a state which is not bound by the Convention, and where a contravention of the principles is likely to occur, or unless the data is in a category of sensitive data which is subject to additional safeguards and the registrar is satisfied that equivalent protection will not be afforded to the data.

Transfer prohibition notices must include a statement of the data protection principles which are alleged to have been contravened; the date on which the notice is to become effective and notice of right to appeal (see below).

(iii) Deregistration Notice

This notice informs a registered person or organization that the registrar intends to revoke a licence. It is used after informal warnings, enforcement notices and possibly prosecution. It is a measure of last resort.

13.9 The Appeals Tribunal

The Data Protection Appeals Tribunal is established under the Act to hear appeals by data users or computer bureaux against the registrar's refusal of an application for registration, or alteration of registered particulars, the revocation of a registration or the issue of a notice.

Further appeal may be to the High Court on a point of law.

13.10 Offences against the Data Protection Act 1984

The following are the principal offences created by the Act. The person or organization who may be liable to prosecution in each case is indicated:

(*a*) Holding personal data without being registered or without having applied for registration (data users only).

(*b*) Knowingly or recklessly holding data (data user); using data, obtaining or disclosing data or transferring data (data users, their servants or agents) other than as described in the register entry.

(*c*) Knowingly or recklessly operating as a computer bureau in respect of personal data without being registered (computer bureau).

(*d*) Not keeping the registered address up to date (data user and computer bureau).

(*e*) Knowingly or recklessly supplying the registrar with false or misleading information on application for registration or change of particulars (data user, computer bureau or their servants or agents).

(*f*) Failure to comply with an enforcement notice (data user, computer bureau).

(*g*) Failure to comply with a transfer prohibition notice (data user).

(*h*) Knowing or reckless disclosure without the data user's authority (computer bureau, its servants or agents).

(*i*) Intentional obstruction of a person executing a warrant (any person).

(*j*) Failure, without reasonable excuse, to give reasonable assistance in the execution of a warrant (any person).

It should be noted that offences (*a*), (*d*), (*f*), (*g*), and (*j*) are offences of strict liability, that is, it is not necessary for the prosecution to prove guilty knowledge or intent. In these cases the Act provides for a defence of 'all due diligence and all reasonable precautions' to avoid the commission of the offence. Offences (*b*), (*c*), (*e*), and (*h*) provide for alternative charges of 'knowingly' or 'recklessly' committing the unlawful act. 'Knowingly' means that the unlawful act was committed with intent and this must be proved by the prosecution. 'Recklessly' is a halfway position between strict liability and guilty intent. It means that the act was committed regardless of the consequences.

13.11 Exemptions

There are numerous exemptions from the requirements of the Act which may be divided into four groups:

(*a*) unconditional exemptions from the Act as a whole;
(*b*) conditional exemptions from the Act as a whole;
(*c*) exemptions from the subject access provisions;
(*d*) exemptions from the 'non-disclosure' provisions.

The effect of an exemption is to automatically exclude the data user or computer bureau from registration or to render an action no longer a criminal offence or to qualify the enforcement powers of the registrar. It is not necessary for application to be made for exemption. It is for each individual or organization to decide, usually with the advice of their lawyers, whether or not the exemption applies to them.

(i) Unconditional Exemptions

These are in respect of:

(*a*) personal data which are required to be exempt for the purpose of safeguarding national security;
(*b*) personal data which the user is required by law to make public;
(*c*) personal data held by an individual and concerned only with the management of his personal, family or household affairs or held by him only for recreational purposes.

(ii) Conditional Exemptions

The conditional exemptions from the Act as a whole are:

(*a*) personal data held for one or more of the following purposes:
1. calculating remuneration or pensions for employment, service etc. purposes;
2. keeping accounts for business purposes etc. by the data user himself.

These conditional exemptions are giving rise to problems of interpretation of the law and some amendments to the Act may be necessary. It is a condition of the exemption that the data be used for no other purpose.

The exemption for payroll data is subject to the qualification that the data must not be disclosed except in the following limited circumstances.

1. to any person responsible for making the payments;
2. for the purpose of obtaining actuarial advice;
3. for research into occupational diseases;
4. where the subject has requested or consented to the disclosure;
5. for audit purposes;
6. to provide information about the user's financial affairs.

Accounts data may only be disclosed:
1. for audit purposes;
2. to provide information about the user's financial affairs.

(*b*) data held by unincorporated member's clubs and relating only to club members;
(*c*) data held only for distribution of articles or information to the data subjects and consisting only of their names and addresses, or other particulars necessary for the distribution.

In respect of exemptions (*b*) and (*c*) above data subjects must have been asked whether they object to these uses of data about them and must not have objected. Moreover, the data may not be disclosed without the consent of the data subject, or in a case where the Act specifically lifts the prohibition on disclosure. Under exemption (*c*) the data must not be used for any other purpose.

(iii) Exemption from Subject Access

Exemption from the subject access requirements of the Act is given in the following cases:

(*a*) data held for the prevention or detection of crime, the apprehension or prosecution of offenders and the assessment or collection of duties or taxes;
(*b*) data held by government departments for making judicial appointments;
(*c*) data to which legal professional privilege may be claimed;
(*d*) data held purely for statistical or reseach purposes provided it is not used for any other purpose and the results do not identify any individual;
(*e*) data whose disclosure is prohibited by law where the Secretary of State orders that such prohibition should override the subject access provisions of the Data Protection Act 1984;

(*f*) data covered by the Consumer Credit Act 1974: Access to such data is provided by that Act and the facility of access under this Act is consequently not required;

(*g*) data held solely for recovery or back-up, for example, duplicate files for security purposes;

(*h*) data held by regulatory bodies discharging statutory functions in connection with the protection of the public against dishonesty, incompetence or malpractice in financial matters;

(*i*) data concerned with physical or mental health or social work.

(iv) Exemptions from the Non-Disclosure Provisions

The following exemptions apply to the non-disclosure provisions of the Act:

(*a*) disclosures made for one of the law enforcement or revenue purposes listed at (*a*) above under the subject access provisions;

(*b*) disclosures required for national security purposes;

(*c*) disclosures required by law or by order of a court for the purpose of obtaining legal advice or in court proceedings where the user is a party or a witness;

(*d*) any disclosure made to the data subject or to someone acting on his behalf;

(*e*) disclosures to the data user's or computer bureau's servants or agents for the performance of their duties on his behalf. Such disclosures do not need to be registered by the data user, but not that the data so disclosed is still governed by the data user's register entry in other respects.

(*f*) disclosures required urgently for the prevention of injury or damage to health of any persons.

13.12 Some Precautions for Business People

Experience under the Data Protection Act 1984 so far suggests some basic precautions which ought to be taken by business people to protect themselves and their customers from possible infringements of the Act. They are:

(*a*) Every business which uses data subject to the Act or is a computer bureau should appoint and train a Data Protection Coordinator. He or she should be responsible for advising the company on registration requirements, advice and guidance to all staff handling data or responding to access requests from data subjects, and the security of data.

(*b*) Keep under review the use and storage of data to ensure that it is kept up to date, accurate etc.

(*c*) Check the exemptions from the Act and eliminate waste in the control system.

(*d*) Check periodically, compliance with the data protection principles.

(*e*) Ensure that the sale, leasing or lending of data to other data users or computer bureaux is only provided to those who are themselves registered (subject to the exemptions).

(*f*) Prepare a proforma contract for dealings in data prohibiting unauthorized copying or disclosure.

(*g*) Ensure that adequate records of all precautionary measures are kept in a form which may be used to establish a 'due diligence' defence if that becomes necessary.

13.13 Mailing Preference Service

In 1984 a mailing preference service was inaugurated jointly by the British Direct Marketing Association, the Association of Mail Order Publishers and the Direct Mail Producers' Association. The scheme permits recipients of mailed advertising to register their desire to have their names removed from or added to mailing lists generally or in particular. Applications have to be made in writing to the service secretariat.

The scheme depends for its success on advertisers joining it and paying a subscription from which it is funded. The service can only ensure that names are removed from or added to lists which are used by registered participants.

The Data Protection Registrar has indicated that he sees the service as being compatible with the data protection principles.

13.14 Telephone Selling

Selling to consumers by telephone is a source of concern to the Director General of Fair Trading and the Consumer Movement. Concern is centred around the risk of unsatisfactory contracts being established, high pressure sales techniques and, most importantly, the invasion of privacy. Most telephone selling is derived from lists of telephone subscribers which indicate their socio-economic status and known interests.

The Director General of Fair Trading has called for greater self-regulation in telephone selling and, in response, the British Direct Marketing Association has produced 'Telephone Selling Guidelines'. In August 1986, however, the Director General warned of the need for more general statutory controls.

The impact of the Data Protection Act on telephone subject lists remains to be seen but the influence of the data protection principles is obvious and predictable.

13.15 Further Information

The Data Protection Registrar publishes leaflets and booklets on the interpretation of the Act and the steps which must be taken for compliance. These include:

(*a*) An Introduction and Guide to the Act (Guideline No 1) (February 1985).
(*b*) Notes to Help you to Apply for Registration (September 1985).
(*c*) Questions and Answers on the Act (September 1985 and February 1986).

Copies of these and other publications may be obtained from the Office of the Data Protection Registrar, Springfield House, Water Lane, Wilmslow, Cheshire SK9 5AX.

14 *Trade bodies and self-regulation*

14.1 The Fair Trading Act 1973

In addition to the responsibilities given to the Director General of Fair Trading in respect of monopolies, mergers and restrictive trade practices (*see* Chapter 12) and those in respect of unfair trading practices (*see* Chapter 8) the Fair Trading Act 1973 seeks to encourage self-regulation through Codes of Practice. Section 124 (3) of the Act places a duty on the Director General to encourage relevant associations to prepare, and to disseminate to their members, codes of practice for guidance in safeguarding and promoting the interests of consumers in the United Kingdom.

The term 'relevant association' means any association (whether incorporated or not) whose membership consists wholly or mainly of persons engaged in the production of supply of goods or in the supply of services or of persons employed by or representing persons so engaged and whose objects or activities include the promotion of the interests of persons so engaged. This definition is not restricted to persons or associations engaged in 'trade'. In theory at least it extends the duty of the Director General to the professions but certain professions enjoy statutory status (the law, medicine, insurance, accountancy and estate agency). In those cases professional codes of conduct with the necessary disciplinary procedures enjoy a special status which would not be affected by the Fair Trading Act 1973.

14.2 Types of Codes of Practice

The use of codes of practice as a means of regulating trade and business is growing rapidly—many observers would say much too rapidly. The promotion of a code of practice has become almost a symbol of respectability for trade and professional bodies and most have them. Some have more than one to deal with different aspects of their members' business. Others confuse the role of 'guidance notes', which are intended to explain legal or trade issues to members, with codes of practice. In the generally accepted sense a code of practice lays down certain principles of fair conduct which the sponsoring body believes are in the interests of their members and their members' customers. They have been dubbed 'exercises in enlightened self-interest.'

14.3 Classification of Codes of Practice

A study of all the codes of practice which exist in 1988 suggests that there are certain common features which permit them to be put into four different groups. These groups are as follows:

(i) Pious Codes of Practice

This rather unflattering classification includes many codes drawn up by trade bodies which have not been endorsed by the Director General of Fair Trading; which do not provide for any remedial procedures to deal with disputes between members and their customers; which do not provide for any disciplinary measures; and which have no status in law. Many of them are little more than an expression of fair trading principles or a vague statement of good intent. Although no doubt well intended their impact on the market place is negligible and they do not merit further comment.

(ii) Codes of Practice Endorsed by the Director General

These are codes which have been discussed with the Office of Fair Trading and which, after a long period of negotiation, have received the Director General's endorsement. There were 20 such codes in 1988 and the Director General had indicated that he considers the first era of code-making to be completed. Although the effectiveness of these codes varies considerably they all have certain common features. First, there are provisions for conciliation and arbitration where disputes between a member and his customer occur. Second, there are prescribed disciplinary measures which can be taken against a member who breaches the code. Third, there are provisions which deal with identified problems occurring within the trade or business concerned.

(iii) Enforceable Codes

These are unique codes which set down rules of conduct and provide for sanctions outside the law which may be applied in the event of non-observance. Such codes can be enforced against traders or businesses which are not members of a sponsoring trade body. The only credible codes in this category are the British Code of Advertising Practice, the British Code of Sales Promotion Practice and the Code of Practice of the Proprietary Association of Great Britain.

(iv) Statutory Codes of Practice

These are codes which are drawn up after discussions with a government department and which are given full or partial status of law after being approved by the Secretary of State or a Minister. Such codes are of increasing importance and many proposals for new legislation currently under consultation make provision for them. A good current example is the Code of Practical Guidance for Packers and Importers which has certain legal status under the terms of Part V of the Weights and Measures Act 1985.

Codes in this category should not be confused with agreements between enforcement authorities and trade bodies about the interpretation of law. Certain agreements between LACOTS (the Local Authorities Coordinating Body on Trading Standards) and trade bodies are known as Codes of Practice but they have no status in law even though they may influence the enforcement of law.

14.4 Codes of Practice Endorsed by the Director General of Fair Trading

These codes must set clear standards of fair trading for trade association members to attain in their dealings with customers. The Office of Fair Trading has developed a set of criteria which must be satisfied before the code can receive the Director General's endorsement. These include the avoidance of any significant restrictions on competition, and a clear statement of the customer's rights at law as they affect transactions in the relevant sector of trade. The code must also set additional rights and benefits on consumers which may be desirable because of problems peculiar to that sector. The trade association concerned is expected to provide a conciliation service in the event of disputes with a cheap, speedy and independent redress scheme, usually based on arbitration.

The effectiveness of such codes also depends on public awareness of them. For this reason the Office of Fair Trading publishes a series of leaflets which include a summary of the provisions of the code and are designed to bring the existence of the code and their principal features to the attention of consumers and their advisers.

The codes in operation in 1988 are as follows:

(*a*) Servicing of domestic electrical appliances (Association of Manufacturers of Domestic Electrical Appliances).

(*b*) Package holidays—travel agents (Association of British Travel Agents).

(*c*) Package holidays—tour operators (Association of British Travel Agents).

(*d*) Electrical appliance servicing by electricity boards (Electricity Boards and Electricity Consultative Councils).

(*e*) Vehicle body repairs (Vehicle Builders and Repairers Association).

(*f*) Electrical appliance servicing by Scottish Electricity Boards (Scottish Electricity Consultative Councils).

(*g*) Motor Industry—motor manufacturers, importers and retailers (Motor Agents' Association, Scottish Motor Trade Association, Society of Motor Manufacturers and Traders).

(*h*) Shoe repairs (National Association of Multiple Shoe Repairers, Society of Master Shoe Repairers).

(*i*) Laundering and dry cleaning (Association of British Laundry Cleaning and Rental Services Ltd.)

(*j*) Footwear retailing (Footwear Distributors' Federation, Multiple Shoe Retailers' Association, Instock Footwear Suppliers Association, British Rubber Manufacturers' Association, Independent Footwear Retailers' Association, British Footwear Manufacturers' Federation).

(*k*) Selling and servicing of electrical and electronic appliances (Radio Electrical and Television Retailers' Association).

(*l*) Mail order publishing—books and records sent by mail order only (Mail Order Publishers' Authority).

(*m*) Furniture and carpets (National Association of Retail Furnishers, British Furniture Manufacturers' Federated Associations, National Bedding Federation).

(*n*) Mail order trading—mail order trading by agents not including direct marketing (Mail Order Traders' Association).

(*o*) Funerals (National Association of Funeral Directors).

(*p*) Photography (British Photographic Association, British Photographic Importers' Association, National Pharmaceutical Association, Association of Photographic Laboratories, Institute of Photographic Apparatus Repair Technicians, British Institute of Professional Photography, Master Photographers' Association, Association of British Manufacturers of Photographic, Cine and Audio Visual Equipment, Professional Photographic Laboratories).

(*q*) Postal services—the Post Office.

(*r*) Party plan selling (Direct Selling Association).

(*s*) Double glazing (Glass and Glazing Federation).

(*t*) Motor cycles (Motor Agents' Association, Scottish Motor Trade Association, Motor Cycle Retailers' Association, Motor Cycle Association).

The foregoing list omits the Code of Practice of the Telecommunications Services which was negotiated with the Office of Fair Trading but following the establishment of British Telecom has now passed to the Office of Telecommunications.

A major weakness in the establishment of new Codes of Practice and the administration of existing ones is the fragmented state of much of British trade representation. There can be no better example than the photographic industry shown above but they have, at least, established a joint code. Other industries are represented by four or more trade bodies with overlapping responsibilities but only one or two of them have drawn up codes of practice. However, it is a fact that these codes have had a beneficial effect on standards of fair trading despite their many weaknesses.

14.5 Conciliation and Arbitration

Most of the Codes of Practice listed above include requirements for conciliation services to be operated by the relevant trade bodies on behalf of their members. Publicity is given to the codes by the Office of Fair Trading and the existence of the conciliation service is communicated to consumers by members of the associations concerned, citizens' advice bureaux, local authorities and other public information bodies. Where a consumer is in dispute with a member of one of the trade bodies and the dispute cannot be settled by negotiation between the parties the matter can be referred to the trade association whose conciliation officer will seek to settle the matter by amicable agreement between the parties.

Where such settlement is impossible the matter is referred to an independent arbitrator appointed by the Chartered Institute of Arbitrators on behalf of the trade association. Both parties agree in advance to accept the arbitrator's award, if any, and appeal to the courts can only take place if the arbitrator has erred in law. The arbitration process is controlled by the Arbitration Acts 1951 and 1979. Such arbitration should not be confused with the 'Small Claims Procedure' of the County Court. This service is available to all litigants with a claim not exceeding £2000 in value. It is not concerned with arbitrations arranged by trade bodies.

The Office of Fair Trading published a consultative document on *Redress Procedures under Codes of Practice* in 1980 which was critical of the services offered by trade bodies. The National Consumer Council published a report entitled *Simple Justice* in 1981 which was also critical and drew attention to the inability of some trade bodies to fulfil their obligations under the Codes. In more recent years the Director General of Fair Trading has frequently expressed his dissatisfaction with the performance of trade bodies in this field. By 1988 some trade bodies had improved their handling of consumer complaints by separating the administration of the codes from their trade representational work. This can be achieved by the creation of a committee to administer the code including non-trade members and an independent chairman. Some trade bodies have also appointed an experienced and skilled code administrator.

14.6 Legal Liability Arising from Codes of Practice

Both criminal and civil liability may arise from adherence to a voluntary code of practice. If the provisions of a code of practice are referred to in a contract then they become binding on the parties to the contract and may be actionable in their breach. Liability may also arise under s.14 of the Trade Descriptions Act 1968 where a trader publicizes his adherence to a code but in a particular case fails to fulfil its requirements. A motor trader was convicted of such an offence in 1980.

14.7 A General Duty to Trade Fairly

The principal weakness of codes of practice as an instrument of consumer protection is that they apply only to members of trade bodies and not to non-members involved in the same business. Reputable businessmen who belong to trade bodies are likely to be those least in need of them and, by virtue of their adherence to the restrictions in a code, may suffer a competitive disadvantage in the market. In 1983 the Director General of Fair Trading published a consultation document entitled *Home Improvements* in which he drew attention to the problems created for consumers by rogue builders and similar traders and suggested that a statutory 'general duty of trade fairly' may be the way forward in this and other problem areas. It would have the effect of making general standards of fair trading, whether derived from codes of practice or not, enforceable against all traders.

The idea created great interest and much support amongst trade bodies and lawyers. In 1986 a further consultative document entitled *A General Duty to Trade Fairly* was published by the Director General into which he incorporated the views of more than 200 individuals and organizations who had responded to the 1983 document.

The concept of general duties in law is gradually developing in a number of fields. Much experience has been gained in respect of the United Kingdom implementation of the EEC 'average quantity' system by the Weights and Measures Act 1979 (now Part V of the Weights and Measures Act 1985). The Act lays down a general duty for packers and importers to comply with the basic rules of the system, that packages should be within a prescribed tolerance of the purported quantity, and the details of the system are contained in a Codes of Practical Guidance which has been approved by the Secretary of State. In the relatively narrow and complex field of quantity control the system has worked well. Later examples are the general duty to sell safe goods to consumers (*see*

Chapter 9) and the new law on misleading indications of price (*see* Chapter 10). The general duty to trade fairly across all trade and business would appear to be a logical development of this trend. Much of the discussion on this topic centres around the question as to whether the general duty to trade fairly should be used as a statutory long stop to deal with traders who do not conform to codes of practice or whether it could fulfil a much wider role. In theory at least, it could replace much of the complex criminal law in such fields as consumer credit and food labelling. It could even, it has been suggested, replace the Trade Descriptions Act 1968.

Whether or not a general duty to trade fairly is ever enacted depends to a considerable degree on the political flavour of government. The left tends to favour a rigid system of criminal law, whereas the right seeks to reduce burdens on business by encouraging self-regulation backed by broad statutory duties.

14.8 Enforceable Codes

In this category of codes of practice we consider codes which have been drawn up voluntarily but which are backed by non-legal or quasi-legal sanctions. The most obvious examples are the two codes drawn up by the Code of Advertising Practice Committee (CAP).

In 1962 the system of voluntary control of advertising by the Advertising Association was replaced by an agreement drawn up by the leading trade and professional associations and institutes in the advertising and media businesses. The Advertising Association, which is a federal body representing the common ground between all advertising bodies, had for many years been administering a code of practice which established basic rules of honesty and decency in advertising. It was generally acknowledged that it had done a good job but something more broadly based and with independent control was required to deal with modern advertising practice. Accordingly, the Code of Advertising Practice Committee was reorganized and its membership broadened and the Advertising Standards Authority was established. The self-regulatory system was further improved under pressure from the government of the day in 1974, and in 1986 an independent committee under a distinguished former civil servant was set up to review the system yet again.

The remit of CAP and the ASA (*see* 14.9 below) is to control all media advertising including posters and cinema advertising but not television or commercial radio which is the responsibility of the Independent Broadcasting Authority (IBA). This division of responsibility for overall control between CAP and the IBA has worked well enough in the past but new areas of advertising, such as Prestel and Ceefax, cable, satellite and direct mail present problems. They do not fit neatly into the responsibilities of either CAP or the IBA and are problems that have been referred to the new review committee.

14.9 The Code of Advertising Practice Committee

The Committee currently consists of representatives of 20 trade and professional bodies and is serviced by an independent secretariat. It draws up and amends from time to time the British Code of Advertising Practice and the British Code of Sales Promotion Practice. It has a series of subcommittees to look at special problem areas such as financial, health, mail order and similar advertising. The Sales Promotion Code is kept under review by a special subcommittee.

In addition to drawing up the codes CAP receives complaints from advertisers about other advertisers where it is thought that their advertisements are in breach of the code. It adjudicates in such disputes and, if the complaints are justified, requires the advertiser concerned to correct his advertising.

The British Code of Advertising Practice is held in high esteem by government and is generally acknowledged as a valuable contribution to consumer protection by the consumer movement. It has been widely copied in other countries. The British Code of Sales Promotion Practice is less well regarded mainly because there are no meaningful sanctions which can be applied in the event of a breach of its provisions (*see* 14.11 below).

14.10 The Advertising Standards Authority

The Advertising Standards Authority (ASA) is a company limited by guarantee set up by the advertising industry to administer the two codes. Its job is to ensure that the codes are observed by all advertisers in the public interest. The ASA has an independent Chairman from outside the advertising industry and the Council of the ASA draws not less than two-thirds of its members from outside the industry. The ASA, whose staff are also the CAP secretariat, seek to enforce the codes by encouraging complaints from the public and by monitoring advertisements.

The ASA and CAP are financed by a levy of 0.01 per cent on all display advertising. The levy is collected by the Advertising Standards Board of Finance which is itself independent of the other bodies within the system.

14.11 Sanctions Against Breaches of the CAP Codes

The philosophy behind the self-regulatory system is that all constituent bodies are committed on behalf of their members to observe the codes in the spirit as well as the letter. Each trade and professional body in membership of CAP seeks to ensure that its members comply with the codes by encouragement, advice and, in the case of serious or persistent breaches, by internal discipline. However, the ASA has available to it two sanctions which it can apply to advertisers who are found to have breached the codes whether the breach is discovered by complaint or as a result of monitoring. They are:

(a) Published disapproval

The ASA publishes a monthly cases report which gives the details of all public complaints and the decision of the Council of the ASA in respect of that complaint.

(b) Media recommendations

In serious cases the ASA can issue a recommendation to the media organizations that a particular advertisement, or advertising generally, should not be accepted from the recalcitrant advertiser until he mends his ways. The media organizations are committed to support such recommendations by virtue of their membership of CAP.

Overall the system works well but it does suffer from inherent weaknesses. In the case of sales promotions and directly mailed advertising, for example, there is no publication of the advertisement by the media and thus the ultimate sanction in the armoury of the ASA cannot be used.

14.12 Legal Status of the Advertising Self-regulatory System

CAP and the ASA have no status in law nor are they immune from the law on restrictive trade practices and defamation. It follows, therefore, that these bodies must take care that the terms of the code and its administration do not create a restriction on trade and their published reports are in no way defamatory.

The ASA can, and occasionally does, pass apparent breaches of the law on to local trading standards officers or the Office of Fair Trading. On the other hand, matters which imply a possible breach of the law may also contravene the codes and the efforts of the ASA to deal with such matters is a source of friction between them and authorized enforcement officers.

14.13 Control of Misleading Advertising Regulations 1986

The implementation of the EEC Directive on Misleading Advertising by the Control of Misleading Advertising Regulations 1988 (*see* 8.24) has fundamentally changed the role of the ASA and CAP. With the injunctive powers of the Director General of Fair Trading in operation they are no longer the sole arbiters of misleading advertising. However, it should be noted that the regulations apply only to misleading advertising and does not extend, as do the CAP codes, to matters of taste and decency. Most independent observers of the advertising control system believe that the statutory powers in these regulations will have a beneficial effect on the control system as a whole. The eccentricities and variability inherent in control systems not based on law should be smoothed out.

14.14 Code of Standards of Advertising Practice of the Proprietary Association of Great Britain

The Proprietary Association of Great Britain represents the majority of manufacturers of medicines available to the public without prescription. It is a condition of membership that all advertisements shall be cleared with the association before publication. The Department of Health and Social Security medicines division recognizes the work of the association as satisfying the requirements of regulations made under the Medicines Act 1968 on the promotion of medicinal products in this class. The Association has, therefore, achieved a unique position by using self-regulation to satisfy statutory requirements.

14.15 Statutory Codes of Practice

These are codes of practice which are approved, recognized or prepared to fulfil a function required by law. In some cases a statutory body, such as the Independent Broadcasting Authority, is required to produce a code of practice for a specified purpose. In other cases the Secretary of State is empowered to approve codes of practice intended to give guidance on or to amplify legal responsibilities. The oldest example of this latter group is the Highway Code but there are many more recent examples in weights and measures, health and safety at work, agriculture, prices, environmental and similar laws.

14.16 Independent Broadcasting Authority

The Independent Broadcasting Authority Act 1973, which consolidated the Television Act 1964 and the Sound Broadcasting Act 1972, establishes the Independent Broadcasting Authority (IBA) and requires it to draw up and maintain rules as to advertisements. Those rules are contained in the IBA Code of Advertising Standards and Practice which applies to both television and commercial radio advertisements. The Code has much in common with the British Code of Advertising Practice and there is close liaison between CAP and the IBA on code content and administration.

All television advertisements are vetted by the Independent Television Companies Association (ITCA) on behalf of the IBA to ensure that they conform to the code. Some, but not all, radio advertisements are also vetted in advance.

14.17 Protection for Consumers in Respect of Money Paid in Advance

The loss of money paid in advance by consumers where the company concerned goes into liquidation before the contract is fulfilled has long been a source of concern to trade bodies. Such money may arise from deposits paid in advance against future delivery or mail order offers where prepayment is a condition of the contract. Conscious of the loss of customer confidence which can arise from such losses a number of trade bodies have set up protection schemes which guarantee, or are supposed to guarantee, that no customer can lose his or her money.

(i) The Newspaper Publishers Mail Order Protection Scheme

The Newspaper Publishers' Association (NPA) operates a guarantee scheme under which any consumer who pays money in advance in response to an advertisement in a national newspaper and loses that money through the bankruptcy of the advertiser can get his or her money back. The NPA Mail Order Protection Scheme is administered by a special body whose function is to ensure that advertisers are financially sound and of good reputation. The scheme is backed by a bonding system from which money is available to reimburse consumers who may lose their money in this way.

The scheme does not extend to regional or local newspapers and does not include classified advertisements. It is recognized as being the best of all the guarantee schemes currently in operation.

(ii) The Periodical Publishers' Scheme

The Periodical Publishers' Association (PPA) operates a set of rules under which members who accept advertisements for publication in their magazines requiring advance payment must satisfy themselves that the advertiser is financially sound. If consumers then lose their money the member is required to reimburse them. The scheme works well enough in respect of the major magazine publishers, but there are numerous magazine publishers who do not belong to the association or who do not support the scheme.

(iii) Trust Funds

A number of trade and professional bodies and individual traders ensure that money paid in advance is put into a trust fund where it remains until the contract is fulfilled. This guarantees that consumers cannot lose their money in the event of liquidation of the trader or professional person concerned.

(iv) Bonded Schemes

Some trade bodies require their members to maintain a bond from which lost payments made by consumers may be recovered. A few trade bodies, such as the Association of British Travel Agents, maintain a bonding system themselves on behalf of members.

14.18 The Insolvency Act 1986

This Act provides that where any director or directors of a company continue to trade beyond the point where they must have known that the company was insolvent they may themselves be held responsible for debts accruing after that point. The Act introduces the concept of 'wrongful trading' which seeks to ensure that company directors are responsible for their own actions within the company. This measure may go some way towards protecting consumers but it falls far short of the recommendations of the Cork Committee on whose report the Act is based.

15 *Institutions and organizations concerned with marketing law and practice*

15.1 Introduction

Having considered the law and self-regulation applicable to marketing in the foregoing chapters it is appropriate to gain some understanding of the departments of central government, local government, *ad hoc* bodies and consumer organizations which make, influence or enforce the law. The structure of self-regulation is discussed in Chapter 14.

15.2 Central Government Departments

(i) Department of Trade and Industry (DTI)

This is the successor department to the old Board of Trade which was the original government body with power to control trading activity through law. Its name has been changed a number of times by successive governments but its functions have remained broadly the same. Its principal current areas of control are as follows.

(a) Weights and measures

This is control of weighing and measuring equipment through the National Weights and Measures Laboratory and the sale of goods by quantity through its consumer affairs division.

(b) Monopolies and mergers and restrictive trade practices

This is by way of liaison with and implementation of Office of Fair Trading recommendations.

(c) Consumer credit

This is the making of regulations under the Consumer Credit Act 1974.

(d) Consumer safety

This is the making of regulations and issuing prohibition orders under the Consumer Protection Acts 1961 and 1971 and the Consumer Safety Act 1978. A special 'safety unit' is maintained to deal with individual cases brought to its attention (usually by local authorities).

(e) General consumer policy

This is the use of powers under the Fair Trading Act 1973, the Competition Act 1980 and related statutes in the public interest.

(ii) Ministry of Agriculture, Fisheries and Food (MAFF)

(a) Food law

This is implementation of the Food Act 1984, regulations made under that Act, food additives and contaminants, horticultural marketing and grading, control of pesticides.

(b) Slaughter and animal welfare

This is implementation of the Slaughterhouses Act 1974, the Slaughter of Poultry Act 1967 and related matters.

(c) Fertilizers and feedingstuffs

This is control of fertilizers of the soil and animal feedingstuffs (including pet animals under the Agricultural Act 1970).

(d) Agricultural and horticultural produce

This covers marketing arrangements, promotion of UK products (by way of Food from Britain), establishment and operation of marketing boards.

(ii) Department of Health and Social Security (DHSS)

(a) Medicines and medicinal products

This is implementation and administration of the Medicines Act 1968 and all orders and regulations made thereunder, also licensing of human medicinal products and medicated animal feedingstuffs.

(b) Food

This is work with the Ministry of Agriculture, Fisheries and Food in respect of the health aspects of food, its treatment and further development.

(c) Poisons

This is control of poisons through the Poisons Act 1972 in liaison with the Pharmaceutical Society of Great Britain.

(iii) Home Office (HO)

(a) Petroleum manufacture and storage

This covers policy and law on petroleum through the Health and Safety Executive (HSE) and local authorities.

(b) Explosives

This covers manufacture and storage of explosives in liaison with the Health and Safety Executive and local authorities.

15.3 Statutory Bodies

(i) Office of Fair Trading (OFT)

(a) General consumer policy

This covers monitoring trading activity to ensure that standards of fair trading are maintained and improved with power to make recommendations to the Secretary of State where action is called for.

(b) Monopolies and mergers, restrictive trade practices and competition

These are investigations, referrals to the Monopolies and Mergers Commission, actions before the courts.

(c) Undertakings and codes of practice

This covers the duty to seek undertakings from traders acting against the public interest and encouraging codes of practice amongst trade bodies.

(d) Consumer credit

This is licensing of credit traders, and supervision of the operation of the Act through local authorities.

(e) Advertising control

This covers injunctive powers against misleading advertising under the Control of Misleading Advertising Regulations 1986.

(ii) Health and Safety Executive (HSE)

(a) Commercial safety standards

This covers enforcement of the Health and Safety at Work Act 1974 through the factory inspectorate.

(b) Explosives and petroleum

This covers enforcement of the Explosives Acts 1875 and 1923 and the Petroleum Consolidation Act 1928 in conjunction with local authorities.

(iii) British Standards Institution (BSI)

This covers the drawing up and maintenance of standards for United Kingdom products. The importance of the Institution has been greatly increased following the announcement of the government's quality accreditation scheme.

(iv) National Physical Laboratory (NPL)

This covers material and product testing to high standards of accuracy, including testing of United Kingdom primary and secondary standards of weights and measures.

(v) National Consumer Council (NCC)

This body has a duty to represent the interests of consumers, and is intended to balance the influence of the trade unions and the Confederation of British Industry (CBI) on behalf of consumers. Financed entirely by government grant, it undertakes consumer surveys and studies into current problems. The NCC has no statutory status but it is influential with government and local authorities.

There are separate Consumer Councils for Wales, Northern Ireland and Scotland.

15.4 Local Government Bodies

(i) Local Weights and Measures Authorities

Non-metropolitan county councils in England and Wales, London boroughs in Greater London, metropolitan district councils in English metropolitan areas and regional councils in Scotland, enforce weights and measures, food, some aspects of medicines, trade descriptions, consumer credit, consumer safety, poisons, petroleum, and related miscellaneous functions. Officers are generally known as 'trading standards officers' or 'consumer protection officers'. They enjoy wide powers of enforcement including the right of entry to trade premises, taking of samples, inspection of goods, examination and seizure of goods and documents. It is an offence to obstruct an officer in the course of his duty.

(ii) Environmental Health Authorities

London boroughs, metropolitan district councils and district councils are responsible for health and hygiene aspects of food law.

(iii) Local Authorities Coordinating Body in Trading Standards (LACOTS)

This was set up by the local authority associations to coordinate the administration of trading standards and some environmental health services. It has no statutory powers and is financed by the local authority associations.

(iv) Association of County Councils

This represents the shire counties in England and Wales, and submits recommendations to government on new and revised marketing law.

(v) Association of Metropolitan Councils

This performs the same function as the Association of County Councils above, on behalf of metropolitan councils.

(vi) Association of District Councils

This performs the same functions as the Association of County Councils (above) but on behalf of district councils.

15.5 Consumer and Voluntary Bodies

(i) Consumers Association

This represents its members in consumer matters. It publishes *Which?* and carries out consumer surveys and reports. It is a powerful parliamentary lobbyist with many successes to its name. It is financed by private subscriptions and profits from sales only.

(ii) National Federation of Consumer Groups

This attempts to coordinate and represent local consumer groups. It is a weak organization with little influence.

(iii) National Association of Citizens Advice Bureaux

This coordinates, represents and trains local citizens' advice bureaux. It is highly regarded and provides much free advice through voluntary workers on legal matters. The National Association is funded by government grants and the local bureaux are funded by local authority grants and private donations.

15.6 Consumer Representation in the Nationalized Industries

(i) National Gas Consumers' Council

Set up by the Gas Act 1972 these bodies represent the interests of consumers with the regional gas boards. They express views on tariffs and service matters and take up complaints from individual consumers through local representatives. With the privatization of the gas industry a new Gas Consumers' Council is to be set up to represent the views of consumers with the new gas companies. The National Gas Consumers' Council coordinates and represents the views of the general councils.

From the total cost of consultative consumer councils for the nationalized industries paid by government under the Statutory Corporations (Financial Provisions) Act 1975 the Gas Councils receive approximately 41 per cent.

(ii) Electricity Consultative Councils (ECCs)

Under the Electricity Act 1947 each area electricity board has a Consumers' Consultative Council. There is no national board as there has been for the gas industry.

The costs of the electricity councils amounts to about 38 per cent of total government expenditure on consumer representation in the nationalized industries.

(iii) Transport Users Consultative Committees

The Central Transport Users Consultative Committee coordinates and represents the views of eleven area committees on the services of British Rail.

The cost of the Transport Users' Council is about 11 per cent of government expenditure on consumer representation in the nationalized industries.

(iv) Post Office Users' National Council

This Council was set up by the Post Office Act 1969 which made the Post Office a public corporation, rather than a government department. There are a number of 'country councils' which are intended to represent the views of consumers on local issues. Because the Post Office is no longer a department of central government the Act requires that the Council be consulted in advance on tariff changes and similar matters.

The cost of the Post Office Users' National Council amounts to about 9 per cent of total government expenditure on consumer representation in the nationalized industries.

(v) Domestic Coal Consumers' Council

This Council was set up by the Coal Industry Nationalization Act 1946 to care for the consumers of domestic coal. It is very weak for there is no requirement for it to be consulted on any matter by the National Coal Board.

The cost of the Domestic Coal Consumers' Council amounts to only 1 per cent of total government expenditure on consumer representation in the nationalized industries.

15.6 Trade and Industry Representation

There is a complex and tangled web of trade and professional bodies representing the views of businessmen to government in the United Kingdom. In most industries attempts have been made to achieve a form of federal structure to ensure that reactions to proposed legislation and government policy on industrial matters are representative of a majority in the business concerned. The most important federal bodies are as follows:

(i) Confederation of British Industry (CBI)

The CBI includes in its membership individual companies and trade bodies. Its Marketing Committee is responsible for ensuring that all legislative proposals from government are properly considered and responded to. Because of its very wide membership base it often has difficulty in finding sufficient common ground between its members to make an effective response to government. It is not uncommon to find the CBI expressing a particular view while a quite different one is being submitted by one of its constituent parts or members.

(ii) Advertising Association

This is the federal body of the advertising industry. It is supported by most of the trade and professional organizations in the advertising and direct marketing business. It has an important role in ensuring that the advertising industry's self-regulation system works well (*see* Chapter 14).

(iii) Food and Drink Federation

Formerly the Food Manufacturers' Federation it was merged in 1984 with the Food and Drink Industry Council to represent the views of all companies in the food and drink industries. Because of the high public profile of the food business and the quantity of legislation affecting the food industry it has a particularly close relationship with government departments.

(iv) British Retailers Association and the Retail Consortium

The Retail Consortium was originally set up in the early 1970s to act as a federation of seven major associations representing retailers. It has gradually declined in prestige and influence as the British Retailers' Association has grown. The BRA is now the dominant force in retail representation and, in view of the power of modern major retailers, is very influential with government.

Further Reading

The following books and publications are recommended for further reading on the subjects covered in this book. Many of them are standard authoritative textbooks written for and used by the legal professions and enforcement officers. Others are written in more general and thus more easily comprehensible terms, and this is indicated where appropriate.

Advertising Standards Authority, *The British Code of Advertising Practice and the British Code of Sales Promotion Practice*

Benion, F., *Consumer Credit Act Manual* (Oyez).

Blair, M. C., *Sale of Goods Act 1979* (Butterworths).

Butterworths Law of Food and Drugs (Butterworths). A very comprehensive six-volume looseleaf textbook.

Chalmers, *Sale of Goods*, 18th edition (Butterworths).

Consumer Law Statutes (Monitor Press, 1988).

Croners Buying and Selling Law (Croner Publications Ltd).

Data Protection Act—Guidelines: Questions and Answers (The Data Protection Registrar).

The Data Protection Act Handbook (Peat, Marwick, Mitchell & Co.).

Encyclopaedia of Product Liability and Safety (Butterworths). A looseleaf volume covering all civil and criminal law on these subjects.

Goode, R. M., *Consumer Credit Legislation* (Butterworths). A two-volume looseleaf textbook.

Harris, B., *Criminal Jurisdiction of Magistrates* (Barry Rose).

Harvey, B. W., *Consumer Protection and Fair Trading* (Butterworths). A very comprehensive and well-written review of the law on consumer protection, containing case studies and examples.

Independent Television Companies Association, *The IBA Code of Advertising Practice*.

Institute of Practitioners in Advertising, *Is it Legal?*

Lawson, R. G., *Advertising and Labelling Laws in the Common Market* (Jordans, 1975).

Lawson, R. G., *Exclusion Clauses* (Longman, 1983).

Lawson, R. G., *Supply of Goods and Services Act* (Longman, 1982).

McLean, I. and Morrish, P., *The Magistrates' Court* (Barry Rose).

Miller, C. J. and Harvey, B. W., *Consumer and Trading Law Cases and Materials* (Butterworths). An easy-to-understand work, contain case studies and examples.

Morrish, P. and McLean I., *The Crown Court* (Barry Rose).

O'Keefe, J. A., *Trade Descriptions Act 1968* (Butterworths, 1968). A two-volume looseleaf textbook.

O'Keefe, J. A., *Law of Weights and Measures* (Butterworths). A two-volume looseleaf textbook.

Rowell, R., *Counterfeiting and Forgery* (Butterworths).

Yates, D., *Exclusion Clauses in Contracts* (Sweet and Maxwell).

Yell N. and West W. T., *The County Court: Practice and Procedure* (Barry Rose).

Index

Law:
  civil, 3–4
  commercial, 4
  common, 3
  company, 4, 5, 6
  of contract, 4, 5, 6
  criminal, 3–4, 103–8, 109–10, 125,
    126–7
  officers, 18–19
  profession, 17–18
  reports, 16–17
  of tort, 4, 5, 6
Legal relationship, 24
Local authorities, 191–2

Mail order, 122, 177, 186–7
Medicines, 120, 127, 168, 185, 189
Mercantile agents, 66
Mergers, 157–8, 160, 188, 190
Misrepresentation, 33–5
Mistake, 31–3
Monopolies, 157, 158–60, 188, 190
Monopolies and Mergers Commission,
  158

Nationalized industries, 193–4
Negligence, 4, 30, 31, 34
Negotiable instruments, 87–102
  and Consumer Credit Act 1974, 102
  definition of, 87
  promissory notes, 101
  see also Bills of exchange
Net Book Agreement, 164, 168

Offers, 21–4
Office of Fair Trading, 190
  see also Fair trading
Ombudsmen, 14

Partnerships:
  and criminal liability, 104
Passing off, 84–6
Patents, 71–5, 161
Poisons, 127, 134, 190
Power of attorney, 55
Prices:
  bargain offers, 138
  codes of practice, 139–43
  control of, 136, 139
  false indications, 137–9
  resale price maintenance, 167–8
  unit pricing, 136–7
  vouchers and coupons, 142

Principal:
  duties of, 61–2
  and third parties, 63–4
Privy Council, 11, 16
Prize draws, 142–3
Products:
  liability for, 125–7
  safety regulations, 127–35
Promissory estoppel, 27
Promissory notes, 87, 101

Registerable agreements, 160–5
Registered designs, 84
Remedies:
  for breach of contract, 37–8
  and copyright infringement, 79–80
  and infringement of patents, 73–4
  against injury by dangerous goods, 125
  against passing off, 86
  and sale of goods, 51–4
Resale price maintenance, 167–8
Restrictive trade practices, 157, 167, 188,
  190
  registerable agreements, 160–5
Retail associations, 195

Safety regulations, 127–35
Sale of goods:
  Acts, 3, 39–40
  and advertising, 109
  buyer's remedies, 51–3
  conditional sale, 39–40, 46
  contracts, 39
  and description, 40–1
  exclusion clauses, 48
  fitness for purpose, 42
  and hire purchase, 39–40, 47, 48
  leasing contracts, 47–8
  lien, 53
  merchantable quality, 41–2
  passing of property, 48–54
  and resale, 54
  retention clauses, 51
  seller's liability, 42
  seller's remedies, 53–4
  stoppage in transit, 53–4
  title to sell, 43–4
  and warranties, 107–8
  without title, 44–7
  see also Trading offences
Service marks, 83
Small claims, 5
Solicitors, 17, 67–8